GOD'S
HOLY
LAW

MATTERS THAT TRULY MATTER!

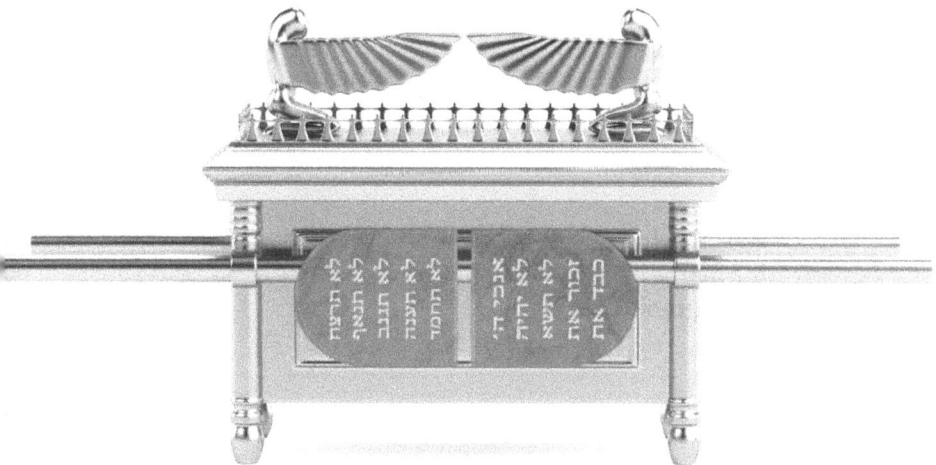

FITZROY BROWN

GOD'S HOLY LAW - Matters that truly matter!

Copyright © 2020 **FitzRoy Brown**

All rights reserved.

ISBN: 978-1-7358137-0-7

Designed by:
INDES PROCOM LTD.
www.indesprocom.com

For any information about the book, please write to:
godsholylaw@gmail.com

DEDICATION

God has given me several breaks in my short life on earth and several people have shown up at different moments to help me through. One pair who have greatly influenced my life aside from my parents (John & Bertha Brown) are my sister Esta Twum and my brother-in-law Kwasi Twum.

I wish to dedicate this book to their honor and to say "Thank you" for being there for me and my family. May God bless and secure your positions in His Eternal Kingdom together with all your children and their families also.

ACKNOWLEDGMENT

I had not set out to write a book - this project started as writing my thoughts after engaging Francis Teye in a conversation regarding the book of Revelation. His thoughts piqued my interest and l started a deeper study into the topic. Had it not been for that conversation and his willingness to share his resources; this project would not have come about. I want to thank him deeply for his insights and desire to share truth with others.

During this period of COVID-19 where all parents are dedicated to helping their children adjust to the new normal of home-schooling; l have been conspicuously absent; putting the burden on my wife to do all the supervisory work with the kids. I am deeply grateful. And to our three beautiful children **A**gyeman, **S**erwah and **K**oranteng **[ASK]** whom I dearly love - thank you for giving me the time and space to finish this work. I love you loads!

My ultimate thanks go to God my creator and redeemer - I have no better words than to borrow those of David - "Who am l that you are so mindful of; that you would be so gracious with me and grant me repentance and a heart to follow you?". To you only l dedicate the rest of my life, to love you and to serve you and to testify of you all the days of my life.

PROLOGUE

ARE GOD'S TEN COMMANDMENTS STILL APPLICABLE TO CHRISTIANS IN THE 21ST CENTURY?

WHAT IS THIS BOOK ABOUT?

In this book, I seek to share my understanding of God's 10 commandments, and why I believe they are still applicable to professing Christians today! In presenting this, I must state that I don't present any new idea - everything contained in this book is very much already known by many - except perhaps, may not have been presented this way, or that you may not have come across it. God's grace has made it possible for me to come to know and understand after several years of living without these truths and failing to honor God the way He expects me. For this, I am most grateful for His pardon, grace and mercy shown me. And now, I feel a strong burden to share with you!

While this is not a scholarly piece, it requires the reader to approach it with humility and a teachable heart and make time to cross-check the different scripture references. You will not get the import of the message if you merely skim through the pages. Only the Holy Spirit can help you discern things of the Spirit, so I ask that you first pray for God to give you wisdom and discernment. The reason this book is full of scripture references is because that's how God teaches us [according to His word] -

> *"Whom will he teach knowledge? And whom will he make to understand the message? ….. For precept must be upon precept, precept upon precept, Line upon line, line upon line, Here a little, there a little."*
> — **Isa 28:9-10.**

We have to study scripture both in context and as well compare with other scriptures so we don't read meanings and make them say what God didn't intend to say. When you read the bible carefully, you will notice that for everything God reveals to us, He repeats it and expands on it (Reveal; Repeat & Expand). So we must at all times, allow the bible to interpret itself.

WHY YOU SHOULD READ THIS?

● To incite personal study & a healthy discussion to build our faith in God & Jesus

● I believe that contrary to what others teach, this topic is salvific and directly bears on whether or not one will make it into God's Heavenly Kingdom. I do believe that we are saved by Grace alone [apart from works] and this saving grace [which forgives sins] leads us to love God, and because we love Him, we obey His commands, and do good works. God has made it clear however that we will be judged by our works - Phil 2:12.

● I also consider that it is very central to Christianity as a belief for our redemption .

- I believe that many sincere believers and lovers of God are in error because they haven't taken time to understand the truth about the Law of God.

WHO WILL BENEFIT FROM THIS BOOK?

All believers and Christians everywhere, [especially] those who teach and or have been taught and are convinced that we no longer need to keep God's law because of grace through faith in the finished work of Jesus for man's redemption. You will find from this study, how that teaching is from the spirit of the Anti-Christ who unfortunately has permeated many Churches, deceiving and leading many to destruction. The book also makes a case for the consideration of anyone who has walked away or is staying away from Christianity due to doubts about its authenticity, to realise that Christianity and the bible are not only true but also very reasonable.

HOW IS THIS PRESENTED?

This book is broken into two parts: Part I will walk us through evidence from scriptures that lead to the conclusion that God's Law is still applicable in the 21st century and that today's Christian must obey the Law fully. Part II will focus on the "forgotten" command of the Sabbath, and how the evil one has sold a counterfeit to modern Christianity leading us to disobey God. The book closes with how we must respond in view of the evidence provided so we can be saved from God's wrath.

PREFACE

My very first trip to China was in the year 2005; but my most recent trip in 2019 helped me to appreciate deeply what the Bible teaches about God's Kingdom. You might be asking - what could possibly draw your attention to God's Kingdom in China? A lot actually, and let me tell you a few.

After several failed attempts at trying to use my whatsapp, gmail accounts and youtube (the apps that I have come to depend on so much); I realized that I was in for some trouble in the few days I was going to be in China. The hotel was unyielding in accepting my US dollar bills for payment, insisting that I pay in Chinese currency - the yuan. It wasn't too long after touching down in Beijing that it became obvious that I was in another territory, where nothing that I had become so dependent on worked.

Because of China's trade war with the USA; most apps developed by Americans didn't work in China - so my gmail, whatsapp, youtube etc were useless in this territory. As though that wasn't enough trouble for me already - I

GOD'S HOLY LAW - Matters that truly matter!

wasn't finding anyone in my hotel who could understand the languages l could communicate in. My phone's battery was about to die and l needed to charge immediately - it was when I tried to use the sockets at the hotel that I noticed that they were different and my charger wouldn't fit in. What am l to do now? I couldn't recollect anyone's number out of memory now that my phone is dead. Even if l were to manage to borrow someone's phone; who will I call to speak to the hotel about my needs - how to get to where my conference location was; where to get a local SIM card and how to get into my email. These were just a few of my immediate concerns. To make it worse, l was hungry and all I had was the US Dollar which was just as "useless" there - until I could find a place to change it into Chinese Yuan.

That's when it hit me - China is a kingdom of its own - if l am going to survive in this kingdom - l must play by it's rules. With so much difficulty, stress and so much wasted time, I finally managed to get help from some Chinese counterparts to show me the ropes. Had it not been for them giving me lessons from which apps I could use and how to change my currency etc; my misery would have lingered much longer than the few days it lasted.

Even before Jesus started His ministry, his fore-runner John the Baptist came preaching the message of repentance - he said the reason why people should repent is because the Kingdom of God is at hand. Jesus came and continued preaching the same message of the Kingdom of God being near and so did the Apostles. Although I have followed the scriptures closely, it was in China that I came to understand the practicality of being in a new Kingdom.

The first lesson for me was that; you couldn't just make a smooth transition from one kingdom to another as I thought. In my naivety and unpreparedness, I carried everything that has been working for me in Ghana to China - not thinking twice about it working there or not. If I had thought deeply about it as I should have; I would have researched prior to my trip; spoken to people who had recently been there and or those I know who live there. If I had done so, I would have carried along Chinese currency, downloaded apps that would work there including an app for translation; and also carried a travel adaptor (at least for starters).

Here is my point - If an earthly kingdom like China, can decide to organize themselves in a way that requires people to approach them with considerable thought and planning; bearing in mind all the requirements to be able to survive there - then how much more will it be in the Kingdom of God? If my experience here in China could make all the things I depend on so "useless" within a twinkle of an eye; could any of these things survive in God's Heavenly Kingdom? What use will my money be? Will it matter who or what I am here on earth; my race, gender, age, socio-economic status - what of my occupation/career and the letters that appear at the end of your name? What of political connections - will the people I know in high places be able to help me? What will really count?

The pages of this book highlight different aspects of the Kingdom of God and we must pay attention to it very carefully so that we will not experience any shock. God's Kingdom has requirements for entry, for becoming a member and rules that pertain to living in there successfully. Have you taken the time to familiarize yourself with these requirements and rules? Or are you making the same mistake 1 made by thinking you can make a smooth transition into His Kingdom - taking the same life you are living in this depraved and soon to fall *kingdom of the devil*; and transporting yourself into God's Kingdom? Do you think you can fall on the same things you depend on in this life in God's Kingdom? Have you asked yourself: "how far will my political connections take me; what would my money be able to buy there; and all the things that I am hustling, fighting and quarrelling for - of what benefit will they be to me there"?

For thousands of years and recently since the days of Jesus; for more than 2,000 years now - everything God has been doing is to prepare us to enter His Kingdom; and we should not in any way make light of that. Let us notice how God does it so systematically by choosing one man and from that one man who is found faithful by obeying all of God's commands *(Gen 26:5)*, God births the nation Israel and gives them His rules and requirements *[Exo 20:1-18]* and now extends all His rules and requirements to the rest of the gentile world - *Acts 17:24-27 I 2 Cor 5:19.*

In his conversation with Nicodemus, notice how Jesus tells him that one needs to be born-again to even see His Kingdom, how one needs to be born of water and the Spirit before being able to enter His Kingdom - *John 3:3-7.* Also notice how Peter on the day of Pentecost opens the door of the Kingdom to over 3,000 people in *Acts 2:38-42.*

Have you been paying attention to the things that truly matter? Someone said; "Of all the years that man would spend on earth; it will never come close in comparison to the eternal [infinite] life that God has promised us in His Kingdom". Knowing this, how should you approach life? Moses prayed - *"Teach us to number our days so we may incline our hearts unto wisdom"* - *Ps 90:12.* Knowing that our days here on earth are short; shouldn't we do whatever it takes to acquaint ourselves with what the requirements of God's Kingdom are and to prepare ourselves to successfully enter and be part of it?

These are the issues that this book concerns itself with - **"matters that truly matter"!**

I would like to take this opportunity to thank you for deciding to read my thoughts and convictions on this subject and I ask that the Lord reward you for your decision. I pray with you that as you turn the pages of this book - "May God open your eyes to incredible truth and insight and fill you with understanding, so that you may be able to apply Godly wisdom to the decisions you make as a result; and be found prepared when He comes to take His saints to the Kingdom that He has prepared for those who love Him". Amen!

FitzRoy

GOD'S HOLY LAW - Matters that truly matter!

GOD'S
HOLY
LAW

MATTERS THAT TRULY MATTER!

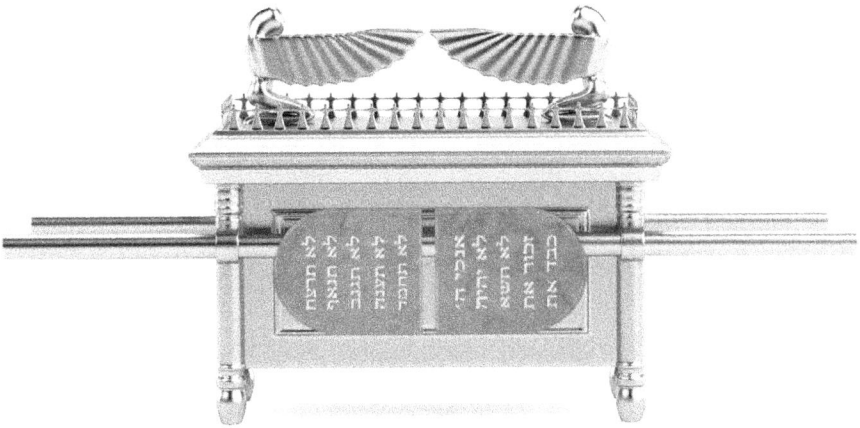

TABLE OF CONTENTS

PART I

TABLE OF CONTENTS

PART II

GOD'S HOLY LAW - Matters that truly matter!

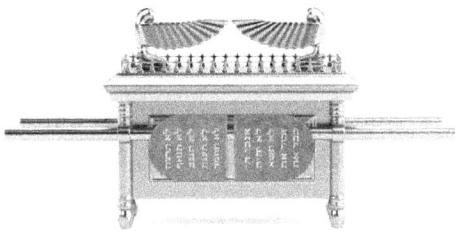

PART
ONE

INTRODUCTION

❝ There is no room for you here, not for you, and certainly not for all those who like you didn't obey my law - now; if you don't mind, please move away so l can shut the door!"

Those were the words of Jesus to him - he had given his life to Jesus when he was only 17, it was his first year of college and he became a disciple just in time before he could get into bad company. Gabby was distraught - he couldn't believe the words he was hearing.

"There must be a mistake somewhere Lord, my surname is Williams", he said as tears started rolling down his cheeks.

"Yes" said the Lord, *"l have it spelt out correctly too - and your middle name Kwasi - your name is not here in the book of life!"*

Yelling now - *"Lord, Lord! You know how much l laboured for you; how many nights l was up praying to you, the 40 minus 1 days l fasted to be filled with your power and to boldly reach out to strangers. The many times l was ridiculed by my colleagues but never gave up my relationship with you - surely they must count for something!"*

"Sorry Sir! The records here show that you denied me; you never had faith in me - you didn't acknowledge me as your creator!"

"*But l spoke of you to all my friends, persuaded Eddie, Josh and Kwame who finally accepted you as Saviour also and made our Music Ministry one of the best - our Church was where everyone wanted to come to - our music was the best and all the youth attended Church.*"

"All I asked was for you to believe that I made you and that l have your best interest at heart, to make me your Lord and accept my will for you - but you chose your own way! Your music entertained people, it showed your talents and you drew people to yourselves - you didn't do it for me…..."

Breaking down at this point - "*Please Lord? You know I loved you and still do.*"

"Then you should have obeyed my commands; it's not just what you say and profess, it is also who possesses you. Isn't faith proven by what you do? Did you do my will?"

* * * * * * *

Imagine you before the Lord on judgment day - how would you like the conversation to go? Know that, not everyone who professes to be Christian is one by God's standard. You know very well that the devil's greatest deception is to make you think that God does not really mean what He has said. Just as the serpent said to Eve in the garden - "*Did God really say…..*". We must be careful not to end up with the words of Eve after they broke God's command - "*The serpent deceived me, and l ate*".

So come with me as we study God's word to find out some truths which you may not have given much attention; but which can dispossess you of your hope of making Heaven! Especially if you desire to hear the Lord say to you: ***"Well done, good and faithful servant - come with me to the place prepared for you!"***. I promise that what you will learn in the following pages will be a blessing to you, even if you disagree with my findings.

And now, as you lay aside all your bias and approach Him in humility, l pray that God grant you wisdom and may the Holy Spirit inspire you to understand everything that He authored in His word so that you can find His truth which will truly set you free. Amen!

April, 2020

1

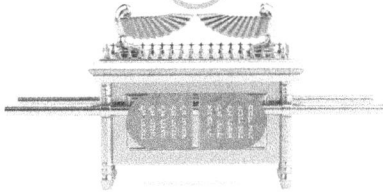

A CASE FOR CHRISTIANITY & THE BIBLE

*Jesus answered, "I am the way and the truth and the life.
No one comes to the Father except through me"*
— **John 14:6 NIV**

Many have questioned and even discredited Christianity and the Bible based on some unanswered questions. Did God create the world in six literal days? If God created only Adam and Eve at the beginning, then who did Cain marry to start a family with? Who did Seth marry? Did the flood in Noah's time destroy the entire earth or was it just a local flood? Is it the same God of the universe who commanded the Israelites to kill other people and stone each other who disobeyed His commands?

We can go on and on - there seems to be a lot more questions than anyone has attempted to offer answers to. However, Jesus quoted the book of Genesis in His teachings, Jesus believed and knew of Adam and Eve from the very beginning - He was the person of the Godhead who was in charge of creation. But I do understand how it can be very fuzzy in the minds of many, how authentic the story of creation especially is when other religions and cultures have similar folklore.

If you would stay with me for a while longer, I would like us to look at the history together and see what we can learn from it.

This chapter is dedicated to all who do not yet believe and or have left the Christian faith because they got confused with some scripture(s) and or thought of the Bible as contradicting itself or are even upset with the seeming fact that Christianity has been used over the years by some unscrupulous people to commit great atrocities including slavery, the crusades and the infamous inquisition of the 12th century.

My goal at the end of this chapter will be to ensure that the reader can understand:

1. Why it is true and reasonable to believe in Jesus as the Son of God who came to redeem you and I;
2. Why Christianity is not a lie or a man-made religion to enslave others;
3. Why Christianity makes the claim of an only God and lastly;
4. Why you should not dismiss the Holy scriptures but accept it as God's gift to you

It is my prayer that by the time I am done with this chapter; you will begin to see the God of the universe not as one fighting for "space" or to be accepted but as a truly loving Father longing for you to return to Him.

* * * * * * *

The Christian movement was not going to go any farther after the death of Jesus - it had come to an abrupt end nearly three years after it began. His death on the cross was a fatal blow to all who believed in Him; even those who secretly followed Him like Nicodemus and Joseph of Arimathea. But here they were, taking down his lifeless body from the cross of Calvary and putting it in a tomb. Over, everything had come to a crushing end - it was all over! What started as a big bang that was so revolutionary didn't last. The hopes of Him being the Messiah [Saviour] of the Jews and the Son of God incarnate was all lost at His death.

His disciples had deserted Him, now hiding behind closed doors - they were scared to death of what was going to happen to them. They were sure the Jews and religious leaders would not spare them if they had not spared Jesus Himself. Being in that locked room was to strategize on their next steps - they were having to face this thought for the very first time because they had indeed believed in Jesus. But alas it was all over!

But wait a minute; not just yet! Sunday came and the women hurriedly rushed to the tomb - the least they could do was to join His mother to embalm His body as they couldn't finish this task for the sake of God's Sabbath command. Little did they know that the story had not yet ended - when they thought all their hopes had been dashed; then Jesus rose from His death. He is Risen - our Lord is risen! You can imagine what it was like. Some had become so dis-illusioned that they had to see the risen Lord face to face before believing Mary's story.

Over a period of 40 days, He appeared to many of His disciples and to several others. It was no secret - to the extent that several people began to write their own account of what they witnessed - not that they heard others tell the story; they wrote what they themselves had seen - a first hand account. How could they not share their testimony; they had touched Him, eaten with Him, talked to Him and then seen Him taken up into Heaven before their very eyes. Such were some of the eye-witness accounts that are recorded for us in the Holy Bible.

The Apostle John was an eye-witness to all that had unfolded; and so was Matthew. The Gospel of Mark records Peter's perspective and the Gentile doctor Luke who knew these men and witnessed the accounts also went on to write his perspective - following on to write the book of Acts [of the Apostles]. You would have to put yourself in the shoes of these men to understand why they wrote what they did - there was no way anyone in Jerusalem had not heard the things that had happened. That a man named Jesus, who claimed to be the son of God had predicted His death and resurrection, and in their very eyes all that He said had come to pass. This sort of "magic" rarely happens!

*"As they talked and discussed these things with each other, Jesus himself came up and walked along with them; [16] but they were kept from recognizing him. [17] He asked them, "What are you discussing together as you walk along?" They stood still, their faces downcast. [18] One of them, named Cleopas, asked him, "**Are you the only one visiting**"*

Jerusalem who does not know the things that have happened there in these days?" [19] *"What things?" he asked. "About Jesus of Nazareth," they replied. "He was a prophet, powerful in word and deed before God and all the people.* [20] *The chief priests and our rulers handed him over to be sentenced to death, and they crucified him;* [21] *but we had hoped that he was the one who was going to redeem Israel. And what is more, it is the third day since all this took place.* [22] *In addition, some of our women amazed us. They went to the tomb early this morning* [23] *but didn't find his body. They came and told us that they had seen a vision of angels, who said he was alive.* [24] *Then some of our companions went to the tomb and found it just as the women had said, but they did not see Jesus."* [25] *He said to them, "How foolish you are, and how slow to believe all that the prophets have spoken!* [26] *Did not the Messiah have to suffer these things and then enter his glory?"* [27] *And beginning with Moses and all the Prophets, he explained to them what was said in all the Scriptures concerning himself." — Luke 24:15-27* [emphasis mine]

Some of the people who wrote these accounts were true eye-witnesses to all that had happened - they were not told by others - they saw everything as the events unfolded.

"That which was from the beginning, which we have heard, which we have seen with our eyes, which we have looked at and our hands have touched—this we proclaim concerning the Word of life. [2] *The life appeared; we have seen it and testify to it, and we proclaim to you the eternal*

life, which was with the Father and has appeared to us. ³
We proclaim to you what we have seen and heard, so that
you also may have fellowship with us. And our fellowship
is with the Father and with his Son, Jesus Christ."
— 1 John 1:1-3.

The disciples who had earlier fled from the scenes when Jesus was being tried and scourged and had locked themselves up were all of a sudden emboldened to stand and even dare speak back to the Religious leaders and before the Sanhedrin. Not afraid of punishment or death - why would these followers of Jesus risk their lives this way if there was no truth in what they had witnessed?

"What are we going to do with these men?" they asked.
"Everyone living in Jerusalem knows they have performed
a notable sign, and we cannot deny it. ¹⁷ But to stop this
thing from spreading any further among the people, we
must warn them to speak no longer to anyone in this
name." ¹⁸ Then they called them in again and commanded
them not to speak or teach at all in the name of Jesus. ¹⁹
But Peter and John replied, "Which is right in God's eyes:
*to listen to you, or to him? You be the judges! ²⁰ **As for us,***
we cannot help speaking about what we have seen
and heard." — Acts 4:16-20 [emphasis mine].

"Many have undertaken to draw up an account of the
things that have been fulfilled among us, ² just as they
were handed down to us by those who from the first were
eyewitnesses and servants of the word. ³ With this in mind,
since I myself have carefully investigated everything from

the beginning, I too decided to write an orderly account for you, most excellent Theophilus, ⁴ so that you may know the certainty of the things you have been taught."
— **Luke 1:1-4**

So we are convinced that there were real people and several of them (not just one or two but many) who saw and talked to Jesus while He was on earth, and witnessed what happened to Him during His life, death, resurrection and ascension. These are the people who wrote what they saw.

Again, notice the account of Paul who converted to become a follower of Jesus a few years down the road. He spoke to believers in the Corinth Church that there were people still living at the time who were eye-witnesses of the life of Jesus and his resurrection - these were not myths or tales; it had truly happened and there were witnesses who were still alive at the time Paul wrote his first letter to the Corinthians.

*"For what I received I passed on to you as of first importance[a]: that Christ died for our sins according to the Scriptures, ⁴ that he was buried, that he was raised on the third day according to the Scriptures, ⁵ and that he appeared to Cephas, and then to the Twelve. ⁶ After that, **he appeared to more than five hundred of the brothers and sisters at the same time, most of whom are still living,** though some have fallen asleep. ⁷ Then he appeared to James, then to all the apostles*
— **1 Cor 15:3-7** [emphasis mine].

We know from the time of Jesus' ministry that his brothers [which included James] didn't believe Him to be the Son of God - **John**

7:5. But this skeptic brother later became one of the pillars of the Church but only after Jesus' resurrection.

So before we dismiss the accounts of the Bible, it is important that we understand how it all came together. When Matthew, Mark, Luke and John wrote their accounts [the Gospels] - as well as the letters of Paul that fill up the New Testament; it is important to note that they didn't sit together or confer with each other to plan to write a book that was to be called the Bible. These individuals wrote accounts of what they had witnessed regarding Jesus. Luke also wrote about how the Apostles carried on after Jesus' ascension in the book of Acts. Paul then records all the events during his missionary journeys and the letters that he wrote to the different Gentile Churches he planted as well as the individuals he mentored. The letters of the Apostles Peter and James also made it in the final canon.

All these were written records or documents or booklets that were preserved and later were collected and put together to form what we have as the Biblical canon - but there was no intention from the start that these individuals were writing what we now have as the Bible. It is also a known fact that there were several other manuscripts by other witnesses that didn't make it in the compilation.

As the Christian movement progressed, Gentiles who got drawn to the lives of followers of the risen Christ joined in - you couldn't hear the events from these eye witnesses and not take a decision to follow Jesus as well. The few who had copies of the writings of these witnesses jealously guarded them and passed them on to other new converts or their children. But in the synagogues where they would assemble every Sabbath and in the various meetings they held in the Temple courts and each others' homes - their readings were taken from the Jewish writings called the Law and the Prophets and the Psalms. It was their admiration of Jesus that caused the new Gentile believers to seek to know more about Him and which led them to study the Hebrew literature - the Law, the Prophets and the Psalms which Jesus himself referred to among His disciples.

> *"He said to them, "This is what I told you while I was still with you: Everything must be fulfilled that is written about me in the Law of Moses, the Prophets and the Psalms"* — **Luke 24:44** [emphasis mine].

The above scripture by itself helps us to see that the Hebrew literature had been preserved and were available and being used in the days of Jesus. We know that Jesus read from them in the synagogue - **Luke 4:16-21.**

It is important to note that the Gentile converts were not necessarily interested in the way of the Jews (circumcision, kosher foods etc) but they wanted to find out more about what the Jewish writings had to say about Jesus. Everywhere they looked - they found Jesus being spoken of or referred to in the pages of these writings and it was clear that Jesus had come in fulfilment of God's promise. How could they who were expecting Him, miss Him? The verdict from the council at Jerusalem recorded in **Acts 15** confirms that Gentile converts did not have to become Jewish in their ways to be accepted as Christians but attending the synagogue meetings and hearing the law of Moses being preached deepened their understanding and knowledge of God. Through their searches of the Jewish writings, they realized that long before - it had been recorded in the pages of the Torah that *"In the beginning, God...."*.

Wait a minute - in the beginning God? You mean to say not gods but God? This was such a BIG revelation and revolutionary to a people who had been raised with the concept of many gods. So realizing that the Jewish text did not make mention of gods but GOD; it aroused their curiosity because in their world; they were used to Polytheism - many gods and not just one.

It must be noted again that what was taught in the assemblies [synagogue meetings] of the early Church were mostly from the Law, Prophets, Psalms and eye-witness accounts directly from the Apostles regarding what Jesus taught them. So the Jewish text was part of the collection of writings that the early Christians considered to be their sacred manual - and what they would refer to in their worship of Jesus their Lord and God who made the universe. It was in the very pages of the Law, Prophets and Psalms (now christened the Old Testament) that they found that; the only One True God who created the universe, made man the pinnacle of His creation to rule over everything else that He made.

This revelation from the Torah that man was to "rule" was another revolutionary idea to the early Gentile Christians who were once used to worshipping images of animals and stones and trees and anything in between?

> *"Formerly, when you did not know God, you were slaves to those who by nature are not gods. ⁹ But now that you know God—or rather are known by God—how is it that you are turning back to those weak and miserable forces? Do you wish to be enslaved by them all over again?"* — **Gal 4:8-9**

Again, following the accounts of creation, the early Christians discovered from the Old Testament how God from choosing Abraham and having a covenant with him, created a Nation for Himself through Abraham and set this nation [Israel] apart to be a model of how He God would want all the nations of the earth to be. God's covenant with Israel was made at mount Sinai which was essentially where the Law (Ten Commandments) was given - which commandments if they followed, God would continue to bless and be with them.

When Israel forsook God's Law and by envying their neighbours even went against God's desire and asked for a king, God sent them prophets to remind them and persuade them to return to Him who created them and delivered them from the hands of their enemies. This went on until they once again found themselves serving under Rome and were at this point looking forward to the Messiah God had promised [through the Prophets]. You notice that the Saviour is who the Jewish nation was waiting for at the time Jesus entered the world and yet the religious leaders failed to recognize Him. They missed the Messiah's visitation probably because they were expecting a military leader who will deliver them from Rome, their physical oppressors. See a few scriptures on Israel awaiting the Anointed One:

"Now there was a man in Jerusalem called Simeon, who was righteous and devout. He was waiting for the consolation of Israel, and the Holy Spirit was on him. [26] It had been revealed to him by the Holy Spirit that he would not die before he had seen the Lord's Messiah"
— Luke 2:25-26

"When John, who was in prison, heard about the deeds of the Messiah, he sent his disciples ³ to ask him, "Are you the one who is to come, or should we expect someone else?"
— *Matt 11:2-3*

"The woman said, "I know that Messiah" (called Christ) "is coming. When he comes, he will explain everything to us." ²⁶ Then Jesus declared, "I, the one speaking to you—I am he….. ²⁹ "Come, see a man who told me everything I ever did. Could this be the Messiah?"
— *John 4:25-26; 29* [emphasis mine]

"Andrew, Simon Peter's brother, was one of the two who heard what John had said and who had followed Jesus. ⁴¹ The first thing Andrew did was to find his brother Simon and tell him, "We have found the Messiah" (that is, the Christ)" — *John 1:40-41*
"You stiff-necked heathen! Must you forever resist the Holy Spirit? But your fathers did, and so do you! ⁵² Name one prophet your ancestors didn't persecute! They even killed the ones who predicted the coming of the Righteous One—the Messiah whom you betrayed and murdered. ⁵³ Yes, and you deliberately destroyed God's laws, though you received them from the hands of angels."
— *Acts 7:51-53 TLB* [Emphasis mine].

Isn't it sad that even to this day; some Jews are still waiting for their Messiah? Their idea of the Messiah was one to destroy the tyranny of Rome and restore the kingdom to Israel - but God had a bigger & better plan - to save the world and redeem it from the hands of the devil. While many are still looking for some wonders to happen in our world; God is rather looking at how we will respond to the invitation of His Son Jesus which is still open to us today - but only for a little more time. God has been patient enough - waiting over two millennia after Jesus' ascension, but that day is coming soon when probation would close and we must all come to give account before His judgment seat - whether we made peace with Him through Jesus or we rejected Him..

So we notice that, it is through Jesus Christ that the rest of the world traced back through the Hebrew literature; to understand the following:

- That there are not many gods as they thought but One God;

- That God made man to rule over the animals, birds and all creation and not to worship them as gods;

- That God's purpose of bringing Jesus was to reconcile the world to Himself. And He did this by first having a covenant with Abraham, then creating for Himself the Nation Israel to be an example of how He wanted all nations of the world to be.

- That God will one day judge the inhabitants of this world as to whether we obeyed Him by choosing or rejecting Jesus

Check out how Apostle Paul puts it in his discourse with the people in Athens:

> *"While Paul was waiting for them in Athens, he was greatly distressed to see that the city was full of idols.*

¹⁷ *So he reasoned in the synagogue with both Jews and God-fearing Greeks, as well as in the marketplace day by day with those who happened to be there.* ¹⁸ *A group of Epicurean and Stoic philosophers began to debate with him. Some of them asked, "What is this babbler trying to say?" Others remarked, "He seems to be advocating foreign gods." They said this because Paul was preaching the good news about Jesus and the resurrection.* ¹⁹ *Then they took him and brought him to a meeting of the Areopagus, where they said to him, "May we know what this new teaching is that you are presenting?* ²⁰ *You are bringing some strange ideas to our ears, and we would like to know what they mean."* ²¹ *(All the Athenians and the foreigners who lived there spent their time doing nothing but talking about and listening to the latest ideas.)* ²² *Paul then stood up in the meeting of the Areopagus and said: "People of Athens! I see that in every way you are very religious.* ²³ *For as I walked around and looked carefully at your objects of worship, I even found an altar with this inscription: to an unknown god. So you are ignorant of the very thing you worship— and this is what I am going to proclaim to you.* ²⁴ ***"The God who made the world and everything in it is the Lord of heaven and earth and does not live in*** *temples built by human hands.* ²⁵ *And he is not served by human hands, as if he needed anything. Rather, he himself gives everyone life and breath and everything else.* ²⁶ *From one man he made all the nations, that they should inhabit the whole earth; and he marked out their appointed times in history and the boundaries of their lands.* ²⁷ ***God did this so that they would seek him and perhaps reach out***

for him and find him, though he is not far from any one of us. [28] 'For in him we live and move and have our being.' As some of your own poets have said, 'We are his offspring.' [29] "Therefore since we are God's offspring, we should not think that the divine being is like gold or silver or stone—an image made by human design and skill. [30] In the past God overlooked such ignorance, but now he commands all people everywhere to repent. [31] For he has set a day when he will judge the world with justice by the man he has appointed. He has given proof of this to everyone by raising him from the dead."—Acts 17:16-31

As Christianity gained grounds or became popular, more and more people denounced idol worship and anyone or thing that they were previously worshipping. You will recall that Jesus had told His disciples and the Pharisees who tried to trap Him to - "give to Caesar what is Caesar's and to God what is His" - worship is supposed to be given God alone - **Matt 22:15-22**. The Christians way of worship aroused the anger of the then civil government how their sect was different in the sense of not paying homage to the Emperor or the gods of the Romans. This caught the attention of the Emperor Diocletian who ruled Rome from 284 - 305 BC. He started the persecution of the Christian sect - leading up to the confiscation of the sacred writings and burning of these texts because it was reasoned that; their scriptures informed their non-conformists nature.

In the first few decades when it began, Christianity was viewed as a sect within Judaism and that was okay until it was realized that

Christianity was a new religion. Under Roman law, new religions were illegal and so it was a crime to be a Christian. And although Rome was known for its pluralistic gods and deities; everyone paid homage to the Roman Emperor as lord. But this growing sect of Christ's followers were not going to worship any human or even less, man-made gods or any creation of God. Not even the threats, confiscation of property or the realities of death could make them denounce their faith or bow to the Emperor and be accepted - thus the persecution that led to many losing their lives and the censorship of the Judeo-Christian writings.

But even persecution didn't stop Christianity from growing - the blood of the martyrs were like seeds that sprouted into many more people - so the more Christians were killed, burnt at the stakes, imprisoned and banished etc - the more Christianity grew. Whether living in joy or suffering, Christ was their identity so nothing else mattered. Also, during this time of persecution; the sacred writings were confiscated, burnt and destroyed.

Later down the line in the 4th century, after Constantine came to power and lifted the ban on persecution of religions - Christian scholars came together openly to collect the writings that had been preserved and survived the days of the persecution. The Old Testament on the one hand and the writings about Jesus which were later referred to as the New Testament on the other hand; were for the first time joined together to make up the complete Christian Bible as we have it today. The first Bible was published in the latin vulgate language in the 4th century; and it was the same Roman Empire that once persecuted the Christians who funded the collection of the sacred writings to form the Bible.

There is no doubt that the Bible shaped western civilization and culture. As you can see, the Bible didn't create Christianity but the event of Christ' death and resurrection created a movement (The Way); that produced records and writings about Jesus and His teachings including the works of His Apostles [the New Testament]. These mostly eye-witness writings caused curious minds to find out more about the origin of Jesus and the prophecies made about Him in Hebrew literature [Old Testament]. It was only later that these two testaments were put together to form the complete Bible.

Following the decline of the Roman Empire and during the period referred to as the dark ages [5th - 15th century]; Papal Rome (i.e. when the Roman Catholic Church was ruling the affairs of the State) censored the Bible and persecuted all whose lives were being shaped by it. During the dark ages, it was actually an offense for the ordinary citizens [laity] to possess, read and or translate the Bible into more known languages. The officials of the Roman Catholic Church said that those who were not in the clergy were untrained and as such their reading of scripture would give rise to misunderstandings and errors. It was therefore thought to be enough for ordinary people to get acquainted with the doctrines of scripture through sermons at Church. The first translation of the Bible into the English language did not get printed until in the early 16th century.

Read the account below which is a portion taken from Wikipedia on Bible censorship by the Roman Catholic Church.

John Wycliffe (1330–1384), a theologian with pre-Reformation views, finished the first authoritative translation of the Bible from Latin into English in 1383. His teachings were rejected in 1381 by the university and 1382 by the Church. For fear of a popular uprising Wycliffe was not charged. The translation of the Bible caused great unrest among the clergy, and for their sake, several defensive provincial synods were convened, such as the 3rd Council of Oxford (ended in 1408). Under the chairmanship of Archbishop Thomas Arundel, official positions against Wycliffe were written in the Oxford Constitution and Arundel Constitution. The latter reads as follows:[30]

[…] that no one in the future will translate any text of Scripture into English or into any other text than book, scripture or tract, or that such a book, scripture or tract be read, whether new in the time of said John Wycliffe written or written in the future, whether in part or as a whole, public or hidden. This is under the punishment of the greater excommunication until the bishop of the place or, if necessary, a provincial council approves the said translation. But those who act against it should be punished like a heretic and false teacher.

Unlike before, translations of liturgical readings and preaching texts (psalms, pericopes from the Gospels and Epistles) were now bound to an examination by Church authorities. Individuals like William Butler wanted to go even further and also limit Bible translations to the Latin language alone. In 1401, Parliament passed the De heretico comburendo law in order to suppress Wycliffe's followers and censor their books, including the Bible translation. At the Council of Constance in 1415, Wycliffe was finally proclaimed a heretic and condemned as "that pestilent wretch of damnable memory, yea, the forerunner and disciple of anti-christ who, as the complement of his wickedness, invented a new translation of the Scriptures into his mother-tongue."[31] His helpers Nicholas Hereford and John Purvey were forced to recant their teachings, and his bones, as determined by the council were finally burned in 1428. However, his translation of the Bible along with 200 manuscripts were secretly preserved and read by followers, and have survived to the present day. However, Wycliffe's Bible was not printed until 1731, when Wycliffe was historically conceived as the forefather of the English Reformation.[32] The next English Bible translation was that of William Tyndale, whose Tyndale Bible had to be printed from 1525 outside England in areas of Germany sympathetic to Protestantism. Tyndale himself was sentenced to death at the stake because of his translation work. He was strangled in 1536 near Brussels and then burned.

Source: https://en.wikipedia.org/wiki/Censorship_of_the_Bible

The story of Jesus has been so worth telling that people lost their lives recording it, preserving it, translating it into common languages and making sure it gets to us. This is why we must be grateful for the Bible and guard it jealously; for soon, I believe the world will go through another period when we won't have the true word of God - see the prophecy in **Amos 8:11-12.** Since the Bible was put together - it has been responsible for pointing man back to God throughout time; and without it - there could have been no civilization and there wouldn't have ever been the knowledge of the one true God. So once again when the Word of God is taken away; "darkness" will cover the entire earth. Christ' followers are indeed the light of the world.

Further, without the Bible, man would have been serving and bowing down to man-made idols that we are to subdue and rule over. Unfortunately - some of this still goes on in our world today and in several parts of Africa and Asia especially. I strongly believe that idol worship debases humans that God has made in His own image and it should not be a way of worship for any human being made of God. God said clearly to the people of old that they should not have any other gods but Him and they should not make for themselves any idol or image to bow down to - the very first two commands.

> *"Have no gods other than Me.* ⁴ *"Do not make for yourselves a god to look like anything that is in heaven above or on the earth below or in the waters under the earth.*
> ⁵ *"Do not worship them or work for them. For I, the Lord your God, am a jealous God. I punish the children, even the great-grandchildren, for the sins of their fathers who hate Me"* — **Exo 20:3-5**

God punished the Israelites for making a calf as a symbol of their worship - **Exo 32.** So that is one sure way of knowing that God doesn't endorse any form of idol worship or bowing to any graven image. Idolatry is a sin and it can never be a way through which we worship God. We need to discard the erroneous notion that we can worship God by going through an idol or any mediums or spiritists.

There are several people who are not fond of Christianity because they argue that; Chrisianity was the way through which Europeans enslaved Africa. They say Europeans demonized the African's way of worship and called it idolatry; then introduced Africans to their made-up Christian religion and a Bible they had carefully written with the sole agenda of taking away it's people, lands and resources. In essence, colonization would not have been successful without the use of the Bible and Christianity to subjugate Africans.

This is where I believe we need to decouple the issues. While the events of slavery and the plundering of Africa are true and unfortunate - we need to understand one thing and separate it right from the onset. The fact that many people have hidden behind the Bible and Christianity to perpetrate the world's worst atrocities doesn't mean they were or are Christians or that; by posing to be Christians - they had any authority from God to do the harm they caused other humans. God respects human life and wants the dignity of humans preserved so unfortunately, man [not God], is responsible for the acts that occur on this part where He gave dominion over to us at creation. It is God's love for humanity that made him send Jesus to come to earth to redeem us even after we disobeyed His commands and handed over our authority of this planet to the devil.

While the Bible has been a tool that some evil persons have used to exploit other vulnerable groups; know that the Bible did not come about nor did God allow it to be put together for such purpose. The Bible today is still a tool just like any other tool like guns, wealth, beauty, fame, race, privilege, etc that give people [or people groups] power and authority over others. All of these tools are not in themselves bad; but they can be used to perpetrate evil on others. In some cases, people have used such tools to threaten, deceive, enslave, frighten, exploit, excommunicate and even kill others or subject them to inhumane treatment.

One thing that is true of the Bible though is that the more of it you know, the less anyone can succeed in using it to enslave or harm you - the Bible is God's word of truth and when you know the truth; it sets you free. Unfortunately, we have so many people who refuse to read it for themselves but depend on some "religious leader" to tell them what is in there - and that's where the majority of the problems stem from.

So it is true that people hiding behind the Church have used the Bible/Church as a vehicle to do harm, but it is not at all difficult to know whether they were God's people; just ask yourself "who was persecuted and why"? In the case of the persecutions of the dark ages perpetrated under Papal Rome by the Roman Catholic Church and State government - it happened mostly because they called others who were not of their "faith and doctrine" heretics and therefore enemies. But let's not allow that to mislead us to think that, calling themselves the Church meant that they were truly the Church of God. Jesus Christ commanded His followers to love all people especially their enemies and to be kind to them - so who do you suppose will do harm to other people because they are different and adhere to different beliefs? Let's not make it any difficult to unmask the real heretics who come in the name of the Church - that's the false Church and not Christ' Church.

A global religious system with power from the devil that portrays itself as God's Church with the intent of deceiving people; and making war against the saints of God. The Prophet Daniel was shown this in a vision of what was to come and history has confirmed who this power is.

> *"The ten horns are ten kings who will come from this kingdom. After them another king will arise, different from the earlier ones; he will subdue three kings. [25]* **He will speak against the Most High and oppress his holy people and try to change the set times and the laws.** *The holy people will be delivered into his hands for a time, times and half a time" — **Dan 7:24-25*** [emphasis mine]

And if we think what they did in the past was bad - wait till you start to experience the worst of its kind in the near future as once again we will see the coming together of Church and State on a global scale. You can read more about this global power of the last days in Revelation 17, where it describes it as "the beast that was and is not and about to be". More on this in later chapters.

So whereas God gave us the Bible and the Church for our good, the devil is also using these same tools to perpetrate harm on humanity. Each of us can make a difference though - the more of the Bible you know, the less likely you will be caught up in the events of the future persecutions and be able to save others from it too. This is why we must not stand aloof but get busy reading and asking the Holy Spirit to give us discernment to understand scriptures.

In all of this, the truth is that; if Jesus hadn't resurrected, there would not have ever been the Bible. Think deeply about this for a moment!

So the story of the Bible is not whether or not you believe the stories in the Bible and are able to make sense of all of it [whether the snake spoke at a point in time or which fruit it is that Eve and Adam ate or how the devil and his agents have used it to execute their own evil agenda]. Rather than get embarrassed by the Bible or the stories in it, understand why and how the holy scriptures came to be instead, what truth it is telling you, and how it seeks to protect you from wrong/harm while pointing you to God.

The story of the Bible is rather to help you ask the question - "Am I at peace with the only one True God in Heaven"? The God who created you after His kind, and even while you have gone astray and lost your bearing from Him, has loved you enough to send His only Son to find you so you may come back into a loving relationship with Him; leading you to His promised Everlasting and Abundant life? That is the reason for the Bible.

And if you are a Christian and you've been disturbed by others claiming the Bible to be false or having contradictions and therefore ridiculing your faith - I encourage you to not allow what they say to shake you, but rather be confident and steadfast. Our response to Christianity and the Bible should be Paul's admonition to the Church in Philippi:

> *"Finally, brothers and sisters, whatever is true, whatever is noble, whatever is right, whatever is pure, whatever is lovely, whatever is admirable—if anything is excellent or praiseworthy—think about such things"* — **Phi 4:8**

This world has nothing that is truer, more noble, right; purer; lovelier, more admirable, more excellent; more praiseworthy than Christianity and the Bible. Meditate on it!

REMEMBERING SOLOMON!

Time will not permit me to talk about five things that God has gifted to man that the devil has used as weapons and weaknesses against men. **W**ill, **W**isdom; **W**ealth, **W**ine and **W**omen - interesting that they all start with **W** - wonder why?

There was a man who lived at one time who possessed more of these things more than any other human can imagine, desire or accumulate in the course of their life. Of his Wisdom, the Bible says that no one will ever come close. And the Will [Power] he had - matchless! He ruled over the entire people of God [Israel], and all the peoples and Nations that had been conquered earlier by his father David.

"So God said to him, "Since you have asked for this and not for long life or wealth for yourself, nor have asked for the death of your enemies but for discernment in administering justice, ¹² I will do what you have asked. I will give you a wise and discerning heart, so that there will never have been anyone like you, nor will there ever be. ¹³ Moreover, I will give you what you have not asked for—both wealth and honor—so that in your lifetime you will have no equal among kings. ¹⁴ And if you walk in obedience to me and keep my decrees and commands as David your father did, I will give you a long life."
— 1 Kings 3:11-14

See also the text in **1 Kings 10** to learn about Solomon's Wisdom, Wealth, Power and splendour. There was nothing he desired that he refused his eyes, and he refused his heart no pleasure. If there was ever a toy he saw that attracted him, he got it - **Eccl 2:10.**

Regarding women - he had 700 wives and 300 "side-chicks" - **1 Kings 11:1-3.** This man also had an encounter with other Gods as his wives led him astray towards the end of his life. Each of his wives had their own god they worshipped and so I guess each one he visited at a particular time introduced him to her god which he didn't turn down.

So there was nothing in life that Solomon did not have a taste of - he experienced everything any human being can ever have the time, energy and means to experience but; at the very end of his life - he stated clearly these words:

> *"Meaningless! Meaningless!" says the Teacher.*
> *"Utterly meaningless! Everything is meaningless."*
> *— Eccl 1:2*

> *"Not only was the Teacher wise, but he also imparted knowledge to the people. He pondered and searched out and set in order many proverbs. ¹⁰ The Teacher searched to find just the right words, and what he wrote was upright and true. ¹¹ The words of the wise are like goads, their collected sayings like firmly embedded nails—given by one shepherd. ¹² Be warned, my son, of anything in addition to them. Of making many books there is no end, and much study wearies the body. ¹³ Now all has been heard; here is the conclusion of the matter:*
> *Fear God and keep his commandments, for this is the duty of all mankind.*
> *¹⁴ For God will bring every deed into judgment, including every hidden thing, whether it is good or evil"*
> *— Eccl 12:9-14*

So remember your Creator during your youth! Otherwise, troublesome days will come and years will creep up on you when you'll say, "I find no pleasure in them,"
— ***Eccl 12:1***

Knowing this, what sort of person should you be? Will you carry on with life and make the same mistakes Solomon has made to arrive at the very same conclusion? But how do you know you will survive to tell the story? Or will you learn from his experiences, change and adopt the advice he gives - to seek God now that you can find Him [before the days of trouble come], to fear God and obey His commands?

Right now, we are all at the fork of a road - one road that seems pleasurable but the end thereof leads to destruction and the other leading to life. What we are certain of is that we will take a step - that step could either be towards Jesus or further away from Him; the way you turn is crucial to how your life ends and perhaps even your children and others around you.

Beloved - please choose wisely!

2

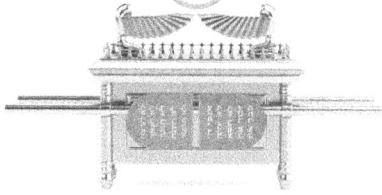

THE CONCEPT OF SIN

Everyone who sins breaks God's law, because sin is the same as breaking God's law"
— **1 John 3:4 CEV**

To establish that one has committed an offense, it is important to first have a standard that points to what is acceptable so as to understand what is not. It can not be said of one to have committed an offense unless it is first established that there is a laid down pattern that the person is being governed by. Paul expresses it this way - "I would not have known what sin is except for the law" **(Romans 7:7)**. The Law is therefore the standard by which God examines or governs how humans live on the earth He created. One is in sin only when it is determined that s/he has transgressed the law/command of God. Something is not sin because we humans think it is, it is sin when our thoughts, motivations and actions are not in conformity to what God prescribes.

An example is in the Garden of Eden when God directed man on what to do and what he could not do. God clearly established that if man does what He has said not to do, then it is sin. In that example, God tells Adam (and Eve) not to eat the fruit from the tree placed in the middle of the garden, and that the day they break that command, they will surely die (**Gen 2:16-17**). Sin entered the garden the moment Adam and Eve broke that command of God and ate the fruit they were not supposed to eat.

That is how sin entered our world but we also know that even before sin entered the garden, the devil who used to be an angel had already sinned. Man was not the first to have sinned but an angel Lucifer - he too broke a command of God and so was cast out of Heaven.

> *"And war broke out in heaven: Michael and his angels fought with the dragon; and the dragon and his angels fought, ⁸ but they did not prevail, nor was a place found for them in heaven any longer. ⁹ So the great dragon was cast out, that serpent of old, called the Devil and Satan, who deceives the whole world; he was cast to the earth, and his angels were cast out with him…… ¹² Therefore rejoice, O heavens, and you who dwell in them! Woe to the inhabitants of the earth and the sea! For the devil has come down to you, having great wrath, because he knows that he has a short time* — **Rev 12:7-12**

When the devil came to Eden - he told Eve (and by extension all humans) that we can have our own standard of right and wrong - and that we don't need God to tell us what is sin according to His law. He said man too can be "God" knowing right and wrong.

The devil's attempt from all time has been to remove God and His Law and replace it with Humanism - using our natural and carnal mind to make judgment in the areas of our lives. Thus, the origin of chaos in the world.

It is instructive to note the following detail in the texts below:

> *"Then God said, "**Let Us make man in Our image, according to Our likeness**; let them have dominion over the fish of the sea, over the birds of the air, and over the cattle, over all the earth and over every creeping thing that creeps on the earth." [27] **So God created man in His own image; in the image of God He created him;** male and female He created them"*
> *— **Gen 1:26-27** [emphasis mine]*

> *"This is the written account of Adam's family line. When God created mankind, **he made them in the likeness of God.** [2] He created them male and female and blessed them. And he named them "Mankind" when they were created. [3] When Adam had lived 130 years, **he had a son in his own likeness, in his own image;** and he named him Seth" — **Gen 5:1-3** [emphasis mine]*

I hope you have noticed the emphasis l am seeking to make with these two scriptures - that while God created the first humans in His image and according to His likeness; man started reproducing according to his own kind and in the image that he had now acquired. Remember that Adam and Eve started having children only after they had broken God's command; this is why humans are born with the tendency to sin. This doesn't mean that we have sinned even by the time we are born [original sin]; but rather that we are born with the genes of sin - we are susceptible to sin. David expresses it this way - *"Behold, I was brought forth in iniquity, And in sin my mother conceived me."* - ***Ps 51:5***. David is not saying that he had committed any sin [broken any command] when he was born but that he was born with the character of a sinner. When we understand this - it is easy to understand why Jesus tells Nicodemus that without being born again, he can not enter the Kingdom of God - **John 3:3-7.**

God doesn't charge you for the sin of your parents or another although you may suffer some consequences as a result of another person's sin; but you are only guilty of sin when you [yourself] have transgressed/broken God's command. You can read much more on that in **Ezekiel 18** and **Ezekiel 33:1-20** where God tells us that; "it is the one who sins who dies".

> *"Then Moses returned to the Lord and said, "Oh, these people have committed a great sin, and have made for themselves a god of gold! 32 Yet now, if You will forgive their sin—but if not, I pray, blot me out of Your book which You have written." 33 And the Lord said to Moses, "Whoever has sinned against Me, I will blot him out of My book"* — ***Exo 32:31-33***

In the above scripture, God emphasizes that His punishment will be on only those who have transgressed His commands and not everyone who was necessarily there.

The Bible says *"For ALL have sinned and fall short of the glory of God"* - **Rom 3:23**. This scripture helps us bring all the others together to understand how even in the case of a new born child, s/he needs God's grace just as much as any adult who has actually transgressed a command of God. This is because, the new child who has been born in the likeness of man has fallen short of God's glory. To have the glory of God is to be born in His likeness (i.e. to have the character of God)' but we see that after Adam and Eve sinned; all children born after them are now being born in the likeness [character] of [sinful] man and no more in the glory of a Holy God. This explains why all of humanity needs a Saviour or to be born again, not according to the flesh but according to the Spirit.

With that in mind, let us consider the Law / commands God gave to His people so that we will know when sin has been committed.

GOD'S HOLY LAW - Matters that truly matter!

3

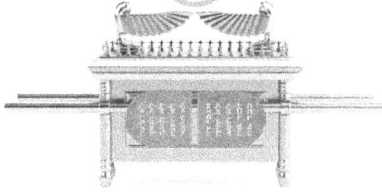

THE OLD COVENANT

Now therefore, if you will indeed obey My voice and keep My covenant, then you shall be a special treasure to Me above all people; for all the earth is Mine"
— **Exo 19:5 NKJV**

We know the story of how God promised Abraham that through his offspring, He [God] will establish a nation for Himself and He will be their God. The sign of that covenant was "circumcision" - God expressed to Abraham that any male child not circumcised will be cut off from his people because the covenant has been breached or broken **(Gen 17:14).** This ceremonial law of circumcision separated Jews from Gentiles. The Jews even made fun of the Gentiles as "uncircumcised" and therefore unclean.

Circumcision became a wall of separation between Jews and Gentiles and we see in **Eph 2:14-15** that Jesus Christ's death, brought down the wall of separation and made the two groups one. This happened because under the new covenant, Israel, the people of God are no longer those that are circumcised physically, but all those who by faith have received Jesus Christ and have therefore passed from death to life. There is therefore no Jew nor Gentile [**Romans 10:12-13; Rom 2:28-29; Gal 3:28-29**]

A pact or a covenant is an agreement between two parties - it specifies what each party is to do under the agreement and also what breaches the covenant. So we see clearly from the agreement between Abraham and God that; as long as Abraham acted satisfactorily; God would also ensure that He establishes him and fulfills His part of the agreement.

Similar to God's covenant with Abraham, God made a covenant with the house of Israel after He delivered them from Pharaoh and the Egyptians - At Mount Sinai, Moses received the ten commandments which were hand written by God Himself - *"And when He had made an end of speaking with him on Mount Sinai, He gave Moses two tablets of the Testimony, tablets of stone, written with the finger of God"* — **Exodus 31:18.** These were the set of commands that were to govern the people of Israel. And as long as the people followed God's commands, He will ensure that they possess the land and He be their God who provides and protects them.

It is also interesting to note how God instructs Moses to ensure that the tabernacle to be constructed was to be the exact pattern that he is shown - *"....who serve the copy and shadow of the heavenly things, as Moses was divinely instructed when he was about to make the tabernacle. For He said, "See that you make all things according* *to the pattern shown you on the mountain." — **Heb 8:5**.* I believe by this, God was showing Moses that He wants things on earth to be done in the very same way as is being done in Heaven. Also look at how Jesus teaches His disciples to pray when they ask Him - **Luke 11:1-4** — *"....May your will be done on earth as it is in Heaven".* Could this be just mere coincidence or was it to tell us that God is the same throughout time and that His Law being one both in Heaven and on Earth will not change for all time? Let's think about it carefully as we read on.

With the establishment of these commands, one could then easily know when sin had been committed - without the Law being established, there was not going to be anything like sin. So what was God's expectation of His people under this covenant and how did He want them to live?

God gave several commands to Moses to guide His people as well as made provisions for how the people could atone for their transgressions. It is important to note the difference between the moral Law which was to govern the people and the ceremonial laws that were mainly ordinances to guide them and as well make [temporary] atonement/restitution for breaches in the moral Law; until the time of the ultimate sacrifice of Jesus. These ceremonial laws are referred to as tutor/guardian in Paul's book to the Galatians.

> *"But before faith came, we were kept under guard by the law, kept for the faith which would afterward be revealed. 24 Therefore the law was our tutor to bring us to Christ, that we might be justified by faith"*
> *— **Gal 3:19-25***

So the question is, what is the moral Law which God gave to His people?

4

WHAT THE TEN COMMANDMENTS ARE

*What should we say, then? Is the Law sinful? Of course not!
In fact, I wouldn't have become aware of sin if it had not
been for the Law. I wouldn't have known what it means to
covet if the Law had not said, "You must not cove"*
— **Rom 7:7 ISV**

Though God had promised Abraham that He would make him into a nation, it was not until centuries later that the fulfilment of the promise came to pass. It was during the time of Jacob that he and his children entered the land of Goshen in Egypt and several years after; God brought them out of Egypt through the leadership of Moses.

When the Israelites got to Mount Sinai, God made a covenant with them and the Law governing that covenant is what is called the Decalogue or the Ten Commandments.

This Law can be found in Exodus 20:1-17 & Moses repeated in Deut 5:6-21

And God spoke all these words, saying,
² I am the LORD thy God,
which have brought thee out of the land of Egypt, out of the house of bondage.
³ **Thou shalt have no other gods before me.**
⁴ **Thou shalt not make unto thee any graven image,**
or any likeness of any thing that is in heaven above, or that is in the earth beneath, or that is in the water under the earth: ⁵ Thou shalt not bow down thyself to them, nor serve them: for I the LORD thy God am a jealous God, visiting the iniquity of the fathers upon the children unto the third and fourth generation of them that hate me; ⁶ And shewing mercy unto thousands of them that love me, and keep my commandments.
⁷ **Thou shalt not take the name of the LORD thy God in vain;**
for the LORD will not hold him guiltless that taketh his name in vain.
⁸ **Remember the Sabbath day, to keep it holy.**
⁹ Six days shalt thou labour, and do all thy work: ¹⁰ But the seventh day is the sabbath of the LORD thy God: in it thou shalt not do any work, thou, nor thy son, nor thy daughter, thy manservant, nor thy maidservant, nor thy cattle, nor thy stranger that is within thy gates: ¹¹ For in six days the LORD made heaven and earth, the sea, and all that in them is, and rested the seventh day: wherefore the LORD blessed the sabbath day, and hallowed it.

*¹² **Honour thy father and thy mother:*** *that thy days may be long upon the land which the LORD thy God giveth thee.*
*¹³ **Thou shalt not kill.***
*¹⁴ **Thou shalt not commit adultery.***
*¹⁵ **Thou shalt not steal.***
*¹⁶ **Thou shalt not bear false witness against thy neighbour.***
*¹⁷ **Thou shalt not covet thy neighbour's house, thou shalt not covet thy neighbour's wife, nor his manservant, nor his maidservant, nor his ox, nor his ass, nor any thing that is thy neighbour's"***
*— **Exodus 20:1-17***

God was very specific in the giving of these commands as those which will govern His people.

> *"The Lord said to Moses, "Come up to me on the mountain and stay here, and I will give you the tablets of stone with the law and commandments I have written for their instruction"*
> *— **Exo 24:12** [emphasis mine].*

Again, God's desire was for the good of the people at all times and so after giving them the Decalogue, He said:

> *"Oh, that their hearts would be inclined to fear me and keep all my commands always, so that it might go well with them and their children forever!"*
> *— **Deut 5:29** [emphasis mine]*

So while these were not the only commandments God gave to His people, God was very careful to place emphasis on these commands like no other commands/statutes He gave to His people.

5

HOW THE TEN COMMAND- MENTS ARE DIFFERENT

These words the Lord spoke to all your assembly at the mountain out of the midst of the fire, the cloud, and the thick darkness, with a loud voice; and he added no more. And he wrote them on two tablets of stone and gave them to me

— **Deut 5:22 ESV**

While God had earlier spoken to people in the past, and also gave several laws or commands even through Moses, the ten commandments given from Mount Sinai were peculiar in many ways.

The first major point is that, there was never a time again as in the giving of the 10 commandments that God spoke directly to His people as a Nation. At all times, God chose a mediator through whom He spoke to His people but on the occasion of giving His moral law, He spoke from Heaven directly to the hearing of ALL His people:

> *"Now all the people witnessed the thunderings, the lightning flashes, the sound of the trumpet, and the mountain smoking; and when the people saw it, they trembled and stood afar off. 19 Then they said to Moses, "You speak with us, and we will hear; but let not God speak with us, lest we die." 20 And Moses said to the people, "Do not fear; for God has come to test you, and that His fear may be before you, so that you may not sin." 21 So the people stood afar off, but Moses drew near the thick darkness where God was. 22 Then the Lord said to Moses, "Thus you shall say to the children of Israel: 'You have seen that I have talked with you from heaven"*
> — ***Exo 20:18-22*** [emphasis mine]

Secondly, God said that His covenant with the house of Israel was based on just the ten commandments - no more was added to them.

> *"And the Lord said to Moses, "Write down these laws that I have given you, for they represent the terms of my covenant with you and with Israel." — **Exo 34:27 TLB***

The list below are a few ways that the Ten Commandments are different from the over 600 commands that is said to have been recorded in Moses book of the law:

a. God spoke the 10 commandments directly to the entire Israelite community Himself and not through Moses -

there is no other command(s) that God gave that wasn't through a mediator - **Exo 20:1; Exo 20: 18-22**

b. Although God gave Moses other commands, His covenant with Moses and Israel was based on none other but the Ten commandments alone - **Exo 34:27.**

c. Moses and the elders of Israel were aware that these commands were being written and given by God Himself for His people **(Exodus 24:9-12)**

d. God was very specific about where He wanted the Law - the tablets of the Testimony were to be put in the Ark under the Mercy seat **(Exo 25:16 & Exo 25:21)** from where God will speak to them. This tells us that the Decalogue was the foundational Law of His ruling, based on these commands, He would either acquit or convict someone.

e. God did not entrust the writing of the 10 commandments to any human - God wrote this set of commands Himself **(Exo 31:18; Exo 32:15-16)**. He wrote them on tablets of stones. Do you realize what humans mean when they say something is written in stone? They mean it is permanent, it can't be undone!

f. When Moses broke the first tablets (at the time when he observed that the Israelites were worshipping the golden Calf - **Exodus 32:19)**; God wrote another set of the Law for them - **[Exo 34:27-28]** indicating how important these particular commands meant to Him and how important it was for His people not to forget these particular commands. Again, notice that there were some commands that God had Moses write down but God wrote these ten commandments Himself (even the second time). He could simply have asked Moses to write them

HOW THE TEN COMMANDMENTS ARE DIFFERENT

but He chose rather to write them all over again Himself.

g. It is interesting to note that these 10 commandments were to be kept in the Ark, in the Sanctuary - **a pattern of which God gave Moses to build on earth (Exo 25:8-9** also **Exo 25:40).** The instructions to build the sanctuary and everything that had to do with it have been recorded in 7 chapters **[Exodus 25 - 31].** To think that God went through the trouble of describing the very fine details of how the earthly sanctuary should be built **(according to the Heavenly Sanctuary - Heb 8:5-6)** also tells us how important and everlasting the ten commandments were.

h. The ten commandments were the set of commands Jesus endorsed or proclaimed that New Testament believers would have eternal life if they lived by them - **Matthew 19:16-22**

i. The Jews recognized the ten commandments as the Law of God - **Matthew 22:36-40**

j. Jesus said that those who obey the ten commandments will have the right to the tree of life in the new Jerusalem - **Rev 22:14**

k. The Ark God gave Moses specifications to build here on earth is just a replica of what is in Heaven, showing the ten commandments are also the commandments used in Heaven - **Rev 11:19**

l. The ten Commandments are forever settled in Heaven - **Psalm 119:89, Psalm 119:151-152**

m. Humanity will be judged by the ten commandments - **James 2:10-12**

n. Unlike the ceremonial laws which required ordinances/ rituals for which the Priests were needed, the moral laws

GOD'S HOLY LAW - Matters that truly matter!

(10 commandments) on the other hand did not have any rituals/ordinances.

It is quite instructive to note that there were several other laws and commands that God gave to Moses; but these other laws, unlike the Decalogue, were recorded and written down by Moses himself.

And Moses wrote all the words of the Lord....[7] Then he took the Book of the Covenant and read in the hearing of the people. And they said, "All that the Lord has said we will do, and be obedient."
— Exo 24:3-7.

"So it was, when Moses had completed writing the words of this law in a book, when they were finished, 25 that Moses commanded the Levites, who bore the ark of the covenant of the Lord, saying: 26 "Take this Book of the Law, and put it beside the ark of the covenant of the Lord your God, that it may be there as a witness against you"
— Deut 31:24-26

Notice also that these other laws/statutes that Moses captured were not placed in the Ark as God had instructed him to do with the tablets, rather, these were put beside the Ark - very big difference.

There is another big lesson for us when we look at the words following the giving of the Ten Commandments as captured in the book of Deuteronomy:

"These words the Lord spoke to all your assembly, in the mountain from the midst of the fire, the cloud, and the

thick darkness, with a loud voice; and He added no more. And He wrote them on two tablets of stone and gave them to me" — **Deut 5:22** [emphasis mine]

Although Moses said in the above scripture that God added no more to the Ten Commandments - we see just a few verses under that God had him wait to be given other commandments and statutes.

"Go and say to them, "Return to your tents." 31 But as for you, stand here by Me, and I will speak to you all the commandments, the statutes, and the judgments which you shall teach them, that they may observe them in the land which I am giving them to possess.'
— **Deut 5:30-31.**

All the above show that God made a very BIG distinction between the Ten Commandments and all other commandments and statutes He gave to His people. The Ten commandments being placed in the Ark of the Covenant which also was itself a copy of the one in Heaven was to show us that it is the very foundation of God's rulership, and thus was permanent and beyond just our stay here on earth.

To that end, though sin was committed when any of God's commands/statutes were broken, the Ten Commandments became the **primary Law** by which God's people for all time and throughout eternity are to live by.

If God had it recorded to show us such a big distinction He made with the ten commands - do you suppose ALL must pay particular attention to it too?

6

REQUIREMENTS OF
THE LAW

> *It came about, when Moses finished writing the words of this law in a book until they were complete, 25 that Moses commanded the Levites who carried the ark of the covenant of the Lord, saying, 26 "Take this book of the law and place it beside the ark of the covenant of the Lord your God, that it may remain there as a witness against you*
> — **Deut 31:24-26 NASB**

After having the Law and therefore knowing when a breach had occurred, the next thing was for the people to know how they could cure a breach - in other words, what was expected of anyone who broke the Law [or any part thereof]? As you will see, other laws were instituted to cleanse the people from their sins - these are the ceremonial laws that required ordinances/rituals - these laws were to be a shadow and were soon going to cease or be abolished after Christ' ultimate sacrifice on the cross - **Rom 10:4; Gal 3:24; Col 2:17; Heb 10:1.**

In **Leviticus 17:11** - God clearly tells us that it is through blood that our sins (breach in or of the Law) can be atoned. This thought is re-echoed in **Hebrews 9:22** where we learn that until blood is shed, forgiveness for sin can not happen. In other words, you had to kill an animal and it's blood sprinkled on the altar so that a person's sin (conscious or unconscious) can be forgiven. This helps us understand why sheep/goats/oxen/bulls/doves etc were sacrificed - these animals without defect needed to be substituted (killed in place of the sinner) for God to forgive the sin that had been committed or the Law that had been broken. God instituted very strict laws and it covered almost everything that was thought to be a breach of the Law. So the Law required that every transgression of a command must be atoned by sacrificing an animal and shedding it's life/blood. In other words, the requirement of the Law was death.

These requirements also meant that there had to be a mediator who would receive the sacrifice, offer it on behalf of the sinner. The sin having been transferred (imputed) to the animal, the animal had to die to satisfy or appease God.

So with the old covenant, we had these four elements: (1) LawGiver **[God]** who is Holy, then we have the standards or the (2) **Law** itself that was to govern the relationship between God and man; then we have (3) **Man** himself who needed to be reconciled to God; and then lastly the mediator between God and man which role was played by the (4) **Priests**. One of the problems this arrangement brought up was with this mediator/priest. The priest himself was a mortal man who was full of weaknesses and sins. He himself had to offer sacrifices for his own sins and get himself cleansed before he could offer sacrifices on others' behalf.

A key role that a priest needed to play was also to be a surety - this meant that he needed to stand in place of the sinner especially in representing him on the day of atonement. Can you imagine the responsibility that being a priest carried? And worse off, the priest being a mortal person, death wouldn't even allow him to continue in his role and thus be trusted by at least one side of the party to the covenant - God couldn't trust the priests' ability to perform such acts satisfactorily. These were weaknesses and imperfections in the entire system that impeded or worked against the achievement of the requirements of the Law in the manner that God required. The requirement of the Law was thus against us, we couldn't ever be in a good position to meet all the requirements all the time and once the requirements are not met, God is not appeased and the relationship between God and man would not be restored to where it needs to be.

So whichever way you look at it, there were imperfections in the system - but these were not as a result of God and neither was it the Law - **Heb 7:11**. There were four elements in the entire system as we have seen [God, Law, Priest and Man] and we know that God is Holy and the Law is also Holy **[Rom 7:12-14]**, it is clear then that the problem with the system was the weakness of man, the sinner but even more the mediator/priest - **Hebrews 8:7-8.**

> *"Now there have been many of those priests, since death prevented them from continuing in office; 24 but because*

Jesus lives forever, he has a permanent priesthood. 25 Therefore he is able to save completely[c] those who come to God through him, because he always lives to intercede for them. 26 Such a high priest truly meets our need—one who is holy, blameless, pure, set apart from sinners, exalted above the heavens. 27 Unlike the other high priests, he does not need to offer sacrifices day after day, first for his own sins, and then for the sins of the people. He sacrificed for their sins once for all when he offered himself. 28 For the law appoints as high priests men in all their weakness; but the oath, which came after the law, appointed the Son, who has been made perfect forever" — **Heb 7:23-28**

In Paul's letter to the Romans, he carefully helps to bring all of these together: *"For God has done what the law, **weakened by the flesh,** could not do. By sending his own Son in the likeness of sinful flesh and for sin, he condemned sin in the flesh, **in order that the righteous requirement of the law** might be fulfilled in us, who walk not according to the flesh but according to the Spirit."* — **Romans 8:3-4.** The verse first establishes where the law was weak and mentions that it was the flesh, in other words, it was the man (priest). He then moves to explain how Jesus has paid the **requirements of the law**.

Notice that he even says that what the law requires is righteous; in other words - God is just to demand that the sinner dies or blood be shed to atone for trespassing the Law. Jesus lived a righteous life but on the cross when he bore the sins of the world (our sins imputed on him); God had to forsake Him as His Son and allow the penalty (righteous requirement of the Law) that results out of sin to be put in effect.

There is a BIGGER lesson here for anyone who takes the mercy of God for granted, but we can come to that another time. **Hebrews 10:26-31** speaks to this. Many just look at God as Merciful father and so will not punish their sins. Such people do not need to look far but look at Jesus on the cross and observe also the Justice of God. If God did not spare Jesus His only begotten Son, do you think you will be spared when you blatantly disregard the commands of God? The same God of mercy is the same God of Justice and He does not play favoritism. If He found Jesus to be deserving of death, then be sure that He won't relent when you transgress any of His Law/commands.

For a further study on the requirements of the Law, I strongly suggest that you study the book of Leviticus regarding the Sanctuary service.

GOD'S HOLY LAW - Matters that truly matter!

7

GOD'S COMMUNICATION STYLE Vs THE WORLD'S

> *"If anyone speaks, they should do so as one who speaks the very words of God......"*
> — **Pet 4:11 NIV**

I just had an aha moment while chatting with my brother Chief. He was advising me to keep short a message I had written and also rather than writing it in a book format, consider podcasts and other audible media which make it easy to reach a mass number of contemporary people. Friend, understand that I believe in brevity but his short advice gave me so much insight into our times. You see, not that being brief is bad or being long is any better - but when that becomes the goal; you can easily miss the point of a message.

On the surface, his advice is very good [that's how business people think]; the advice focuses on the need/want of the consumer much more than the need of the supplier/author. Emphasis is placed on the one who is going to receive the message; and it is the clients bidding that must be done. That's what I learnt in business too. But when it comes to God - that is not the criteria He uses to communicate. In the bible, we learn that the Prophets who wrote scriptures followed along as the Holy Spirit led them -

> *"knowing this first, that no prophecy of Scripture is of any private interpretation, 21 for prophecy never came by the will of man, but holy men of God spoke as they were moved by the Holy Spirit"* — **2 Pet 1:20-21.**

We also see that on the day of Pentecost, the disciples didn't say what they wanted to say but what the Holy Spirit led them to say - **Acts 2:4**

When you analyse the scriptures, you see that the sequence the author [Holy Spirit] used can be categorised into two sets. The first set of three are:

1. The purpose [WHY]
2. The message [WHAT]
3. The target audience [WHO]

After these key priorities - those that are the core essentials, then comes the next set of three which are:

1. The media [WHERE]
2. The format [HOW], and last but not least,
3. The timing [WHEN].

This latter sequence may change because it is not the core.

So when you put them all together, the sequence flows something like this:

WHY → WHAT → WHO → WHERE → HOW → WHEN.

Let's test this by looking at a few examples in scripture:

The Great Commission:

> *"Then Jesus came to them and said, "[WHY] All authority in heaven and on earth has been given to me. [19] [WHAT] Therefore go and make [WHO] disciples of all nations, [HOW] baptizing them in the name of the Father and of the Son and of the Holy Spirit, [20] and teaching them to obey everything I have commanded you. And surely I am with you always, to the very end of the age."*
> *— Matt 28:18-20*

The Decalogue:

"2 [WHY] I am the Lord your God, who brought you out of Egypt, out of the land of slavery. 3 [WHAT] "You shall have no other gods before me....."— *Exo 20:1-17.* Please take time to read up to vrs 17 for the entire 10 commandments, to further identify all the parts.

What we see in both texts is that it all begins with God having all authority - The Purpose is established as HE being the one in charge, the one who has all authority. It is because of this [WHY] that we must listen to [WHAT] He has to say.

In the world however, the customer is king so the focus is never on the author/supplier - "He who pays the piper calls the tune". Does that sound familiar in your industry?

So the sequence in communicating in the business world is completely different from how God communicates. The sequence in the world often looks like this:

WHEN → WHO →WHERE →HOW →WHAT → WHY

Let's use an example so you see how this sequence is captured in a practical way:

"Because of the current COVID-19 pandemic [WHEN], majority of the people [WHO] are working from Home [WHERE], so we have to increase our advertisements via Social Media [HOW] so we can sell a lot of our masks [WHAT] which are sitting in our factory [WHY]".

As we have seen, God doesn't communicate the same way the world does - *"For my thoughts are not your thoughts, neither are your ways my ways," declares the Lord. 9 "As the heavens are higher than the earth, so are my ways higher than your ways and my thoughts than your thoughts"* — **Isa 55:8-9**. In God's communication, HE alone is KING and the emphasis is on Him. God communicates with authority and it is the same way with those who bring God's message - *"Now when they saw the boldness of Peter and John, and perceived that they were uneducated and untrained men, they marveled. And they realized that they had been with Jesus"* — **Acts 4:13**. Again see; *"And they were astonished at His teaching, for He taught them as one having authority, and not as the scribes"* — **Mark 1:22**

Sadly, because of the influence from the world, many approach God and the Bible in a very wrong way; in just the same way the world communicates. For example, they come first looking for which translation is easy to read.

"Considering how busy I am [WHO], which is the quickest way [HOW] I can get on with this bible study [WHAT] so I can move on to other important things, Which of the translations is easy and current?"

When you look critically, even the way they ask puts them as the primary focus - as "King" and unfortunately the purpose [WHY] and the message [WHAT] is considered last, only as an afterthought. In bringing this same approach used in the world, people end up looking for watered-down translations of the bible which may not render the message the author intended, accurately. In doing a bible study, our key priority should be to ask; "Which translation best renders the author's intended message"?

We need to remember that Publishing is a business - and the bottom-line for businesses including [some] who publish the Bible is to make profit. So they do their market research to understand what the market wants and then publish to meet the demand - it is purely business. They may have identified that today's contemporary reader is not looking for the details but just a quick skim through and so [some] contemporary bibles focus on how easy and nice the text is rendered. Look at how the Bible warns us of this: *"For the time will come when they will not endure sound doctrine, but according to their own desires, because they have itching ears, they will heap up for themselves teachers; 4 and they will turn their ears away from the truth, and be turned aside to fables"* — **2 Tim 4:3-5.**

In the next chapter, we will look at examples of how some bible verses have been translated and the harm this has caused in Christianity - how the devil is leading many astray as a result.

Sadly, some Churches are no different in their ways from businesses - rather than render truthfully God's message, they have conformed to the world's way and their messages and style of communications are to appease the customer - not the KING of all kings. Paul warned the Romans - *"And do not be conformed to this world, but be transformed by the renewing of your mind, that you may prove what is that good and acceptable and perfect will of God"* — ***Rom 12:2-3.*** Today, [most] Churches plan their services around what the pastor wants to say; what the congregations want to hear; how much time people are willing to stay; the kind of entertainment that will draw people; and even what sort of ambience, lights and decor people want. So in most Churches, no longer is God King, but the pastor and the person who attends Church is who is VIP.

What do you look for in a Church or ministry to attend? Do you look for a Church that makes it easy and convenient for you to attend; the kind that has the building and decor you like [the packaging], the one that accepts you the way you are and won't challenge you; the Church that has all the sound equipment and the best entertainment? Are you in the Church because that's where you are likely to meet some suitors or rub shoulders with the Joneses? Are you in the Church because it connects you to the movers and shakers of the country? Are you in your current Church because the "Prophet/man of God" is telling you lies that you believe are true? Do you look for the Church and messages that say what your itching ears want to hear?

Or is your goal for Church to look for one that presents the Timeless Truth of God? Please hear the words of Solomon - "[1] *Guard your steps when you go to the house of God. Go near to listen rather than to offer the sacrifice of fools, who do not know that they do wrong.....² God is in Heaven, you are on Earth........⁷ Therefore Fear God" — Eccl 5:1-7* [Emphasis mine].

Back to my conversation with my brother - I thanked him for his advice and said to him "I am not looking for readers but seekers". Let me tell you the difference - Seekers will read to find out why God is saying what He is saying and dig deep for the gems hidden in the message for them. Readers [like Church-goers] on the other hand don't necessarily seek for the why and what of the message. Instead, they look at it to see how short the material/message is; how much time reading it will take; will it entertain; is the cover attractive; is the message the type and kind that speaks to my world view and bias; does the speaker say it the way I like; where is this speaker/author from and what's his/her background etc.. etc..?

My brother, my sister, please don't approach God's word and Church that way. Learn from this scripture that says, *"There is a way that seems right to a man, but it's end is the way of death" — Prov 14:12.*

If you are up for a little challenge, let me give you an assignment with the text below so you can identify the parts of this communication and to help you deepen your conviction on God's style of communication:

> *"Many people did believe in him, however, including some of the Jewish leaders. But they wouldn't admit it for fear that the Pharisees would expel them from the synagogue. 43 For they loved human praise more than the praise of God. 44 Jesus shouted to the crowds, "If you trust me, you*

*are trusting not only me, but also God who sent me . 45 For when you see me, you are seeing the one who sent me. 46 I have come as a light to shine in this dark world, so that all who put their trust in me will no longer remain in the dark. 47 I will not judge those who hear me but don't obey me, for I have come to save the world and not to judge it. 48 But all who reject me and my message will be judged on the day of judgment by the truth I have spoken. 49 I don't speak on my own authority. The Father who sent me has commanded me what to say and how to say it. 50 And I know his commands lead to eternal life; so I say whatever the Father tells me to say." — **John 12:42-50.***

8

MIS-INTERPRETATION OF SOME SCRIPTURES

Paul writes about this in all his letters. Sometimes there are things in Paul's letters that are hard to understand. And some people explain these things falsely. They are ignorant and weak in faith. They also falsely explain the other Scriptures. But they are destroying themselves by doing that
— ***2 Pet 3:16 ICB***

I t is worth mentioning that even in Paul's days, there were slanderous reports being made about him. Some of these reports purported that; Paul was preaching that the Law had been abolished - see **Romans 3:8** and **Acts 21:20-25**. This was all because [and as Peter puts it], unstable people were twisting what Paul was saying because some of the things he said were hard for them to understand - **2 Pet 3:15-16.** Knowing this, it should therefore not be surprising to us that 2000 years later, there would be more people even more confused about Paul's teaching on the Law.

In the next 12 to 24 months after a vaccine has [hopefully] been found for the **COVID-19** pandemic [that hit the world late 2019] and applied to most people on planet earth; we will begin to take off our facial masks. I believe the likely answer that people would give to the question: "What have you done with your masks" will be - "I shred it up"; "l flushed it down my toilet"; "l tossed it in my garbage bin" and others like such. Now, please understand that it would not mean they have done this literally nor would it mean that what necessitated our need to wear the masks in the first place is no longer there, it could only mean that the world has found a better way to protect ourselves from the **Coronavirus** infection. This will never mean that COVID-19 has been flushed down the toilet or tossed into the garbage bin; but rather **the requirements of COVID-19** (wearing of facial masks, need for social distancing etc) is what we would have done away with.

With that in mind, let's look at some scriptures that l believe are mis-interpreted.

COLOSSIANS

The text in **Col 2:14** reads:

NIV

having canceled the charge of our legal indebtedness, which stood against us and condemned us; he has taken it away, nailing it to the cross.

NKJV

having wiped out the handwriting of requirements that was against us, which was contrary to us. And He has taken it out of the way, having nailed it to the cross.

NLV

We had broken the Law many ways. Those sins were held against us by the Law. That Law had writings which said we were sinners. But now He has destroyed that writing by nailing it to the cross.

NLT

He canceled the record of the charges against us and took it away by nailing it to the cross.

HCSB

He erased the certificate of debt, with its obligations, that was against us and opposed to us, and has taken it out of the way by nailing it to the cross.

Unfortunately, many Christians quote **Colossians 2:14** to say that Jesus nailed the Law to the cross. But with the COVID-19 example above; I want us to read the context so we can understand what Paul is saying. The text says that it is the "requirement of the law" or the demands/obligations of the law that has been nailed to the cross - this is not the same as saying the Law has been nailed to the cross. It is that which the Law required of us (to make atonement, to sacrifice an animal, to shed blood) which has been taken and nailed to the cross. This also explains why it is recorded in **Matthew 27:51** that on the cross when Jesus died, the veil in the temple was torn into two signifying an end to the animal sacrifices for our atonement. So there is no scripture that even remotely suggests or supports the idea that the Law was nailed to the cross. **God still very much expects us to obey his Law.** *"Circumcision is nothing and uncircumcision is nothing, but keeping the commandments of God is what matters." — 1 Cor 7:19*

Further, they also cite **Col 2:16 & 17** to claim that we are no longer supposed to observe the Sabbath command. Such way of taking scripture out of context is very harmful. First, we need to examine the context and see how Paul's immediate audience understood what he was saying before we apply it to ourselves. A careful study of the passage helps us to see the issue at hand - in **vrs 8** as well as in **vrs 20-22**; we see that the people trying to lure these disciples in Colosse were not the Judaizers as in the case of the Galatian Gentile disciples.

Paul mentions that their message is based on Philosophy and Legalism and are commandments of men. These people have an ascetic doctrine or practice. In **vrs 16**, we see that these people most likely are telling the disciples to abstain from food/drinks that are served at some festivals including Sabbaths. Paul is telling the disciples to not let this group of people cheat them from what they could freely enjoy and which would have no effect on their spirituality - it was a reward they could benefit from and was harmless to their faith.

There is nothing in that passage that slightly or remotely suggests that Paul is telling the disciples to abstain from Sabbath observance. Unless of course you read this scripture in one of the more contemporary translations such as say: NLT, TLB, CEV, AMP, EXB etc which [in my humble opinion] inaccurately translates this scripture from its original Greek context. You may want to compare how the different bible versions translate **Col 2:16** here. It is just unfortunate that many may read these translations and therefore draw the wrong conclusions.

NOTE: A good advice as you study the bible: Always make it a practice to use/read/check different translations - some translations render the scriptures more accurately than others and gives you an undiluted rendering of what the author [Holy Spirit] said. Some translations focus rather on the contemporary reader's understanding and not necessarily what the author is saying. Watch out for such translations.

As an example, see below how Col 2:16 is captured in different Bible translations:

NIV

Therefore do not let anyone judge you by what you eat or drink, or with regard to a religious festival, a New Moon celebration or a Sabbath day.

NKJV

So let no one judge you in food or in drink, or regarding a festival or a new moon or sabbaths,

NLV

Do not let anyone tell you what you should or should not eat or drink. They have no right to say if it is right or wrong to eat certain foods or if you are to go to religious suppers. They have no right to say what you are to do at the time of the new moon or on the Day of Rest.

NLT

So don't let anyone condemn you for what you eat or drink, or for not celebrating certain holy days or new moon ceremonies or Sabbaths.

TLB

So don't let anyone criticize you for what you eat or drink, or for not celebrating Jewish holidays and feasts or new moon ceremonies or Sabbaths.

CEV

Don't let anyone tell you what you must eat or drink. Don't let them say that you must celebrate the New Moon festival, the Sabbath, or any other festival.

EXB

So do not let anyone •make rules for [or criticize; judge; or condemn] you about eating and drinking or about a religious •feast [festival], a New Moon Festival [2 Kin. 4:23; Neh. 10:33], or a Sabbath day [religious observances that false teachers pressured the Colossians to keep].

AMP

Therefore let no one judge you in regard to food and drink or in regard to [the observance of] a festival or a new moon or a Sabbath day.

If you took time in checking out how this verse is rendered in the different translations above, you may have noticed that for instance the NLT, TLB, CEV, EXB and AMP translations directly make it seem that Paul is saying it is wrong to observe such festivals. However, the NKJV, NLV and NIV do not convey that meaning at all.

In reading scripture, it is important that we choose a translation that tells us what the author intended for us to know and not one that translates scripture into what a contemporary reader wants to hear. Unfortunately, it is not only true that we will have false teachers in the last days; but I dare say that some translations are quite mis-leading in the way they render some of the scriptures, to the extent that what the Holy Spirit authored is not what they have captured. We therefore need to be careful even with the choice of bible translations we use.

There's a story that Jesus tells in **Matt 7:21-23** which is quite instructive if we would look into it. These "Christians" or "men of God" must have heard that no one is required to obey the law(s) of God any longer so they showed up at judgment believing that they had everything they needed to be allowed entry into God's Heavenly Kingdom. Jesus' answer is quite surprising especially when you look at their credentials - they prophesied, they cast out demons and were miracle workers too - plus they claim they did it all in Jesus' name.

Why should Jesus stop such people from entering God's Kingdom; if not for nothing; at least why not consider what they had done? But the text says Jesus said: "I never knew you". It is not that these guys later became corrupted; the text would have indicated that but it says; I never knew you. So how did they attain their salvation - what sort of gospel did they hear? Realize that Jesus tells them that they are lawbreakers (transgressors of the law, you who practice lawlessness - **NKJV**). These guys must have been following the preachers who were promising freedom from God's Law - **See 2 Pet 2**

Let's also look at a few more of what Paul wrote regarding this subject of the Law. Beginning with his letter to the Romans - Paul takes his time to explain the importance of the Law. In Rom 3:31 - He tells us that faith is what helps us to appreciate and then uphold the Law - and that without faith, we couldn't in any way appreciate our relationship with Jesus to the extent of obeying the Law. According to John 14:15, Jesus teaches us that the way to demonstrate our love for Him is by obeying His commands.

Further in **Rom 6:2-5** - Paul emphasizes the purpose of our baptism, that it was to remove (purge us from/forgive) our sins [breaking or transgressing the Law] so we can walk in a new life. Where would be the logic to seek for pardon from sin and then turn-around to live in sin again? Why do that? This is the same point Peter seeks to make in **2 Peter 2:18-22.** In **vrs 22**, he says: *"A dog comes back to what he has vomited, and a pig is washed only to come back and wallow in the mud again - TLB".* The end of such people are worse off than when they didn't know the truth/ God. Also look at how the Hebrew writer puts it:

> *"Dear friends, if we deliberately continue sinning after we have received knowledge of the truth, there is no longer any sacrifice that will cover these sins. [27] There is only the terrible expectation of God's judgment and the raging fire that will consume his enemies. [28] For anyone who refused to obey the law of Moses was put to death without mercy on the testimony of two or three witnesses. [29] Just think how much worse the punishment will be for those who*

have trampled on the Son of God, and have treated the blood of the covenant, which made us holy, as if it were common and unholy, and have insulted and disdained the Holy Spirit who brings God's mercy to us -
— **Heb 10:26-29**.

GALATIANS

Others also quote portions of scripture from the book of Galatians to support their stance that modern Christians are not to observe the Law and that the Law was only meant for the Jews and not Gentile Christians. Again, a critical look at the book of Galatians shows that there were some Jewish believers who were teaching that Gentiles had to become Jews in order to become followers of Jesus [Disciples]. This issue was addressed in **Acts 15** at which the elders in the Church closed the case by saying that the Gentiles need not become Jews.

Looking at his letter to the Galatians, Paul's foremost goal is to first affirm his ministry of apostleship and call to the Gentiles by Jesus; and secondly - he is defending the truth that one is justified through faith alone and apart from the Law. Some Judaizers were trying to get the Gentile converts to be circumcised before accepting them as true believers - these were the Jews who believed that one could only become a Christian by first following the Jewish covenant of circumcision. This was the main issue that Paul was dealing with because to some extent, the Judaizers had convinced the Gentile believers of the need to become Jews (by circumcision) for the sake of righteousness. Earlier though, God had allowed Peter to see a vision where He explained to Peter that the Gentiles (who the Jews thought of as unclean) had been cleansed and made ready for salvation - **Acts 10:9-15**.

One should read carefully and thoughtfully through the entire book of Galatians to understand what Paul is saying. The following portions are worth noting: **Gal 2:15-16; Gal 2:21**; It must be understood that the point Paul was stressing to these Gentile believers is that they could not attain salvation by becoming circumcised - no one could; circumcision had not of itself helped the Jews to obey the Law and thus be saved. The Jews had now gladly accepted salvation by faith alone. And if the circumcised Jews could not live by the Law to attain salvation, why would Gentiles think circumcision could help them become justified? And why would the Gentiles accept such a message when the Jews enticing them to be circumcised were themselves not justified by circumcision unto salvation?

We too should make a clear distinction between attaining salvation by means of the Law and **abiding by the Law because we have been saved**. One needs to understand this difference when it comes to the book of Galatians; if you get that twisted, you might easily mis-interpret what Paul is saying to the Gentile believers in Galatia.

But what of when Paul talks about their observance of special days, months and years in **Gal 4:8-11**; was he not referring to their keeping the Sabbath also? This idea is so far fetched to think that Paul was chastising the Galatians for keeping the Sabbath. In the first place, remember that during his first missionary journey, Paul actually visits some places in the region of Galatia and shows up at the Synagogues where Jews and Gentiles alike gather on the

Sabbath - could Paul be so hypocritical enough to tell these same people to not observe the Sabbath even after he had done so in their midst?

Also, remember that the Galatian believers were mostly Gentiles so for Paul to say they are returning to their old way of life *[9 But now that you know God—or rather are known by God— how is it that you are **turning back** to those weak and miserable forces[a]? Do you wish to be enslaved by them **all over again?**]*- the old life of these Gentiles (before they came to know God); couldn't have been observing Jewish festivals? Paul was here referring to pagan festivals that these Gentile converts were once accustomed to - see vrs 8 where he actually mentions that they were following idols [8 Formerly, when you did not know God, you were slaves to those who by nature are not gods]. Sabbath observance was not one of those festivals when they didn't know God and so Paul couldn't have been referring to the Sabbath in this scripture widely quoted to support non-adherence of the Sabbath.

Again, you only get that 'error' depending on the Bible translation you are using, let's compare a few here:

NKJV

⁸ But then, indeed, when you did not know God, you served those which by nature are not gods. ⁹ But now after you have known God, or rather are known by God, how is it that you turn again to the weak and beggarly elements, to which you desire again to be in bondage? ¹⁰ You observe days and months and seasons and years. ¹¹ I am afraid for you, lest I have labored for you in vain.

NIV

⁸ Formerly, when you did not know God, you were slaves to those who by nature are not gods. ⁹ But now that you know God—or rather are known by God—how is it that you are turning back to those weak and miserable forces[a]? Do you wish to be enslaved by them all over again? ¹⁰ You are observing special days and months and seasons and years! ¹¹ I fear for you, that somehow I have wasted my efforts on you.

TLB

⁸ Before you Gentiles knew God you were slaves to so-called gods that did not even exist. ⁹ And now that you have found God (or I should say, now that God has found you), how can it be that you want to go back again and become slaves once more to another poor, weak, useless religion of trying to get to heaven by obeying God's laws? ¹⁰ You are trying to find favor with God by what you do or don't do on certain days or months or seasons or years. ¹¹ I fear for you. I am afraid that all my hard work for you was worth nothing.

EXB

⁸ In the past you did not know God. You were slaves to gods that were not real. ⁹ But now you know the true God. Really, it is God who knows you. So •why do [how can] you turn back to those weak and •useless [bankrupt; poor] •rules [or spiritual forces; or elementary principles/powers; v. 3] you followed

before? Do you want to be slaves to those things again?
10 You still follow teachings about [are observing/
keeping] special days, months, seasons, and years
[probably Jewish Sabbaths and festivals, which Paul's
opponents claimed must be observed to be saved]. 11
I am afraid for you, that my work for you has been
wasted.

Look carefully at these translations - see how for instance the TLB and EXB have captured this piece of scripture and compare it to the other much older versions like the NKJV and even the NIV. If anyone reads from one of such contemporary translations, obviously you will be very confused as to what Paul is saying. I hope these examples will quicken your resolve to want to check different translations as you study scriptures.

Regarding circumcision which distinguishes Jews from Gentiles, Paul spends time to explain that in Christ, it was not about being Jewish (circumcision of the flesh) but rather having a circumcised heart **(Rom 2:25-29)**.

The verdict from the meeting with the elders in Jerusalem was that; all Gentiles **NEED NOT** be circumcised to become Christians. It is instructive to note that James ends this meeting by saying that the law of Moses is taught in the synagogues every Sabbath - **Acts 15:19-21**. [Hold on to this thought, we will come back to it shortly to emphasise a point]

We also know that Jesus prayed for unity among all his disciples - the one mark He said the world will observe and come to faith is when they saw the unity, that the dividing wall of hostility had been taken away and that all Christians irrespective of their race, gender and or status were one in Christ - **Gal 3:28-29 [John 17:20-23]**.

Do you imagine then; that in the early Church that had both Jewish and Gentile Disciples, the Gentile Christians had separate meetings from the Jewish Christians? Well, the verdict is that scripture rather supports that these two groups were together in the synagogues on the Sabbaths **(Acts 13:42; 44-48; Acts 17:1-4)**. The Apostles and deacons in the first century Church were all Jewish people as well as the Synagogue rulers; they were the ones who knew enough to start and lead the Church(es).

It will be absurd to think that the Apostles after all that they had heard directly from Jesus, and the vision of Peter before Cornelius' conversion and the success of Paul and Barnabas' ministry to the Gentiles, would have sought or encouraged a division among the two groups of believers contrary to Jesus' teaching/prayer on unity. Paul particularly lashes out at the Corinthians on this matter in **1 Cor 1** and **1 Cor 3**. If division was going to be allowed on the basis of race, the idea of separate meetings would have come up at that time. Paul further goes on in **1 Cor 12** to describe how the entire body of Christ (the Church) which includes Jews, Gentiles, slaves and those who are free all together make up the one body connected to each other.

So back to my point on why James will end his talk by saying that the law of Moses was being preached in all synagogues on the Sabbath. I hold the view that James believed that all that could not be said or was not said in this meeting regarding the new life for the Gentile believers will be made known to them once they attend the Sabbath convocations. Remember that in their days, there were no printed Bibles as we have now, they only had the books of Moses and the writings of the Prophets on scrolls which many did not have personal copies of at the time. It was only at their meetings usually on the Sabbath that these readings were heard. Having been converted, the Gentile converts were also going to be part of the Sabbath convocations to enable them hear/learn all that they needed to about the Way. Otherwise, how do you suppose the Gentile converts were taught concerning the way?

WHAT OF ROM 14:1-6?

Another passage that is quoted to support the argument that Sabbath was no longer observed by the early Church is **Romans 14:1-6** especially vrs 5. The scripture states:

> *"One person esteems one day above another; another esteems every day alike. Let each be fully convinced in his own mind"* — **Rom 14:5**

It is instructive to know that Paul nowhere in the entire chapter brings up Sabbath per se but many seem to say that is the only day he could have been referring to.

Here is why I believe Paul would not have made that argument. A study of the passage shows us that Paul was referring to matters that are disputable - if he discussed the Sabbath, then he would have put the Sabbath into the category of disputable things. If that's how Paul felt about the Sabbath, it would have been clear from various other scriptures but we don't find that; rather we see that it was his custom to observe the Sabbath - **Acts 17:2**. Paul also tells the disciples in Corinth to imitate him as he imitates

Christ - **1 Cor 11:1**. We see clearly that it was the custom of Jesus to observe the Sabbath - **Luke 4:16**. And we are certain that anyone who follows Christ will never be lost because of this, He said: *"I am the way, the truth, and the life. No one comes to the Father except through Me"* — **John 14:6**.

It is very improbable from the following that Paul would say elsewhere that the Sabbath is a disputable matter. Was he asking these Gentile disciples [and every other disciple for that matter] to follow him and Christ except in the area of Sabbath observance?

Further, there is no doubt that the 7th day is a day that God set apart right from creation. God didn't make all days equal at creation; He deliberately set the 7th day apart [made it Holy] and blessed it - **Gen 2:1-3**. We know that God's blessings are without repentance, that is, when God blesses; it remains forever - **2 Sam 7:29** and **1 Chron 17:27**. Also, God's calling is irrevocable - **Rom 11:29**.

Finally, let's see what the Psalmist says about when God speaks so we can tie all of this together. *"My covenant I will not break, Nor alter the word that has gone out of My lips"* - **Ps 89:34**. So we can be very certain that God blessing the Sabbath day and making it Holy can never change until the end of time - it will be so forever notwithstanding what man says or does.

In discussing this scripture therefore, it is very important we begin with that background because this is what Paul and the Apostles also knew about God and also about the Sabbath. When you look at **Rom 14:5** with this lens/background - you can be very sure it was not the Sabbath day that Paul was referring to in this passage.

In conclusion; Paul at no point hid his identity as a Jew - he grew up in Jewish tradition and observed the traditions when he could and whatever his tradition required of him, that he did - **Philippians 3:4-9**. His philosophy however was to become all things to all men so that he might win some (**1 Cor 9:19-23**). There was no one who understood grace as Paul did (**1 Tim 1:12-17**), he felt undeserving of what God had done for him because of his past way of life (persecuting the Church) - this made him appreciate God even more and work tirelessly to ensure that many would come to the saving grace of our Lord Jesus. Paul was not a hypocrite either and could not have been living a double life - telling the Gentiles to break the Law of God when he was upholding the Law. It is important for one to check all of Paul's writings to see the consistency and not just mis-interpret a few to suit whatever you are leaning towards.

Equally important is to re-emphasize that the problem that God found with the first covenant was not that the Law was bad - but He found fault with humanity - read **Hebrews 8:7-13**. Particularly in **vrs 8a**, God mentions the problem that the first covenant had - *"But God found fault with the people and said…. NIV"* The fault with the first covenant was with the people. Again see vrs 9b: *"because they did not remain faithful to my covenant, and I turned away from them, declares the Lord."* It needs to be very clear that God never found fault with His Law and neither did the Apostles; therefore it presupposes that if anything needed to change in the new covenant, the change would also have to help the people to obey - not that the commands were going to be different, but how God could make it possible for the people to obey. Thus, God introduces Grace. Let us therefore understand what Grace is and what it does under the new covenant.

GOD'S HOLY LAW - Matters that truly matter!

9

THE NEW COVENANT

You show that you are a letter from Christ, the result of our ministry, written not with ink but with the Spirit of the living God, not on tablets of stone but on tablets of human hearts
— **2 Cor 3:3 NIV**

We can not have a full grasp of the new covenant unless we understand what Grace is and what it does for us. It is also important that we understand what God is trying to achieve or the problem He is trying to solve by this new covenant. Simply put - Man was struggling to meet his side of the covenant; to remain a people of God meant that he fully obeys the commands and meets it's requirements.

When you read carefully what is said in **Hebrews 8:10 & 11** - you see that the new covenant was going to have a new location. Rather than it be on tablets of stone, it was going to be written on our **minds and our hearts**. The Hebrew writer goes on to say in vrs 11 that *"There won't be need to teach or remind each other"* - Could that perhaps mean that one of the problems with the old covenant was **ignorance of the Law** (not knowing what the Law required) and **forgetfulness** [of the Law itself]? Otherwise, why would God specifically say He would now write the same Law on our minds and hearts?

One of the scriptures that God has put in His Holy word to warn us His people, the Christian community usually quote it way out of context and apply it to everything except the very purpose for which God says it. Let's examine together what God is trying to teach us in **Hosea 4:6** which says: *"For lack of knowledge my people perish"* - what knowledge do you suppose God is speaking of here through the Prophet? Have you ever taken time to read the entire chapter to understand it's context? Let's do that together while we are at it.

> *1 Hear the word of the Lord, You children of Israel, for the Lord brings a charge against the inhabitants of the land: "There is no truth or mercy Or knowledge of God in the land. 2 By swearing and lying, Killing and stealing and committing adultery,*
> *They break all restraint, With bloodshed upon bloodshed. 3 Therefore the land will mourn; And everyone who dwells there will waste away with the beasts of the field and the birds of the air; Even the fish of the sea will be taken away. 4 "Now let no man contend, or rebuke another; for your people are like those who contend with the priest. 5 Therefore you shall stumble in the day; the prophet also shall stumble with you in the night; and I will destroy your*

mother. 6 My people are destroyed for lack of knowledge. Because you have rejected knowledge, I also will reject you from being priest for Me; Because you have forgotten the law of your God, I also will forget your children. 7 "The more they increased, The more they sinned against Me; I will change their glory into shame. — **Hos 4:1-7**

In vrs 1, God tells them that He has a charge against them because they do not know Him. In vrs 2, He tells them what they were doing for which He has a charge against them (also look at from vrs 11) - take your time and go through the list and compare to the 10 commandments [**thou shall not swear, thou shall not lie, thou shall not commit adultery, thou shall not murder, thou shall not worship other gods, thou shall not bow down to any image etc etc**]. God is reminding them of His Law. In vrs 3-5, God tells them the consequences, interestingly, He also mentions that even those who are supposed to be His priests and therefore know the truth are guilty of not upholding His Law.

Now you get to the Church' favourite part in vrs 6 and God says that the reason His people are perishing is because they have forsaken His Law - the knowledge God is referring to is His Law that has been **forgotten, set aside, rejected.** Very sad indeed, this scripture is speaking to our generation more than any other but these days, l hear so many people quote the scripture out of context - even so called Priests and Prophets. They think it is knowledge of some deep secrets to success which we are to know or go after - but right there, just a sentence away, God explains what the knowledge we have forsaken is - His Law *[......Because you have forgotten the Law of your God]!*

If the Priests who served in the temple as mediators could forget God's Law, doesn't it stand to reason that God would want to change them when coming up with a new covenant? So basically, in the new covenant - what had to change was (a) the mediator/surety and (b) the Law now being written on **our minds and hearts.**

There is something else that comes with the new covenant, it is ushered in through the Holy Spirit which enables us to live the new life of obedience to God. We are unable to live out the life that God expects in our flesh except by the Holy Spirit. As many as are led by the Spirit, they are the children of God **[Rom 8:14]**.

So to put them all together in understanding what made up the system under the 2nd covenant, we have (1) the Law-giver [God]; we have the (2) **Law,** then we have (3) the mediator/surety/priest of this new covenant **[Jesus Christ]** who gives (4) **Man** the Holy Spirit to enable us obey God's Law.

The Spirit reminds us of God's Law that is now written on our minds and hearts. It is the same Spirit that also convicts us of sin, of judgment and of righteousness **[John 16:8-11]**. This is perhaps the reason God said: "no longer will a man have to teach his neighbor…" - Heb 8:11. The Holy Spirit does this work for us.

When Jesus started His ministry, He was emphatic that He had not come to abolish the Law - **Matt 5:17-19.** How could we miss what Jesus said? How could we turn Paul against Jesus [assuming our interpretations of what Paul said were even true]. And further, let's even assume Paul and Jesus had opposing views of the Law and it's application - do we dare take what Paul said and ignore Jesus' words?

Rather than think that the commandments were abolished under the new covenant as many think and preach - we realise that Jesus rather gave us the full meaning or if I could put it this way - stretched the meaning of the commandments for us. Let us study together what Jesus says in **Matt 5:21-48**.

The Law was **given** through Moses and Grace and Truth **came** through Jesus Christ **[John 1:17]**. Many people therefore see grace as a license to a life free of the Law, but Jesus takes the expectation under the dispensation of grace [2nd Covenant] higher than in the time of the 1st Covenant.

For instance, Jesus tells us that murder starts when you are angry with your brother without cause; adultery starts when you look at a woman lustfully; and swearing begins when you don't stop at your "Yes and No" but go a step further to make oaths. It means therefore that under the 1st Covenant, conviction of sin happens when or after you break the Law but under the 2nd Covenant, you are convicted of sin by your thoughts and motives even before the actual act of transgressing the command occurs. This is also why God says that under the new covenant, He will write His Law on our minds and in our hearts **(Heb 8:10)**. You can see clearly that the way the Law operates under grace (Jesus) is much higher than that of when God introduced the Law through Moses.

Am I saying therefore that we should obey/keep the Law so as to be saved? Certainly not. There is no way keeping the Law can bring us the salvation that can only come through God's promise made to Abraham **[Gen 17]** at which time the Law had not yet been given. Realise that the Law was given some 430years after this promise to Abraham and at the time when the 4th generation of Israelites who entered Egypt ([1st generation] 12 sons of Jacob generation - [2nd generation] Josephs' sons Ephraim, Manasseh and Levi's son Kohaths' generation - [3rd generation] Kohath's son Amrams generation - [4th generation] Amram's son Moses' generation) came out of Egypt in the exodus; just as God had promised in **Gen 15:16.** Lastly on this, the Law and the Prophets all point to Christ - thus, the ultimate purpose of the Law is for men to look to Christ for their righteousness and not by keeping the Law to attain righteousness. "For Christ is the end of the Law unto righteousness to everyone who believes" - **Romans 10:4.**

What then am I saying in regard to the Law? While we are not reckoned righteous by keeping the Law, but only by faith in the finished work of Jesus - we need to understand that Jesus righteousness is imputed to us at baptism (participation in the death, burial and resurrection of Jesus), so that when we come out of the waters of baptism, we are filled with the Holy Spirit (which also raised Jesus from death) to enable us live righteously (according to God's standard/Law). This is the thought that Paul so clearly emphasizes in Rom 3:31 (TLB): *"Do we then make void the law through faith? Certainly not! On the contrary, we establish the law"*. Paul also asks the question in **Rom 6:1-4:** "Shall we continue to break the Law [sin] so that grace may increase? Certainly not, we made a commitment to stop breaking God's Holy Law when we participated in Jesus death, burial and resurrection; how can we go back to that way of life [the life of breaking God's Law]? - (my paraphrase).

Christians are therefore reckoned righteous by accepting the grace that Jesus' offers - but now having been forgiven of our sins through nothing that we have done and or deserve; we are commanded to go and live a life that is devoid of the sins that we once used to live in. This is the difference between obeying the law to be saved and obeying the law because we have been saved. Christians are supposed to be of the latter group who follow God's command because He has in His mercy freely saved us from our past sins. This is the 2nd Covenant that we are living under.

GOD'S HOLY LAW - Matters that truly matter!

10

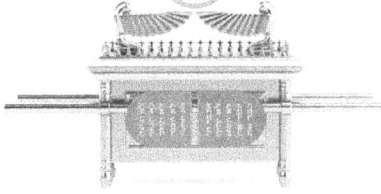

A WORD CAN MAKE
A WORLD OF DIFFERENCE

I am certain you have come across some literature and writings where the presence or omission of a single punctuation changes the entire meaning of what is written. When you have been a victim of this error, you tend to become a lot more careful. Sometimes, no matter how careful you are, you still end up missing one or two things. While some mistakes can be glossed over; other errors make a world of difference where what you miss or include changes the meaning of your text in its entirety.

In some cases we are going to look at; the mis-understanding of a single word can make a difference between truth and error; life and death or the particular doctrine that we embrace leading up to whether we live our lives in conformity to scriptures or otherwise.

So although we are talking about very little things such as punctuations, where a comma should have been rather than a full stop or a single word - we will notice that it can change the entire meaning of the text. This is why Jesus was emphatic that not a jot or tittle will disappear from the Law until everything in it is fulfilled - **Matt 5:18 NKJV**

Take for example the texts below; taking particular notice of where the punctuation mark is.

1. I tell you, today you will be with me in Paradise.
2. I tell you today, you will be with me in Paradise.

In the former, it connotes the idea that on that very day - the persons referred to will be together in Paradise; whereas in the latter, the promise of being together was being made today - however the realization of the promise is not known. As simple as both texts are - where the punctuation mark is placed is what makes the difference in it's meaning.

So what conclusion can we draw? As small as punctuation marks are [jots & tittles as Jesus describes it] - they truly can make a world of difference when it comes to what the author intended. This calls us to be very careful especially when it comes to the Holy scriptures - because they will inform our interpretations of the text and our very lives will depend on such interpretation.

If punctuation marks can make such a BIG difference, then what do you suppose the introduction or omission of a word or phrase could do to the meaning of a text? In this chapter, we are going to look at a couple of examples from scripture.

In previous chapters, I have tried to show the distinction between the Law and the Requirements of the Law so we now know that these are not one and the same. Just to refresh our memory; the Law refers to the moral code [Ten commandments] which God wrote Himself on tablets of stone in His own handwriting and requested that they be put inside the Ark. The requirements of the law on the other hand refer to the ceremonial laws recorded by Moses in a book and put on the side of the Ark.

Throughout scripture - references are made to each of them separately and that which usually distinguish them may be a word or a phrase. When you do not pay attention to such words or phrases, you can confuse yourself as to which of these [moral or ceremonial law] is being referred to.

You might have heard the phrase - "Christ is the fulfillment of the law" - I must admit that when you hear or see it put this way; it is challenging to know which is being referred to and this is where a lot of sincere people often get confused.

First of all, the scripture(s) being referred to do not render the text this way as is often quoted. Let's look at the different passages that this text could have been quoted from.

1. **Rom 8:4**
2. **Rom 10:4**

As we have learnt to do - we will take each of these scriptures and look at them in the various translations, but since Rom 8:4 is in the middle of the sentence, let's look at it from the previous verse so we can capture clearly what Apostle Paul was saying:

ASV

³ For what the law could not do, in that it was weak through the flesh, God, sending his own Son in the likeness of sinful flesh and for sin, condemned sin in the flesh: ⁴ that the ordinance of the law might be fulfilled in us, who walk not after the flesh, but after the Spirit.

AMP

³ For what the Law could not do [that is, overcome sin and remove its penalty, its power] being weakened by the flesh [man's nature without the Holy Spirit], God did: He sent His own Son in the likeness of sinful man as an offering for sin. And He condemned sin in the flesh [subdued it and overcame it in the person of His own Son], ⁴ so that the [righteous and just] requirement of the Law might be fulfilled in us who do not live our lives in the ways of the flesh [guided by worldliness and our sinful nature], but [live our lives] in the ways of the Spirit [guided by His power].

CEB

³ God has done what was impossible for the Law, since it was weak because of selfishness. God condemned sin in the body by sending his own Son to deal with sin in the same body as humans, who are controlled by sin. ⁴ He did this so that the righteous requirement of the Law might be fulfilled in us. Now the way we live is based on the Spirit, not based on selfishness.

NIV

³ For what the law was powerless to do because it was weakened by the flesh, God did by sending his own Son in the likeness of sinful flesh to be a sin offering. And so he condemned sin in the flesh, ⁴ in order that the righteous requirement of the law might be fully met in us, who do not live according to the flesh but according to the Spirit.

ESV

³ For God has done what the law, weakened by the flesh, could not do. By sending his own Son in the likeness of sinful flesh and for sin, he condemned sin in the flesh, ⁴ in order that the righteous requirement of the law might be fulfilled in us, who walk not according to the flesh but according to the Spirit.

As you can see, by the time you read from the previous verse, the text becomes much clearer as to what it is referring to. We already have learnt the weaknesses in the law which were mostly:

- The sinfulness of the earthly high priest;
- The mortality of the high priest - death not making him stay in office forever;
- The blood of animals not being able to perpetually take away man's sins.

These were areas that the law was weak in so God made a new covenant by replacing the high priest with Jesus whose blood has paid for man's sins for all time.

So Paul explains to us that by replacing the earthly high priest with Jesus - God doesn't take away the Law but that Jesus will better meet the demands of the law being;

- A High Priest who is tempted in every way but without sin;
- A High Priest who lives forever to intercede for us; and a
- High Priest whose blood cleanses our sins for all time

So there's a BIG difference between the law and the requirements. Christ' becoming our High Priest through his death has fulfilled the **requirements** of the law. The law was the standard by which man is expected to live, that is what governs man - but the requirements of the law was blood/sacrifice/death which man had to pay when he transgressed the moral law. Jesus death on the cross accomplished [fulfilled] the requirement of the law (sacrifice of blood).

Now let's also look at the other scripture in **Rom 10:4:**

ASV

For Christ is the end of the law unto righteousness to every one that believeth.

AMP

For Christ is the end of the law [it leads to Him and its purpose is fulfilled in Him], for [granting] righteousness to everyone who believes [in Him as Savior].

CEB

Christ is the goal of the Law, which leads to righteousness for all who have faith in God.

NIV

Christ is the culmination of the law so that there may be righteousness for everyone who believes.

ESV

For Christ is the end of the law for righteousness to everyone who believes.

This scripture though similar to the first can be a little tricky [if] you stop at the "law". And I believe that's where most people do and often quote. However, you will notice from all the translations that it speaks of the "law of righteousness" or "law unto righteousness" or "law that leads to righteousness" (depending on which translation you use). In other words; it refers to the law that makes one righteous. It is when a person has met the requirements of the law that his sins are forgiven and righteousness is imputed to him.

Under the old covenant, it was the animal sacrifice through which the sinner became righteous, but under the new covenant - it is through Jesus' sacrifice or death on the cross that righteousness is imputed on the sinner. When you have that background; it is clear to then understand what Paul means by his statement - that **"Christ is the end of the sacrificial system through which sinners were justified"**.

I think it is also very important to understand the word "fulfilment" because our interpretation of it affects what we believe.

Fulfilment in the Oxford dictionary says: "the achievement of something desired, promised or predicted. It also says it is the meeting of a requirement, condition or need. Fulfill or fulfilment doesn't necessarily mean to end something. So when something is fulfilled; it means it has been achieved but it doesn't mean to "set aside" or to "abolish" or to "end" it - but to actually meet a standard that has previously been set.

The word is used by Jesus when He speaks to John the Baptist about being baptized. *"Jesus replied, "Let it be so now; it is proper for us to do this to fulfill all righteousness." Then John consented"*— **Matt**

3:15*. [emphasis mine]. Notice in the text that Jesus doesn't set-aside baptism when He speaks of fulfilment of righteousness but rather He participates in the ordinance of baptism. This further suggests that fulfillment doesn't mean to set-aside or abolish as some may think but rather to achieve or meet the requirement.

For those who have a wrong understanding of the word fulfill, two mistakes are often made when they stop at hearing the [mis] quote "Jesus is the fulfilment of the law". The first mistake is to realise that the text doesn't just end there [but continues to add - "... end of the law **for righteousness** ...." as seen in the full verse **Rom 10:4**]. The second mistake is to interpret the word "fulfill" to mean to "end". This is why some conclude that the scripture may be saying - "Jesus is the end of the law". Now, hopefully it is clear that is not what the scripture says at all.

GRACE

Another word that l believe we need to understand clearly is the word "Grace" as it relates to the chrisitan belief. For some reason, people believe and or have been taught that Grace has come to abolish the law. Often, you will hear people quote scriptures such as:

> *"For the law was given through Moses; grace and truth came through Jesus Christ"* — ***John 1:17***

The scripture above has two parts and the first part only tells us that; it is through Moses that God announced His standards for man's living to us. God also gave Moses the requirements of the law so we can understand how our sins can be atoned for. The requirements of the law (which were the priestly duties and the animal sacrifices) was that which man did to become right with God - it was man's work towards reconciling with God. So the first part of the scripture tells us that God gave the law and it's requirements through Moses.

Then the second part of the scripture moves on to say that it is through Christ that we have grace and truth. Grace is the work of God Himself through which we can be reconciled to Him. It is not what we do, but rather what God has done - this is why we can not boast about our justification under Christ - for it is unmerited; it is all what He has done; man simply has to accept what God/Jesus has done to set us free from the bondage of sin. So Grace is - that which we haven't worked for and thus don't deserve.

This scripture is not setting Jesus against Moses, nor is it comparing their achievements - it is only affirming to us which part each person played in God's work; Moses setting the standard [Law]; and Christ making atonement for where we fall short. It doesn't mean that Christ has come to set aside what Moses did - not at all.

This is why Paul poses the question - *"Shall we continue in sin that grace may abound?"* — **Rom 6:1.** And the answer is - Certainly not; because anyone who has been baptized [become a Christian] has affirmed that s/he will now turn to God in repentance and live according to the standard of God - no longer as an enemy who breaks God's commands [which is what sin is - sin is living against the standards of God]. It is absurd to think of anyone who shows remorse for breaking God's commands and then turn again to live the very life that s/he claims to have repented of.

Let's look at an example from everyday life to help understand what Grace means.

Suppose you are on a highway driving at a speed of 80mph where the speed limit is 60mph. Unfortunately for you, the Police stops you and shows you that you have broken the speed limit [Law]. You however ask the Police to pardon you because you were rushing to the Emergency Room where your child has just been rushed from an accident scene. This Police-man having lost his son at the same hospital earlier sympathises with your situation and let's you go without charging you [Grace]. Does the Police allowing you to go mean that the law is no longer in force?

Similarly, I am sure you can see that being pardoned and not charged for your sin (breaking the law) doesn't in any way take away the law. Yet, some are teaching that Jesus has introduced grace so as to abolish the law. But in His very first public sermon [the sermon on the mount] - Jesus clearly says that He did not come to abolish the law.

In conclusion, words are very important to having a clear understanding of scriptures - and we need to pay very close attention to what is being said and how it is being said also; ensuring that we don't read our own meanings into what God is saying to us. If we take away the law of God, there will be no sin, and if there is no sin, then there will be no need for a savior - in that case, Jesus' painful death is meaningless and has achieved nothing. Is that what you believe?

So where exactly is this teaching of the law being abolished, being set aside or having come to an end coming from? Your guess is as good as mine.

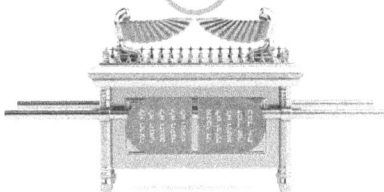

11

DID JESUS BREAK THE SABBATH?

> *For our high priest is able to understand our weaknesses.*
> *He was tempted in every way that we are, but he did not*
> *sin*
> **— Heb 4:15 ICB**

irst of all, if we ever conceive that Jesus broke the Sabbath - then we are saying He didn't live a perfect life (a life free of sin) as the bible tells us - **Heb 4:15**. What is absurd about that thought is the fact that Jesus death' would not have been accepted by God as a ransom if he sinned while on earth. To say that Jesus sinned (broke the Sabbath law) would also mean that God accepted a blemished sacrifice. Recall that any sacrifice for sin had to be a lamb without blemish - **Exodus 12:5; Deut 17:1; 1 Pet 1:19.**

But rather than Jesus desecrating the Sabbath, scripture tells us that He actually observed it. *"So He came to Nazareth, where*

He had been brought up. And as His custom was, He went into the synagogue on the Sabbath day, and stood up to read" — **Luke 4:16.** So here we see clearly that it was His custom to observe the Sabbath command.

But let's study the scriptures so we can be further convinced that Jesus never broke the Sabbath. Some quote **Matt 12:1-8** to support the assertion that Jesus broke the Sabbath. Before we even dig into that passage, let's first acquaint ourselves with Jesus' description of the Pharisees in **Matthew 23** and also **Matthew 15:1-14.** These passages [and others plus history] help us to understand that the Pharisees had their own laws and traditions some of which nullified (put out of effect / neglected) God's Law. Very terrible if you think about it; for humans to elevate their own traditions and side-step or denigrate what God has said - but that was what the Pharisees were known for - that was the judgment Jesus passed on them.

With that background, let's now dig into Matt 12:1-8

At that time Jesus went through the grainfields on the Sabbath. And His disciples were hungry, and began to pluck heads of grain and to eat. ² And when the Pharisees saw it, they said to Him, "Look, Your disciples are doing what is not lawful to do on the Sabbath!" ³ But He said to them, "Have you not read what David did when he was hungry, he and those who were with him: ⁴ how he entered the house of God and ate the showbread which was not lawful for him to eat, nor for those who were with him, but only for the priests? ⁵ Or have you not read in the law that on the Sabbath the priests in the temple profane the

Sabbath, and are blameless? ⁶ Yet I say to you that in this place there is One greater than the temple. ⁷ But if you had known what this means, 'I desire mercy and not sacrifice,' you would not have condemned the guiltless. ⁸ For the Son of Man is Lord even of the Sabbath." — **Matt 12:1-8**

First, in **vrs 7** - Jesus accuses these Pharisees of falsely condemning His disciples - that tells us that their accusation was wrong. How so? It could only be that the Pharisees had added to the law of the Sabbath, and it was their own traditions that had been added to the command which they were accusing Jesus' disciples of breaking. Earlier in **Matt 11:28-30**; you notice Jesus telling people who have become weary and burdened to come to Him for rest - people of the day were burdened due to all the commands the Pharisees had added to God's simple command of which Jesus said: "my yoke is easy and my burden is light". Contrary to God's Law, the rules/regulations, commands and traditions of the Pharisees were man-made rules and difficult to follow and they themselves were unable to bear them nor were they willing to carry them. Jesus could not be judged by what humans expected of him - **John 5:41-44.**

Further, what is even more interesting is that according to scripture, not only did Jesus observe the Sabbath during His life but even in His death, He rested on the Sabbath.

"⁵³ Then he took it down, wrapped it in linen cloth and placed it in a tomb cut in the rock, one in which no one had yet been laid. ⁵⁴ It was Preparation Day, and the Sabbath was about to begin" — **Luke 23:53-54.**

Another scripture where we find Jesus being accused of breaking the Sabbath is:

> *"Therefore the Jews sought all the more to kill Him, because He not only broke the Sabbath, but also said that God was His Father, making Himself equal with God"*
> — *John 5:18 NKJV*

We have to make up our minds on whether we will agree fully with the Pharisees on both counts because we can't uphold one and forego the other. For instance, we can't say Jesus broke the Sabbath but He is not guilty of blasphemy because He is Son of God - that wasn't the position of the Pharisees who laid these two accusations on Him. It is interesting when Christians come to the defense of Jesus that He indeed is God's Son but go silent and often even join in accusing Him of breaking the Sabbath. Sometimes, our misunderstanding of His words "The Son of Man is also Lord of the Sabbath" makes us think that Jesus is acknowledging that He broke the Sabbath.

On the contrary, what Jesus meant by that statement was that; being Master of the Sabbath, He should be the better qualified person to interpret and or judge what was a breach/transgression to the command; more than those who felt they could judge Him.

Although God had instructed them not to add to His commands, the Pharisaic Rabbi's had elevated their own [man-made] traditions making them equal to the commands of God; and so, it was their own added commands they were accusing Jesus of breaking.

"Do not add to what I command you and do not subtract from it, but keep the commands of the Lord your God that I give you" — **Deut 4:2**

I believe that when we all come to understand the length Jesus went in keeping the Sabbath [even at His death]; we will not accuse Him again of breaking it. Because He was obedient both in life and unto death - scripture tells us that He was perfect - **Heb 5:8-9**.

GOD'S HOLY LAW - Matters that truly matter!

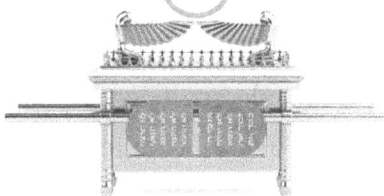

12

HOW GOD JUDGES

> *For we must all appear before the judgment seat of Christ,*
> *so that every person may receive the works of his body,*
> *according to what he has done, whether it be good or bad*
> — **2 Cor 5:10 NMB**

Perhaps, it is important to establish God's consistency when it comes to the area of His judgment so we don't leave this to our own imagination. Throughout the Bible, you will notice that God is very consistent in His approach towards judgment - we will look at a few examples through creation; in the antediluvian world (the world before the flood in Noah's day); in the days when the Law was given to Moses and lastly also under the New covenant so we can predict with higher accuracy what the end time judgment would look like with the support of scripture.

First, let's look at Adam. In Genesis 2, God gives commands to Adam - He shows His generosity by telling Adam all that He can have except for fruit from one particular tree. To understand all the options that Adam had, just begin to list the number of fruits we have in this world - too numerous to count. So first, God allows Adam to have them all except for one, then He adds the consequences to breaking His command. We learn from the story that Adam and Eve through the deception of the serpent breaks God's command and eats of the fruit - how does God approach this. In **Gen 3:9-19**; we first see that God summons Adam to appear before Him (**court session**), God then seeks to find out (**investigation / cross-examination**) and gives Adam an opportunity to **defend himself.** Through this proceeding, Adam is found guilty (together with Eve and the serpent); it was only then that God tells them what will happen as a result of their sin (**judgment is pronounced**). After judgment is pronounced, we see that they are sent away to begin life under the new conditions (**execution of judgment**).

This gives us five (5) stages of God's judgment process; (**1**) God issues His Law or a command and adds what the consequences of breaking His Law/command will be; (**2**) Summoning of the accused; (**3**) Investigate / Cross-examine to ascertain whether wrong has occurred and giving the accused an opportunity to defend him/herself; (**4**) Judgment is pronounced; and lastly (**5**) Execution of the judgment.

To show God's consistency, let's look at other examples in the scriptures. Let's take Cain in **Gen 4:3-12**. When you look at this story, you notice that God must have given them a command to bring an offering to Him, or Adam and Eve may have carried out their responsibility as parents to raise these boys with all the commands of God including to bring freewill offerings and not to murder. vrs 7 - *[7 "If you do well [believing Me and doing what is acceptable and pleasing to Me], will you not be accepted? And if you do not do well [but ignore My instruction], sin crouches at your door; its desire is for you [to overpower you], but you must master it."* - AMP]* corroborates this point. Further, we see that God talks to Cain (**summoning**); and **investigates/cross-examines** him to establish that indeed wrong has been done. God then passes the **judgment** which we know from the story is **executed** as planned.

Another example we can look at is the story of the tower of Babel. After the flood, we see in **Gen 9:1** how God [1[**commands** for the earth to be filled. When you read the account of **Gen 11**, the people had decided against God's command to fill the earth - *[4 And they said, "Come, let us build ourselves a city, and a tower whose top is in the heavens; let us make a name for ourselves, **lest we be scattered abroad over the face of the whole earth"]*. So God comes down to check it out for himself (**[2] summoning**); he observes what is being done (**[3] investigates/cross-examines**), then He [4] **passes judgment and also** [5] **executes the judgment** by giving them different languages so they won't understand each other and then scatters them on the surface of the earth.

Let's take another example, this time years after the Law was given to Moses. Let's read the fine account in **Joshua 7**. In this account, we see that the Israelites are defeated in a battle that they were very confident of winning - the covenant they have with God is that as long as they obey God's commands, God will be with them and cause them to defeat all their enemies **(Deut 28:1-14)**. When Joshua goes to God to find out what could be wrong, God tells him exactly what he must do - **Josh 7:9-26**.

¹⁰ So the Lord said to Joshua: "Get up! Why do you lie thus on your face? ¹¹ Israel has sinned, and they have also transgressed My covenant which I commanded them. For they have even taken some of the accursed things, and have both stolen and deceived; and they have also put it among their own stuff. ¹² Therefore the children of Israel could not stand before their enemies, but turned their backs before their enemies, because they have become doomed to destruction. Neither will I be with you anymore, unless you destroy the accursed from among you. ¹³ Get up, sanctify the people, and say, 'Sanctify yourselves for tomorrow, because thus says the Lord God of Israel: "There is an accursed thing in your midst, O Israel; you cannot stand before your enemies until you take away the accursed thing from among you." ¹⁴ In the morning therefore you shall be brought according to your tribes. And it shall be that the tribe which the Lord takes shall come according to families; and the family which the Lord takes shall come by households; and the household which the Lord takes shall come man by man. ¹⁵ Then it shall be that he who is taken with the accursed thing shall be burned with fire, he and all that he has, because he has transgressed the covenant of the Lord, and because he has done a disgraceful thing in Israel.' "¹⁶ So Joshua rose early in the morning and brought Israel by their tribes, and the tribe of Judah was taken. ¹⁷ He brought the clan of Judah, and he took the family of the Zarhites; and he brought the family of the Zarhites man by man, and Zabdi was taken. ¹⁸ Then he brought his household man by man, and Achan the son of Carmi, the son of Zabdi, the son of Zerah, of the tribe of Judah, was taken. [19] *Now Joshua said to Achan, "My son, I beg you, give glory to the Lord God of Israel, and make confession to Him, and tell me now what you have done; do not hide it from me."* [20] *And Achan answered Joshua and said, "Indeed I have sinned against the Lord God of Israel, and this is what I have done:* [21] *When I saw among the spoils a beautiful Babylonian garment, two hundred shekels of silver, and a wedge of gold weighing fifty shekels, I coveted them and took them. And there they are, hidden in the earth in the midst of my tent, with the silver under it."* [22] *So Joshua sent messengers, and they ran to the tent; and there it was, hidden in his tent, with the silver under it.* [23] *And they took them from the midst of the tent, brought them to Joshua and to all the children of Israel, and laid them out before the Lord.* [24] *Then Joshua, and all Israel with him, took Achan the son of Zerah, the silver, the garment, the wedge of gold, his sons, his daughters, his oxen, his donkeys, his sheep, his tent, and all that he had, and they brought them to the Valley of Achor.* [25] *And Joshua said, "Why have you troubled us? The Lord will trouble you this day." So all Israel stoned him with stones; and they burned them with fire after they had stoned them with stones.* [26] *Then they raised over him a great heap of stones, still there to this day. So the Lord turned from the fierceness of His anger. Therefore the name of that place has been called the Valley of Achor to this day.* — **Josh 7:9-26**

So, Joshua **[2] summons** all the people to appear before God, then there is the [3] **investigation** where **Achan** is found out - he is also given an opportunity to defend himself, after which **[4] judgment is passed** and swiftly **[5] executed**.

Now let's take another example, this time from under the New Covenant. In **Acts 5:1-11**, a story is told about a couple who out of their own good will decided to bring freewill offerings for God's people. They didn't have to, but voluntarily chose to be a blessing to their community. This couple like all the disciples knew exactly God's commands about lying (together with all the other commands). Having chosen to bring an offering to God, they were to conform to the provisions of God's commands, seeing to it that none was broken even though they meant well. [This story also helps us to understand that the end doesn't necessarily justify the means as we often say]. Under the guidance of the Holy Spirit, Ananias is summoned for cross examination.

"But a certain man named Ananias, with Sapphira his wife, sold a possession. ² And he kept back part of the proceeds, his wife also being aware of it, and brought a certain part and laid it at the apostles' feet. ³ But Peter said, "Ananias, why has Satan filled your heart to lie to the Holy Spirit and keep back part of the price of the land for yourself? ⁴ While it remained, was it not your own? And after it was sold, was it not in your own control? Why have you conceived this thing in your heart? You have not lied to men but to God." ⁵ Then Ananias, hearing these words, fell down and breathed his last. So great fear came upon all those who heard these things. ⁶ And the young men arose and wrapped him up, carried him out, and buried him. ⁷ Now it was about three hours later when his wife came in, not knowing what had happened. ⁸ And Peter

answered her, "Tell me whether you sold the land for so much?" She said, "Yes, for so much." ⁹ Then Peter said to her, "How is it that you have agreed together to test the Spirit of the Lord? Look, the feet of those who have buried your husband are at the door, and they will carry you out." ¹⁰ Then immediately she fell down at his feet and breathed her last. And the young men came in and found her dead, and carrying her out, buried her by her husband. ¹¹ So great fear came upon all the Church and upon all who heard these things". — Acts 5:1-11

The picture is much clearer when Sapphira is [2] **summoned**, she's given an opportunity to respond during her [3] **cross-examination**, when it is established that she has sinned, [4] **judgment is passed** and the [5] **execution of the judgment** swiftly follows.

Lastly, let's look at a few passages for what Jesus says will happen at the end of the age:

"There is a judge for the one who rejects me and does not accept my words; the very words I have spoken will condemn them at the last day" — John 12:48

Jesus tells us that it is his words/commands that we will be judged by on the last day [paraphrased]. This means that it is our obedience to what we've been commanded to do that will acquit or condemn us on the last day.

Matt 7:21-23

> "Not everyone who says to Me, 'Lord, Lord,' shall enter the
> kingdom of heaven, but he who does the will of My Father
> in heaven. [22] Many will say to Me in that day, 'Lord, Lord,
> have we not prophesied in Your name, cast out demons in
> Your name, and done many wonders in Your name?' [23]
> And then I will declare to them, 'I never knew you; depart
> from Me, you who practice lawlessness!'

Isn't it interesting what Jesus tells these people? "I never knew
you, you are lawless, you who do not obey my laws".

Matt 25:31-46

> "When the Son of Man comes in His glory, and all the
> holy angels with Him, then He will sit on the throne of
> His glory. [32] All the nations will be gathered before Him,
> and He will separate them one from another, as a shepherd
> divides his sheep from the goats. [33] And He will set the
> sheep on His right hand, but the goats on the left. [34] Then
> the King will say to those on His right hand, 'Come, you
> blessed of My Father, inherit the kingdom prepared for you
> from the foundation of the world: [35] for I was hungry and
> you gave Me food; I was thirsty and you gave Me drink; I
> was a stranger and you took Me in; [36] I was naked and you
> clothed Me; I was sick and you visited Me; I was in prison
> and you came to Me.' [37] "Then the righteous will answer
> Him, saying, 'Lord, when did we see You hungry and feed
> You, or thirsty and give You drink? [38] When did we see You
> a stranger and take You in, or naked and clothe You? [39] Or

*when did we see You sick, or in prison, and come to You?'
⁴⁰ And the King will answer and say to them, 'Assuredly, I
say to you, inasmuch as you did it to one of the least of these
My brethren, you did it to Me.'⁴¹ "Then He will also say to
those on the left hand, 'Depart from Me, you cursed, into
the everlasting fire prepared for the devil and his angels: ⁴²
for I was hungry and you gave Me no food; I was thirsty
and you gave Me no drink; ⁴³ I was a stranger and you
did not take Me in, naked and you did not clothe Me,
sick and in prison and you did not visit Me.' 44 "Then
they also will answer [b]Him, saying, 'Lord, when did we
see You hungry or thirsty or a stranger or naked or sick or
in prison, and did not minister to You?' ⁴⁵ Then He will
answer them, saying, 'Assuredly, I say to you, inasmuch as
you did not do it to one of the least of these, you did not
do it to Me.' ⁴⁶ And these will go away into everlasting
punishment, but the righteous into eternal life."*

Again, notice the sequence:

[2] Summoned before God *[All the Nations will be gathered before
Him]*
[3] Investigation / Cross-examination *[I was hungry and you gave
me food.....]*
Also notice how everyone is given an opportunity to defend
themselves [Lord, when did we see you hungry and feed you,
.......]
[4] Judgment is passed *[Come, you who are blessed by my Father;
take your inheritance, the kingdom prepared for you since the creation
of the world]*

[5] Execution of Judgment *[Then they will go away to eternal punishment, but the righteous to eternal life]*

What l am trying to establish is that, at all times God's procedure for judgment has not only been fair but also repeatable, consistent and thus predictable - He never rushes into judgment but takes His time to first investigate the issue and give us an opportunity to defend ourselves. If a transgression of his command is found, then He passes judgment and also executes it. God does this so that no one can ever question His judgment. See how Paul describes it in **Rom 2**, In **vrs 9**; he says that there will be tribulation, anguish, affliction, distress, misery, suffering for everyone who sins (breaks or transgresses God's law, works iniquity) in spite of what their background is - whether they were religious or not [my paraphrase]. You can trust God's judgment because as quoted in vrs 6: *"God will repay each person according to what they have done."*

When we study the books of Daniel and Revelations, we see the same pattern of God's judgment - check for instance **Daniel 7:9-28, Daniel 12:2-3** and also **Rev 20:11-15**.

There's considerable proof all through scripture that God's judgment in the last day will be very much like how He has approached judgment throughout history. The Righteousness of God means that He is a God of both Justice and Mercy - see **Ps 89:14**. For instance, in God's great Mercy, He sent Jesus to die on the cross in our place, taking the curse that was due us so that we could have His blessing of eternal life by believing in Him. In the same way, God's Justice would not allow Him to spare a sinner; so when Jesus carried the sin of the entire world, God had to see to it that the righteous requirement of the Law was met - therefore

Jesus paid the penalty/wages of sin [death]. God's character will not allow Him to clear the guilty of wrongdoing as described in Exodus 34:7.

Friend, perhaps you are counting on the mercy of God and forgetting that the other side of that coin is His justice. Having shown us how He treats sinners (including His ONLY begotten son Jesus); we should have no doubt in our minds as to how God will judge us when we are found guilty of breaking His Law. If you don't want to be caught unawares, then you need to come to terms with God's expectation of acting justly, loving mercy and walking humbly with Him - see **Micah 6:8**.

Please pay attention to Jesus admonishment in these scriptures:

> *"The servant who knows the master's will and does not get ready or does not do what the master wants will be beaten with many blows. ⁴⁸ But the one who does not know and does things deserving punishment will be beaten with few blows. From everyone who has been given much, much will be demanded; and from the one who has been entrusted with much, much more will be asked"* — ***Luke 12:47-48***

> *"Anyone who hears my words and does not •obey [keep] them, I do not judge, because I did not come to judge the world, but to save the world. ⁴⁸ There is a judge for those who •refuse to believe in [reject] me and do not accept my words. The word I have •taught [spoken] will •be their judge [judge them] on the last day"*
> — ***John 12:47-48 EXB***

GOD'S HOLY LAW - Matters that truly matter!

13

CHRISTIAN
BY BIBLE STANDARDS

*Tekel, you have been weighed in the balances and found
wanting*
— **Dan 5:27**

I grew up in the days when one of the questions on most forms you'd have to fill at almost all organisations included your religion - and you'd have to choose one of the options listed depending on whether you are Christian; Moslem; African Traditional Religion (ATR); Jewish, Hindu or you state if any other. I must confess that several years before I ever became a Christian or understood it's true meaning, and without thinking; I would always tick Christian. I did this because in my mind - my mom was affiliated to a Church and she used to take us to Church. We even had devotions some mornings in our home and I prayed regularly to God. So I really believed I was a Christian until one day in the year 2000, someone studied with me for the very first time and showed me what it meant to be a Christian according to the Bible.

These days you don't see forms requesting for your religion - however, the options for gender include a lot more than what we know God created in the beginning - Male or Female. Now you find LGBTQi and yet still, others. I don't allow that to confuse me - my simple way is to remember that God made them male and female at creation, and anything beyond that is not what God has made. The text clearly says: "God finished all His work of creation and rested [ceased] from His work of creation on the seventh day" - **Gen 2:1-2** [Paraphrase mine]. This is how we know with certainty that God didn't create any other gender after He was done creating male and female. But let's suppose you believe something differently - what do you think God thinks of your claims that you have faith in Him?

All of that reminds me of a parable Jesus told where the servants of the master asked - did we not only sow good seed - where are the weeds from?

"Jesus told them another parable: "The kingdom of heaven is like a man who sowed good seed in his field. 25 But while everyone was sleeping, his enemy came and sowed weeds among the wheat, and went away. 26 When the wheat sprouted and formed heads, then the weeds also appeared. 27 "The owner's servants came to him and said, 'Sir, didn't you sow good seed in your field? Where then did the weeds come from?'
28 "'An enemy did this,' he replied. "The servants asked him, 'Do you want us to go and pull them up?' 29 "'No,'

he answered, 'because while you are pulling the weeds, you may uproot the wheat with them. ³⁰ Let both grow together until the harvest. At that time I will tell the harvesters: First collect the weeds and tie them in bundles to be burned; then gather the wheat and bring it into my barn.'"
*— **Matt 13:24-30*** [emphasis mine].

What is important to note in Jesus' parable is the fact that; being on the field didn't make the weeds to be wheat - just as being part of a Church or even being born to Christian parents doesn't make one a Christian. Secondly, He tells the origin of the weeds - "an enemy did this" - they were not planted by the owner. Thirdly, Jesus makes it plain that the weeds will remain with the wheat until the time of the harvest. This calls for serious eyes and understanding on our parts so we don't mistaken what is weed for wheat - often, the weeds can look so much like wheat that you may not recognise it except with time and at the harvest, the weeds do not produce the right fruit. The other ways to distinguish the two are by subjecting everything to the right test so you know and lastly by spiritual discernment. In the same way, Jesus says that by their fruit you will know them - whether they are of God or the enemy planted them. But to wait till the time of the harvest to see the fruits may be too late, so how about we explore the other two options - by testing and spiritual discernment?

I can't begin to describe all the emotions I felt when I came to understand what it meant to be a Christian according to God's word - I was elated I had come to know the truth but I was also very shocked, disappointed and very angry that I hadn't known this earlier, even though I spoke in tongues [or thought I did];

and had even been part of prayer groups and participated in evangelism campaigns. I was particularly angry with the Church I used to attend and with the pastor because I wondered why he never showed me the truth all along but had happily accepted me as a Christian and part of his congregation.

But now, I have come to know that there are many; including pastors and religious leaders; who have no clue what it means to be a Christian or Christ' follower. It is very troubling when those who are supposed to help you get saved are themselves not even saved according to the standard and word of God. Only when we turn to God's word for direction will we find truth. But we must approach this issue of our salvation in humility and be poor in spirit (coming empty and prepared to learn); we must truly hunger and thirst for righteousness if we are to find it; and we must be diligent and seek God with all our heart if we are to find Him - **Matt 5:3-6 : Jer 29:13**. God never forces Himself on anyone, and our pursuit of Him is the only way we prove that we desire to have a relationship with Him.

So in this chapter, I invite you to come with me as we study what it means to be a true Christian according to the standard of the bible. We will put our Christianity under check via the lens of scriptures which can truly test to see whether we are wheat or weed. The bible [word of God] says of itself that it is the only tool that is able to sharply and correctly divide truth from error or right from wrong.

"For the word of God is living and active and full of power [making it operative, energizing, and effective]. It is sharper than any two-edged sword, penetrating as far as the division of the soul and spirit [the completeness of a

person], and of both joints and marrow [the deepest parts of our nature], exposing and judging the very thoughts and intentions of the heart. [13] And not a creature exists that is concealed from His sight, but all things are open and exposed, and revealed to the eyes of Him with whom we have to give account". — Heb 4:12-13 AMP

I like how the **Living Bible translation** renders this text - it says - "God's word exposes us for what we really are". This means we can't hide when we put our lives under the lens of the bible - we will know clearly without a doubt whether we are wheat or weed. And I think that should encourage us - because at least we will know for sure and not be "fooling" ourselves. That is what l got excited about when I came to know the truth that all my life when I thought l was a Christian - I was only fooling myself. I was taking part in everything that **Christians** do, but I wasn't a **Christian**. What of you - could that be your story too? Would you like to find out?

This chapter like the others in this book is very practical; and l would like you to indulge me by reading the scriptures and answering the questions that follow. I believe I owe it to others, to point out what God was gracious enough to show me through a brother who reached out to me at that point in my life. He rescued me from the lies and deception going around even in some Churches; and by some sincere and zealous [but not too well knowing] preachers and religious leaders who misunderstand God's grace.

So as we begin this study, please lay aside all your biases and everything you think you know; and pray that the Holy Spirit will guide you into all truth as you open up your life and your heart for Him to lead you.

PRAYER

Righteous Father - thank you for this opportunity to come before your Holy presence - please release your Spirit to come and be with me and draw me to yourself. l agree with your word in **Jer 17:9-10** which says that my heart is deceitful and desperately wicked and only you can search, expose, heal and save me. Lord l lay all that l am before you today and ask that you do what only you can do. As I go through your word, show me where I fall short and guide me into your truth - that I may forever dwell in your tabernacle and be counted as your child. Help me not to fight you but be grateful for all that you show me and help me to be quick to turn to you according to your word. Thank you for answering my heart's deepest need to be with you - I pray this in the name of your Holy Son Jesus. Amen!

BEGIN STUDY

1. Please read the following passages **Romans 7:7, 1 John 3:4 and Isaiah 59:1-8**

According to these passages - What is sin and what is its effect on you?

_____

_____

_____

_____

_____

_____

2. Please read **Romans 3:23**

_____

_____

According to this passage - Who has sinned? _____

_____

3. Read these scriptures to identify some sins - **Gal 5:19-21; 2 Tim 3:1-5; James 4:17**

_____

_____

_____

_____

_____

_____

- Are you guilty of any sin?_____ _____

   _____

- Which ones? _____

   _____

   _____

   _____

   _____

4. What happens to you when you sin according to **Rom 6:23**

_____

_____

_____

_____

- What type of death? Read **Gen 3** for a clue to the type of death being referred to and compare to **Isa 59:1-2**

_____

_____

_____

_____

_____

5. Please read **Mark 9:43-47**

- Why do you suppose Jesus says it this way?

_____

_____

_____

_____

- What attitude does Jesus want you to have regarding your sins?

_____

_____

_____

_____

- Are you dealing with your sins the way Jesus expects you to? If not why?

_____

_____

_____

_____

6. Please read - 1 **Tim 2:3-5**

- According to the passage - What is God's will for all humanity?

- What does God want us to be saved from?

- How many mediators exist between God and man?

- Would you like Jesus to be your mediator?

7. Please read - **Heb 9:16-22**

_____

_____

_____

_____

_____

- According to the passage - How can our sins be atoned for or forgiven?

_____

_____

_____

_____

_____

8. Please read - **Hebrews 10:1-18**

- According to this passage - Why could the blood of animals not atone for our sins?

_____

_____

_____

_____

_____

- What was wrong with the animal sacrifice?

_____

_____

_____

_____

- Whose blood can truly forgive us our sins for all time?

_____

_____

_____

_____

_____

9. Please read - **Acts 4:10-12**

- According to this passage - In whom can salvation be found?

_____

_____

_____

_____

- Can any prophet; spiritual guru or religion or it's leader save you? Explain

_____

_____

_____

_____

If you believe Jesus is your only answer and way to be saved; then listen to what He says and do it.

10. Please read - **John 3:1-12**

- Who was Nicodemus?

_____

_____

_____

_____

_____

● Why did he come to Jesus at night?

_____

_____

_____

_____

● What did he want from Jesus?

_____

_____

_____

_____

● In **vrs 11**; although a teacher/preacher - did Nicodemus know how to be saved? If he wasn't saved himself - do you think he could have helped others get saved?

_____

_____

_____

_____

● Do you think there could be Pastors/Preachers/Prophets etc today who don't know the true plan of salvation? How can you be sure?

_____

_____

_____

_____

● What did Jesus tell Nicodemus to do to be saved? See **vrs 3-5**

_____

_____

_____

_____

● Do you really want to be saved like Nicodemus wanted - if so, what must you do?

_____

_____

_____

_____

_____

11. Please read - **Matthew 16:13-19**

What did Jesus appoint Peter [and the other Apostles] to give them special authority/role to play?

_____

_____

_____

_____

_____

● What are keys used for?

_____

_____

_____

_____

_____

12. Please read - **Acts 2:36-41**

- Where was Jesus when this incident happened? For a clue, read **Acts 1:1-11**

_____

_____

_____

_____

_____

- What did Peter ask the first set of converts after Jesus' ascension to do?

_____

_____

_____

_____

- Who else did Peter say will be saved through this same way? **Acts 2:39**

_____

_____

_____

_____

- How did Peter use the keys Jesus told him he is giving him in **Matt 16:19**

_____

_____

_____

_____

● What is repentance?

_____

_____

_____

_____

_____

● In what ways is repentance different from stopping sin?

_____

_____

_____

_____

● What are you to repent of? See **Matt 3:7-10**

_____

_____

_____

_____

● According to **Acts 26:20** - how do you prove that you've repented?

_____

_____

_____

● What happens when you repent? Check **Acts 3:19**

_____

_____

_____

● At what point is a person's sin forgiven according to **Acts 2:38**

_____

_____

_____

_____

● According to **Acts 2:38** - What if you repent but you don't get baptized; will your sins be forgiven? And will you be saved?

_____

_____

_____

_____

● According to **Acts 2:38** - What if you get baptized without repenting; [still living the same old way] - will your sins be forgiven? And will you be saved?

_____

_____

_____

_____

● According to **Acts 2:38** - What if you get baptized without repenting; [still living the same old way] - will you receive the Holy Spirit that enables you to live the Christian life?

_____

_____

_____

_____

- So what must you do for your sins to be forgiven and be saved?

_____
_____
_____

13. Let's read about a few people who became Christians after Jesus' ascension into Heaven.

- Read **Acts 8:34-39** - The Ethiopian Eunuch
- Read **Acts 16:29-34** - The Jailer
- What did these people do to be saved?

_____
_____
_____
_____
_____

- How would you describe their attitude towards salvation? Clue **Acts 8:36-37 & Acts 16:33**

_____
_____
_____

- How did they feel after they were baptized? Clue **Acts 8:39 & Acts 16:34**

_____
_____
_____

● What does Salvation bring to us or do for us?

_____
_____
_____
_____

14. Please read - **1 Peter 3:20-21**

● According to this passage - through what were people in the past saved?

_____
_____
_____
_____
_____

15. Do you know about any person who was saved any other way in the New Testament except through Repentance and Baptism?

_____
_____
_____

16. Please Read **Luke 23:39-43**

How do you explain Jesus saving the thief on the cross?

_____
_____
_____
_____

● Read **Matthew 9:1-6 / Mark 2:10** - [Notice that Jesus had the Power to forgive sin while on earth].

_____

_____

_____

_____

_____

● Read **Heb 9:16-22** - Jesus was still living (he hadn't died yet) when he forgave the sins of the thief. Jesus had to die before the 2nd covenant of baptism could come into effect. But after He died, everyone who ever got saved had to go through Repentance & Baptism.

_____

_____

_____

_____

_____

17. Are there people in scriptures who were saved by praying Jesus into their hearts?

_____

_____

_____

_____

18. Do the scriptures say anywhere that when you ask Jesus to come into your heart, He does?

_____

_____

_____

_____

19. Please Read - **John 8:30-32**

● How did Jesus refer to those who believe in Him and do as he teaches?

_____

_____

_____

● We notice from this scripture that - It is not those who believe in Jesus who are His disciples but those who obey and follow His teachings. Do you see the difference?

_____

_____

_____

● When we start to obey and follow Him is when we will know the truth. Notice that we don't get to know the truth by just believing that Jesus is the son of God.

_____

_____

_____

● And until you know the truth - will you be free?

_____

_____

_____

_____

_____

● It is only people living as disciples of Jesus who are truly free. Conversely, if you are not a disciple of Jesus - you are never free.

20. Please read - **Acts 11:25-26**

_____

_____

_____

_____

_____

● Who are the people who were given the nickname "Christian"?

_____

_____

_____

● What were they called before they were given their new name/nickname?

_____

_____

● Why do you think they were given the nickname Christian?

_____

_____

_____

● If you are not living as a Disciple of Jesus, can you be called a Christian?

_____

_____

_____

21. Let's look at some attributes of those who were disciples of Jesus?

a. 1 John 2:5-6

Does your life prove you imitate the life of Christ? What would you do to imitate Him?

_____

_____

_____

_____

_____

b. Acts 2:42-46

Have you been devoting yourself to scriptures (reading and obeying), fellowship of believers and Prayer, meeting the needs of others by any means possible? What do you need to change?

_____

_____

_____

_____

_____

_____

c. Luke 9:23-27

NOTE: In the early Church; being a Christian was in violation of the dictates of the Roman Emperor and the punishment was death. To follow Jesus meant carrying your cross [death] and those who made Jesus their Lord and were baptized were certain that as soon as it was known by the authorities; they would face death often by beheading.

Are you prepared to deny yourself, take up your cross [die to yourself] daily and not look for a world of comfort, and not be ashamed of Jesus Christ? What do you need to do?

_____
_____
_____
_____
_____
_____

d. Luke 9:57-62

Do you understand that with Christianity you should have no excuse for not following, and that the desires of Jesus must always come first in your life? Are you ready for this?

_____
_____
_____
_____
_____
_____

e. Luke 14:25-32

The priority when it comes to Christianity is Christ, and you must not allow any person or thing to be a distraction or stop you from following Jesus. Are you ready to surrender everything for the cause of Jesus? What do you need to give up to do this?

_____

_____

_____

_____

_____

f. John 13:34-35

Will you love one another as Jesus commands you, in spite of what the other person(s) are like or have done to you?

_____

_____

_____

_____

_____

g. 1 Peter 4:7-11

Do you use your gifts to serve others? What do you need to change in this area?

_____

_____

_____

_____

_____

h. Romans 12:9-21

In what ways do you prove your love? How do you compare to what the bible teaches?

_____
_____
_____
_____

i. Matthew 28:18-20

- The one purpose for Jesus' disciples is to make disciples; and notice that this is the Lord's command, not a suggestion - how have you done in this area?

_____
_____
_____
_____

- Are you prepared to make "disciple making" your life's most important objective; obeying Jesus' command to go and find ways to bring others to Christ always?

_____
_____
_____
_____

- Have you been taught to obey ALL of Jesus' commands? And are you obeying them ALL?

_____
_____
_____
_____

_____

_____

● According to the scripture, who are to be baptized? The command says - Make disciples and baptize them. That means we are to baptize those who repent of their old ways and start living as disciples. If a person is not living as a disciple, should they be baptized?

_____

_____

_____

_____

● If a person is not baptized - will their sins be forgiven? If their sins are not forgiven - are they saved? Refer to **Acts 2:38** above.

_____

_____

_____

_____

● On what condition does Jesus promise to be with us even to the very end?

_____

_____

_____

● If you are not a disciple and don't make disciples - will Jesus be with you to the very end?

_____

_____

_____

22. What conclusion can you draw from all that you have read about being a [true] Christian?

_____

_____

_____

_____

_____

_____

You may have by now noticed that - you don't become a Christian by:

- Being born into a Christian family;
- Going to Church,
- Reading your bible and praying;
- Singing Christian music and praising God;
- Believing in Jesus, Loving God/Jesus;
- Telling others about God/Jesus;
- Speaking in tongues or prophesying or working miracles;
- Being a good and moral person;
- Being generous and philanthropic;
- Answering an altar call once or many times;
- Praying Jesus into your heart once or many times.

A Christian according to the Bible is one who has been saved by relying on the blood of Christ:

1. By repenting of sin (No longer living as an enemy of God)

2. By having been baptized for the forgiveness of sins and to receive God's Spirit

3. And is being empowered by the Spirit to imitate Jesus and to live a new life of:

- TOTAL Obedience to ALL of God's commands,
- Fellowship or be in the company of other saved people,
- Denying self daily and putting Christ first in all things and at all times,
- Continuously surrendering everything to God
- Devoting oneself to Studying God's word; Prayer and Evangelism
- Loving other people just as Christ loved you and
- Always helping others to become Christians

FINAL QUESTIONS

- Have you been living your life as a disciple of Jesus according to the scriptures?

_____

_____

_____

_____

_____

- Did you repent of your sins and get baptized?

_____

_____

- Are you saved if you did not do both?

_____

_____

_____

- If you did not repent and get baptized - are you certain you have the Holy Spirit?

_____

_____

_____

- If you don't have the Holy Spirit - can you live the Christian life by your strength or by any other means?

_____

_____

_____

- Will Jesus call you His disciple? If Yes, on what basis? If No, why not?

_____

_____

_____

_____

- If you are not a disciple, are you qualified to have the Christian title/nickname?

_____

_____

_____

- What would you like to do now that you know where you stand?

_____

_____

_____

_____

If you diligently did this study - I have no doubt that the Holy Spirit has revealed the truth about where you stand with Jesus and whether or not He will call you His disciple and therefore a Christian. Please know that it is not about the world's definition of a Christian but about meeting the standard that Jesus teaches in His word. I encourage you to keep seeking the path that He has made available to you, and to further deepen your understanding and walk with Jesus by finding a Church that practices sound theology according to the word of God and as the Holy Spirit directs you.

God bless you!

"Turn to me and be saved, all you ends of the earth; for I am God, and there is no other" - **Isaiah 45:22**

14

CONCLUSION

For we must all appear before the judgment seat of Christ, so that every person may receive the works of his body, according to what he has done, whether it be good or bad — **Eccl 12:13-14 TLB**

For judgment to occur (i.e. be it to convict us of sin or what we refer to as the final judgment), there has to be established a basis on which one can be acquitted or condemned; this is called the Law. Without such Law/commands, there can be no indication that it has been followed or transgressed/broken; and therefore there can be no talk of sin. *"Whoever commits sin also commits lawlessness, and sin is lawlessness"* — *1 John 3:4.* The Law is therefore essential in God's procedure of judgment. God must also have established with man the consequences of breaking such Law prior to the day of the judgment.

Throughout the Holy Scriptures, we have observed through the different dispensations that; God first gives people His Law to follow, He warns us of the consequences of breaking His Law/ commands. And when He comes to judge, He gives people an opportunity to defend themselves before judgment is passed and the sentence executed.

When Christians say we no longer have the Law to obey, then God does not have any basis on which to judge us. When we say the Law is no longer applicable; what we are also saying is that we **can not** sin [how can you break a Law that is not there or doesn't exist?]; and if we **can not** sin, then on what basis is God able to pass judgment? It will therefore be unfair for God to pass judgment on us. And if God does pass judgment on anyone, then God is not acting right and fair; [look at Abraham's discourse with God regarding judgment of Sodom and Gomorrah - Abrahams says to God - *".....Shall not the Judge of all the earth do right?"* - Gen 18:25]. But if God were unfair and His judgment not right, then the creator of the universe is also a liar [Yet we know it is impossible for God to lie - **Heb 6:18**]. And if we make God to be a liar, then we **can not** trust anything else He has said, be it the hope of Heaven for those who obey and are justified or the fear of the 2nd death for those who disobey His Law.

Assuming the foregoing analysis were true, then the basis of the Christian doctrine is also very hollow, deceptive and faulty. And if faulty, then such hope of resurrection is also baseless - see **1 Cor 15:12-19.**

Simply put, Christianity is a belief based on the redemption of **sinful man** and bringing that man back into a **relationship** with a **Holy God** through **Jesus Christ the mediator and propitiation.** For this to happen, man has to admit his sin (trespass based on a command/law); and also know that, without his sin being atoned for to appease God, he can no longer be connected to the Holy God.

But how can there be sin if there is no law? And if there is no law, then there can be no sin. And of what purpose would forgiveness/grace be if there is no sin? And if no need for Grace, then there is no need for Jesus - then his death would be meaningless. And if Jesus' death has no meaning, then He didn't have to come to earth at all. And if Jesus didn't come to earth, then there would be no Christianity because Christianity is based on Christ Jesus. And if no Christianity then why are we even having this conversation? The moment you throw out the Law, there will be no need for Christ!

This is how far the discussion at hand goes, we must thus be careful in promoting a doctrine of Christianity without regard to the Law. This is called antinomianism - a system that promotes lawlessness. Does this ring any bell? The devil is called the man of lawlessness and scripture has already warned us that in the last days, he will set himself in God's temple as God. Please read 2 **Thess 2:1-12** for deeper understanding. The spirit of the anti-Christ is already at work in many Churches deceiving and leading astray many sincere men/women of God. We are in the days of the apostate Church.

To bring it all to a close, let me draw your mind to a parable that Jesus told in relation to the Kingdom of God and how everything I have discussed fit together.

Jesus spoke to them again in parables, saying,
² "The kingdom of heaven may be compared to a king who gave a wedding feast for his son. ³ And he sent his servants to call those who had [previously] been invited to the wedding feast, but they refused to come. ⁴ Then he sent out some other servants, saying, 'Tell those who have been invited, "Look, I have prepared my dinner; my oxen and fattened calves are butchered and everything is ready; come to the wedding feast."' ⁵ But they paid no attention [they disregarded the invitation, treating it with contempt] and went away, one to his farm, another to his business. ⁶ The rest [of the invited guests] seized his servants and mistreated them [insulting and humiliating them] and killed them. ⁷ The king was enraged [when he heard this], and sent his soldiers and destroyed those murderers and burned their city. ⁸ Then he said to his servants, 'The wedding [feast] is ready, but those who were invited were not worthy. ⁹ So go to the main highways that lead out of the city, and invite to the wedding feast as many as you find.' ¹⁰ Those servants went out into the streets and gathered together all the people they could find, **both bad and good***; so the wedding hall was filled with dinner guests [sitting at the banquet table]. ¹¹ "But when the king came in to see the dinner guests, he saw a man there who* **was not dressed [appropriately] in wedding clothes,**
¹² and he said, 'Friend, how did you come in here without wearing the wedding clothes [that were provided for you]?' And the man was speechless and without excuse.
¹³ Then the king said to the attendants, 'Tie him hand and foot, and throw him into the darkness outside; in that

GOD'S HOLY LAW - Matters that truly matter!

place there will be weeping [over sorrow and pain] and grinding of teeth [over distress and anger].' [14] For many are called (invited, summoned), but few are chosen."
— **Matthew 22:1-14 - AMP**

In this parable, Jesus tells us that an open invitation was given to all and several people were brought to the wedding feast because they accepted the invitation. The story actually specifies that those who showed up came from different backgrounds - some were good and others were bad; perhaps some were religious and others were not; but that was not the measure that was used for who would be allowed to enter the hall where the wedding feast was being held. *All who accepted the invitation* were made to enter the hall. In other words, the invitation was by grace - not that anyone deserved to be there. However, prior to the start of the feast, we see the master come in for an inspection or investigation - His focus is to ensure that everyone there is wearing the [1] appropriate garment. He finds there is someone in there who is not properly clothed and so He [2] summons the fellow, [3] investigates / cross examines him, allows the fellow to defend himself, when the person couldn't give any good reason for not being garbed appropriately, the master [4] passes judgment that he should be thrown out - and swiftly, the servants [5] execute the judgment. In this parable, again we see how God's judgment is always fair and consistent.

But there's something else I want to point out from this scripture - did the person who is thrown out know the appropriate garment he should have worn and the consequences of not putting on the right garment? Did he think the Master would overlook it simply because he had been invited [shown grace] and or even gained entry into the banquet hall? And what could this garment be by the way?

Let's look at another scripture to help us find out what the expected garment is [allow scripture to interpret itself].

> *⁶ Then I heard something like the shout of a vast multitude, and like the boom of many pounding waves, and like the roar of mighty peals of thunder, saying,*
> *"Hallelujah! For the Lord our God, the Almighty, [the Omnipotent, the Ruler of all] reigns.*
> *⁷ Let us rejoice and shout for joy! Let us give Him glory and honor, for the marriage of the Lamb has come [at last] and His bride (the redeemed) has prepared herself."*
> *⁸ She has been permitted to dress in fine linen, dazzling white and clean—**for the fine linen signifies the righteous acts of the saints** [the ethical conduct, personal integrity, moral courage, and godly character of believers].*
> *⁹ Then the angel said to me, "Write, 'Blessed are those who are invited to the marriage supper of the Lamb.'" And he said to me [further], **"These are the true and exact words of God."***
> *¹⁰ Then I fell down at his feet to worship him, but he [stopped me and] said to me, "You must not do that; I am a fellow servant with you and your brothers and sisters who have and hold the testimony of Jesus. Worship God [alone]. For the testimony of Jesus is the spirit of prophecy [His life and teaching are the heart of prophecy]."*
> *— **Rev 19:6-10 - AMP***

In this vision that was shown the Apostle John of what would happen in the last days, we notice that it describes the same wedding feast that Jesus Christ spoke about in His parable. Vrs 8 describes the fine linen, the appropriate garment which was expected of those invited to the wedding feast, and the scripture explains what it is by saying: *"for the fine linen signifies the **righteous acts** of the saints"*. But if faith in Jesus alone is what is required for our participation in the wedding feast, then why would the scripture be talking about another requirement - righteous acts? Is there any chance, or the slightest possibility that this scripture is teaching us that - "faith in Jesus [Grace through His invitation] may bring us into the wedding hall but to partake of the feast, you need to have lived a righteous life"? If so, then what do you suppose the righteous acts that one must perform are?

> *"I desire to do your will, my God; your law is within my heart."*
> — *Ps 40:8*

What do you suppose God's will is? The Psalmist says God's will is to obey His Law.

Dear friend, if the criteria for those who are chosen and allowed to stay and partake in the wedding feast is based on something they must do - how important is it that we look for it? And how much of your energy would you like to spend to find it out? Is it worth all your time?

James, the brother of Jesus, seems to believe that there is a law by which we will be judged. Check out what he says concerning this: *10 For whoever shall keep the whole law, and yet stumble in one point, he is guilty of all. 11 For He who said, "Do not commit* adultery," also said, "Do not murder." Now if you do not commit adultery, but you do murder, you have become a transgressor of the law. 12 So speak and so do as those who will be judged by the law of liberty." — **James 2:10-12**. What might James be referring to as the law of liberty that we will be judged by in **vrs 12?** When you read carefully from vrs 10; he seems to be referring to God's moral laws simply because he also names some of them - adultery and murder.

Further in that passage **vrs 14-26**, James teaches on how we prove that we have faith - there he mentions that faith which is not accompanied by works is dead.

> [14] Blessed are those who do His commandments, that they may have the right to the tree of life, and may enter through the gates into the city. [15] But outside are dogs and sorcerers and sexually immoral and murderers and idolaters, and whoever loves and practices a lie.
> — **Rev 22:12-16.**

One day, His disciples asked Him what the sign of His second coming will be. In His response, He tells them that it will be like in the days of Noah. You can read the story in **Matthew 24.** In this story, Jesus again leaves a very big clue for us that we must pay attention to. Do you recall where Noah was telling people to go for safety; where they will be protected? Yes, the Ark - it was that which preserved the lives of those who were not taken by the destruction of the flood. Noah preached to them saying: "If you want to save your life, enter the Ark". Friend, if Jesus says to look at the days of Noah, I believe the Ark is very significant and we should keep our eyes on it. We have learnt earlier that

God's law [the 10 commandments] is kept in no other place but in the Ark of the Covenant - **Exodus 25:21**. I do not think that God specifically had Moses place the tablets of the covenant in the Ark for decoration. Not at all, rather; God has given us enough evidence and clues in His word to show that His law is very applicable throughout History and most certainly in these final days prior to the end of this world.

Dear friend, let's not make any mistake - just like in the days of Noah, the only ones who will be **saved** in these last days, will be those people who **enter His Ark to obey His commands.**

Let me make it extra clear that legalistic obedience of the commandments can never save you. I believe and scripture is very clear that we are saved by God's grace [alone]. *"For by grace you have been saved through faith, and that not of yourselves; it is the gift of God, 9 not of works, lest anyone should boast".* — **Eph 2:8-9.**

But when God saves us, He expects us to go and not sin again (in other words, don't continue in a life of lawlessness; stop breaking His commands). That's what happened in the story of the woman who was caught in the act of adultery. The Law required that she be stoned to death but Jesus saved her by grace (she didn't work for it; didn't earn it; she couldn't pay for it and didn't deserve to be spared). Jesus **freely** gave her the **gift of salvation**. But now notice what Jesus told her - *"......Go and sin no more"* — **John 8:11.** Jesus' expectation of this woman [and for all who God has redeemed by the same Grace]; is to live a life of gratitude and appreciation by no longer breaking the commands. He expects that as a result of the love He has first shown us, we would love Him back by obeying the Law - See also **Rom 3:31**.

Therefore, a Christian doesn't keep the Law to earn salvation, rather a Christian keeps the Law because they have been saved. Obedience to the Law is therefore a natural response to what God has done for us. *"And He died for all, that those who live should live no longer for themselves, but for Him who died for them and rose again"* — **2 Cor 5:15.**

It is my hope and prayer that anyone who calls him/herself a Christian will decide to **personally** look into this matter and not leave it to their Church or pastor. And I pray, that this write-up will incite further study and discussion across Christian Churches, fellowships and small groups - and that God will guide us to know the whole truth and **be set free** by **His truth**.

May God's name be forever praised and glorified.

Shalom!

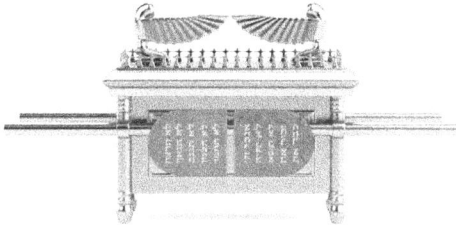

PART TWO

INTRODUCTION

In **PART I** I share my convictions about the Law being operational even in the 21st century [in the life of a follower of Jesus]. If you haven't read it already, I encourage you to take time to do so before you continue. In this part, I will continue my thoughts and to now write as though the moral law of God [10 commandments] is applicable.

Apart from the 2nd commandment regarding the worship of idols which is believed to have been eliminated by the Roman Catholic Church from their set of commandments *[I touch on that briefly later in this chapter]*, there isn't much controversy about the 10 commandments themselves among almost all Christian denominations and even Jewish folk - except when we come to the 4th commandment on the Sabbath. So I will devote the majority of my time here to focus on that.

* * * * * * *

I mentioned in **PART I** that Jesus stated emphatically at the beginning of His ministry that; He didn't come to do away with the Law but to ensure that it is adhered to. He further went on to teach how under the 2nd covenant, sin happens when it is thought of or conceived in the heart even before the action itself occurs. As such, Jesus came with a higher standard of the Law than was known from the days of Moses. For example, He says; *"²⁷ You have heard the commandment that says, 'You must not commit adultery. ²⁸ But I say, anyone who even looks at a woman with lust has already committed adultery with her in his heart."* Read the full account in **Matthew 5:17-48 NLT**

> *¹⁷ "Don't misunderstand why I have come. I did not come to abolish the law of Moses or the writings of the prophets. No, I came to accomplish their purpose. ¹⁸ I tell you the truth, until heaven and earth disappear, not even the smallest detail of God's law will disappear until its purpose is achieved. ¹⁹ So if you ignore the least commandment and teach others to do the same, you will be called the least in the Kingdom of Heaven. But anyone who obeys God's laws and teaches them will be called great in the Kingdom of Heaven......*

In His last message to His disciples before He ascended into Heaven, Jesus parting words included His instructions to teach everyone everything He had commanded:

"²⁰ Teach these new disciples to obey all the commands I have given you..." — Matthew 28:16-20 NLT.

Also in His final message to us before He returns to judge the world, in what He revealed through John in the book of Revelation, Jesus tells us *"¹⁴ Blessed are those who do His commandments, that they may have the right to the tree of life, and may enter through the gates into the city. ¹⁵ But outside are dogs and sorcerers and sexually immoral and murderers and idolaters, and whoever loves and practices a lie.* — Rev 22:12-16

So what we see here is that in the three most important parts of His Ministry;

(1) When Jesus starts His ministry;
(2) When He is leaving the earth and;
(3) Prior to His 2nd return to earth;

His message to us is centred on God's Law. Can we thus conclude that God's Law is very central to Jesus teaching?

"If you keep my commandments, you will abide in my love, just as I have kept my Father's commandments and abide in his love" — John 15:10 NRSV

So far, with even those that I have personally come across who claim that we are no longer living under Law, none will say something as - *"Because we are no longer under the law, we can steal; or we can commit sexual immorality; or we can worship idols; or we can covet our neighbors wife/belongings; or that we can practice idolatry".* That's why I am baffled as to the number of people who come with a defensive attitude regarding the command to *"Remember the Sabbath and keep it Holy"*. I have come to the very sad realization that; mostly, the whole reason people argue that we are no longer supposed to observe the Law [in its entirety] is because of the Sabbath command. It is the one command that people are mostly offended by or are quick to conclude that God has changed without ever being able to support it with scripture. They usually base the reason for the change on the fact that Jesus rose on Sunday - *"Early on Sunday morning, while it was still dark,*

Mary Magdalene came to the tomb and found that the stone had been rolled away from the entrance. ² She ran and found Simon Peter and the other disciple, the one whom Jesus loved. She said, "They have taken the Lord's body out of the tomb, and we don't know where they have put him!" — **John 20:1-2.** While the fact remains that Jesus rose on a Sunday, there is nothing in scripture that says that God changed His command.

Many have attempted to quote scripture showing that the disciples got together on the first day of the week to support such change. Below are a few of scriptures they quote:

> *"So when it was evening on that day, the first day of the week, and when the doors were shut where the disciples were, for fear of the Jews, Jesus came and stood in their midst and *said to them, "Peace be with you."*
> — **John 20:19**

> *"On the first day of the week, when we were gathered together to break bread, Paul began talking to them, intending to leave the next day, and he prolonged his message until midnight.*
> — **Acts 20:7**

> *"Now regarding your question about the money being collected for God's people in Jerusalem. You should follow the same procedure I gave to the Churches in Galatia. 2 On the first day of each week, you should each put aside a portion of the money you have earned. Don't wait until I get there and then try to collect it all at once.*
> — **1 Corinthians 16:1-2**

*"I was in the Spirit on the Lord's day, and I heard behind
me a loud voice like the sound of a trumpet,*
— **Revelation 1:10**

I am not sure that the fact of the early Church deciding to meet
on any particular day nullifies God's command to observe the day
on which He commanded men to rest. The scriptures don't say
much about what was happening; besides there are passages that
suggest that the disciples met at the temple courts and in each
other's homes everyday — **Acts 2:46-47.** Why should the few
scriptures pointing to their meeting on a Sunday cancel out God's
supreme command? The Psalmist says *"....all thy commandments
are righteousness"* - **Ps 119:172.** When he says "all" - I believe he
means ALL. Which one out of the lot do you suppose we are
allowed to erase or take out?

QUICK SIDE NOTE:

I would like to add that these have not been my convictions for
all time, so I am not sharing from a position of strength, nor am I
accusing anyone who hasn't known these in the past. When God
reveals truth to us, He doesn't do so to embarass or to condemn
us; but to cause us to repent so He will save us. God in His mercy
has chosen to open my eyes to this and I want to share them with
you in all humility, in the hope that you may also consider what
I believe a lot of sincere God loving men and women of God are
wrong about — **1 Cor 2:10-16.** So, please consider my thoughts
just for this moment and then debate it further. After all, the
bible encourages us to *"......test all spirits to see whether they are of
God"* — **1 John 4:1.**

15

THE SABBATH

> *Keep my Sabbaths holy, and they will be a sign between me and you, so you may know that I am the Lord your God* — **Eze 20:20**

[The ONLY day God **set apart** from the beginning of time and **blessed** to be a memorial [reminder] of His works of creation — **Gen 2:1-3**]. Also a sign between God and His people — **Eze 20:12**

Jesus is not at odds with the Sabbath as some make it seem. Scripture clearly tells us that Jesus is the creator of the world - *"All things were made through Him, and without Him nothing was made that was made"* — **John 1:3; Col 1:15-16; Heb 1:1-2.** So when scripture tells us that He rested from all the work of creation on the seventh day and He blessed the seventh day and set it apart - we know that it was Jesus the scripture refers to.

In giving the Law at Mt. Sinai to Moses, the Sabbath command is the only command that begins with **"Remember"** - and yet, that's the only command that most people (even some Christians) say we are to **"forget"** about in the entire commandments of God. No born-again New Testament Christian will ever tell you to dishonor God, nor will they refute the commands "do not murder, do not steal, do not commit adultery, do not covet your neighbours wife and property"; yet these same people make all efforts to prove that the Sabbath command that God tells us to remember have been abolished.

All the other commands obtain their validity from the 4th commandment of the Sabbath. When you tell anyone *"Do not kill, do not steal, do not lie, do not commit adultery, do not bow down to any image, don't use my name in vain, don't have any other god except me"* - the question arises - why should anyone obey the law-giver? Interestingly, that answer can only be found in the 4th commandment - "because in six days the Lord created the Heavens and the earth…". We (the creatures) obey God because He is our creator. The Sabbath command is therefore the root of all the other commands and makes all of the commands valid; without it, the other commands won't stand.

When God created the world and everything in it, man was not present to witness God at work. Even when God created woman, He put man to sleep so man really didn't see anything being created. He had to have faith in what God was saying - *"In the beginning God created the Heavens and the Earth"* — **Gen 1:1**. Man has no other way of verifying whether this is true or not? *"By faith we understand that the worlds were framed by the word of God, so that the things which are seen were not made of things* *which are visible"* — **Hebrews 11:3.** To those who believe God created the world, it is only through faith - and there can be no other way! This is also why there are people who don't believe the story of creation - because humanly speaking, there is no way to verify, others also choose to believe in the theory of Evolution. The Sabbath is the only way to distinguish between those who believe God as creator and those who don't - Yes, the Sabbath is a BIG deal!

To an extent, we can say that God intentionally instituted the Sabbath to test man's faith in Him? In doing this, God simply states that man would have to observe the Sabbath as a reminder to him that God was the creator of the Heavens and Earth and everything in them. Remember that our faith in God will be tested - indeed the scriptures tell us that faith that is not tested is no faith at all and can not be trusted - **1 Pet 1:7.** So God will bring situations our way to test whether or not we believe in Him as the creator. I believe thus, the Sabbath command is a test in itself.

> *"Remember the Sabbath (seventh) day to keep it holy (set apart, dedicated to God).* ⁹ *Six days you shall labor and do all your work,* ¹⁰ *but the seventh day is a Sabbath [a day of rest dedicated] to the Lord your God; on that day you shall not do any work, you or your son, or your daughter, or your male servant, or your female servant, or your livestock or the temporary resident (foreigner) who stays within your [city] gates.* ¹¹ ***For in six days the Lord made the heavens and the earth, the sea and everything that is in them, and He rested (ceased) on the seventh day.***

That is why the Lord blessed the Sabbath day and made it holy [that is, set it apart for His purposes]".
— **Exodus 20:8-11 AMP.** [emphasis mine].

Pay particular attention to what it says in **vrs 11**. Observing the Sabbath means worshiping God because you believe that God was indeed the creator of the world [it's as simple as that]. Further, **those who desecrate the Sabbath are unbelievers** - they do not believe that God is the creator of the Universe as He says. They can also be referred to as those who practice falsehood or lies - because they have accepted a teaching not from God but man. When the Apostle John is shown what is to come in the book of Revelation, Jesus tells him that those who don't make it into the new Jerusalem will include the **unbelieving and liars**, together with idolaters, sexually immoral, murderers etc — **Rev 21:8** also **Rev 22:15**. Seeing how important the Sabbath is therefore - do you imagine that the devil would sit idly-by and watch people in all Nations worship God the Creator or do you think that he will rather attack God's rule and authority and attempt to change the day?

In the future, in the new Jerusalem that God will create after the final judgment and destruction of this present world; the Bible clearly tells us that we will be observing the Sabbath - *"23 And it shall come to pass That from one New Moon to another, And from one Sabbath to another, All flesh shall come to worship before Me,"* *says the Lord"* — **Isaiah 66:22-23**. Let me pose a question - "On which day do you think we will be observing this Sabbath - will it be the same day God instituted from creation on which He rested or do you think it will be another day chosen by man"? Do you imagine God will change the day that He says He rested on? He tells us - *"For I am the Lord, I do not change...."* — **Mal 3:6**. Though **Malachi 3** is mostly only known for the verses that speak of robbing God of tithes and offerings, I recommend that you read the chapter through to see how God is calling us back to His ordinances, to repent and to return to His Law that we have not kept.

> *"Thus the heavens and the earth, and all the host of them, were finished. ² And on the seventh day God ended His work which He had done, and He rested on the seventh day from all His work which He had done. ³ Then God blessed the seventh day and sanctified it, because in it He rested from all His work which God had created and made* — **Gen 2:1-3**

The Sabbath is not only a reminder/memorial of creation but also a memorial of redemption. Notice, Moses tells the Israelites to observe the Sabbath and allow their servants rest as a reminder to them that they themselves were slaves in Egypt.

> *"Observe the Sabbath day, to keep it holy, as the Lord your God commanded you. ¹³ Six days you shall labor and do all your work, ¹⁴ but the seventh day is the Sabbath of the Lord your God. In it you shall do no work: you, nor your son, nor your daughter, nor your male servant, nor your female servant, nor your ox, nor your donkey, nor any of your cattle, nor your stranger who is within your gates, that your male servant and your female servant may rest as well as you. ¹⁵ And remember that you were a slave in the land of Egypt, and the Lord your God brought you out from there by a mighty hand and by an outstretched arm;*

therefore the Lord your God commanded you to keep the Sabbath day"— **Deut 5:12-15**.

You may say that you are not a Jew so this doesn't apply to you. But the truth is that we are all in bondage to sin and need a redeemer. Just as God led the Israelites out of bondage from Egypt, we as Gentiles are also being freed from the bondage of sin through Jesus finished work on the cross. That is also why Jesus observed the Sabbath even in his death when He was taken from the cross and placed in the tomb — **Luke 23:53-54**.

So as we can see, the Sabbath observance is an important memorial for us, of the facts that we were [1] created by God and as well, we have been [2] redeemed by God. Do you think all of humanity falls into one or both categories? God is saying to us - "Observe the Sabbath; If you were created by, and or have been redeemed by God". Our failure, reluctance or whatever reason for which we don't obey this command, shows that - notwithstanding what we profess, we do not believe God is indeed who He says He is - Creator & Redeemer. And yet, notice; our God is called **"I AM who I AM"**.

Sabbath is not a day to lounge about doing nothing - the command says we should keep it holy. We can't make any day holy, only a Holy God can, so ours is to keep it holy. Not that we can't worship God any other day; but keeping it Holy is a sign between God and His people just as circumcision was the sign of God's covenant with Abraham. Where God says we should keep it holy, he adds that He has given us six days to labor and do all our work but on the Sabbath - He wants us to reserve it for His purpose only. So with anything that we want to partake in on the

Sabbath - we have to ask ourselves; how does God feel about me doing this on His special day?

THE SECRET OF THE LORD

When we come to understand the underlying meaning of the Sabbath and why God has decreed that we observe it - we will no longer be tossed left and right by any wind of doctrine. *"But without faith it is impossible to please Him, for he who comes to God must believe that He is, and that He is a rewarder of those who diligently seek Him"* — **Hebrews 11:6 NKJV**. This scripture helps us to understand the nature of God - He doesn't want any of us approaching Him who doesn't believe that He is who He says He is. There is no point because He doesn't allow a relationship with those who don't trust Him.

It seems that of all God's commands, the Sabbath command is that which is central - it is the core of all the other commands, and the one that holds it all together. When you check the covenant promise [I will be your God/Father and you will be my sons/daughters]; you will understand that at it's very root and heart, it speaks of a relationship. Two can not walk together except they agree. God can not claim to be God and you not believe Him and still be able to carry on in a relationship with Him. It is only when we trust God fully that we can accept Him to be our God, then we will not worship other gods before Him or bow down to graven images; it is then also that we will commit to do whatever else He instructs us to do [*do not murder; do not commit adultery; do not lie; do not covet your neighbours wife/property etc*]. This is why the Sabbath is the secret to having a thriving relationship with God. No one can ever please God unless you first take Him at His word; and the way He has chosen to test our faith is with the Sabbath. I firmly believe that - "Out goes the Sabbath, and out goes our hope in ever being in a relationship with God".

Who do you share your secrets with? Secrets are valuable to us, we don't go about letting everyone at all know. We keep them from open view and guard them so only the people we want to know will find it. It is the same with God - If God were to make His secrets known, I believe David would surely be one who would qualify - God called him "a man after His own heart". David tells us the kind of people God reveals His secrets to - *"The secret of the Lord is with those who fear Him, And He will show them His covenant"* — **Ps 25:14.** God's covenant [law/decree/statute] is His secret - wait a minute; why should God make this a secret, and why would He only show those who fear Him?

To fear God means to trust Him besides no other - just like you will have to trust the person you share your secret with. Apparently, God doesn't waste His time showing His truths to everyone; He reveals Himself to those who have decided in their hearts to obey and follow Him, to those who completely trust Him - not those who are only curious for the sake of knowing.

Paul also agrees with this assertion as he says - *"It is only after we have first given ourselves as living sacrifices that we will find out what God's purpose for our life is"* — **Rom 12:1-2** [Paraphrase mine]. Many want to know what God would have them do before they decide whether they want to follow Him or not, but that's not how God operates. He asks us to first give ourselves to Him, only then will He tell us what He wants us to do. Look what Jesus said to the Jews when they questioned His insight - *"If any of you really* *determines to do God's will, then you will certainly know whether my teaching is from God or is merely my own"* — **John 7:17 TLB.**

It takes a lot of trust [faith] to commit yourself to a course prior to knowing all that is involved - but that's how God wants us to come to Him - in total faith! Jesus told the story of a persistent widow who had faith [even] in an unjust judge - at the end of the parable, He asks: *"Nevertheless, when the Son of Man comes, will He really find faith on the earth?"* — **Luke 18:1-8.**

Do you remember the story of Daniel and his friends when King Nebuchadnezzer put them in training preparing them for roles in Babylon? Isn't it interesting that their wisdom was found to be 10 times more than all those who chose to drink the wine from the king's table — **Dan 1:8-20?** And do you realise how as a result of having faith in God, they were the only ones who God showed Nebuchadnezzer's dream to and gave them understanding to interpret it? At the end, they were the ones through whom all the wise men of Babylon were saved from the king's decree to annihilate them. After this incident, would you trust the magicians and sorcerers of Babylon or would you rather trust those who have devoted themselves to God? Read this beautiful story in **Dan 2.** As a result of their faith in God, a pagan king bowed before them and acknowledged that their God is indeed God.

"Then King Nebuchadnezzar fell on his face, prostrate before Daniel, and commanded that they should present an offering and incense to him. ⁴⁷ The king answered Daniel, and said, "Truly your God is the God of gods, the Lord of kings, and a revealer of secrets, since you could

reveal this secret." ⁴⁸ Then the king promoted Daniel and
gave him many great gifts; and he made him ruler over the
whole province of Babylon, and chief administrator over
all the wise men of Babylon. ⁴⁹ Also Daniel petitioned the
king, and he set Shadrach, Meshach, and Abed-Nego over
the affairs of the province of Babylon; but Daniel sat in [p]
the gate of the king" — **Dan 2:46-49**.

This story confirms that; God reserves insight, wisdom and understanding to only those who have faith in Him - indeed He only shares His secrets with the ones who are faithful to Him. Is your faith practical? Does your faith cause others to know God and worship Him?

God is pleased to share His secret with us, He only wants us to be resolved in our hearts; to trust and follow [obey] Him no matter what it takes. Jesus also calls us to follow Him so we won't have to walk in darkness.

"I am the light of the world. Whoever follows me will never walk in darkness, but will have the light of life."
— **John 8:12 NIV**

Will you follow Jesus?

GOD'S HOLY LAW - Matters that truly matter!

16

JUSTIFIED BY WORKS

You know that if you do what is right, I will accept you. But if you don't, sin is ready to attack you. That sin will want to control you, but you must control it.
— **Gen 4:7 ERV**

What of those who say they have faith in God and that they truly believe He is who He says He is [the creator of Heaven and Earth and everything in them]? James the brother of Jesus uses many words to encourage us to understand that our **faith by itself without works will never save us**. It is not enough for you to just voice out faith; God doesn't want that kind of faith. The faith God wants from us is the faith that has action. Of this Paul says, *"when our hearts believe, our mouths should confess so that we will be saved"* — **Rom 10:9-10** [paraphrase mine]. We are not saved with just our hearts believing - our mouths must confess as well.

Suppose I deposit a thousand dollars into an account for you, but you never go to withdraw it, will the [unclaimed] money benefit you? You can believe alright that the money is there - but to have it work/benefit you, you would have to go and claim it. In the same way, believing that God is creator should move us to observe His commandment to prove that we truly believe He is who He says He is; that's how we will be saved - "Faith without works is dead" — **James 2:14-26**

When Abraham believed God, he acted and that is why righteousness was credited to him. Abraham had a faith that acted, his faith in God was so strong to make him believe that God could bring Isaac back alive and so he went ahead to offer Isaac when he was tested — **Heb 11:17-19**.

The line-up in **Hebrews 11** records several heroes of old who were acknowledged because of their faith in God. In each of their cases, the faith of these heroes prompted them to act. From Abel, through Enoch, Noah, Abraham, Sarah, Isaac, Jacob, Joseph, Moses, Rahab, Gideon, Barak, Samson, Jephthah, David, Samuel, and the Prophets - each of these heroes were acknowledged because of what they did. In fact, their faith would not have been noticed if not for what that faith caused them to do.

Just as the heroes of faith were reckoned because they acted on their faith - Sabbath observance proves to God that we believe He is Creator - that's what His word teaches us to do. He decided to choose that as the sign and we His creatures can't do anything about it - it is settled! The relationship between creator and creature is obedience - we rest because He asks us to.

Yet, rather than obey what our creator says; man tends to question Him as though He is unfit for the position of Creator of the Universe or that we can do a better job. Let's take a quick dive into the book of Job for his interaction with God so we understand our place before the Almighty. I encourage you to read all through **Job 38 - Job 42**.

> *"¹ Then the Lord answered Job out of the whirlwind and said,*
> *² "Who is this that darkens counsel [questioning my authority and wisdom] By words without knowledge?*
> *³ "Now gird up your loins like a man,*
> *And I will ask you, and you instruct Me!*
> *⁴ "Where were you when I laid the foundation of the earth? Tell Me, if you know and have understanding.*
> *⁵ "Who determined the measurements [of the earth], if you know?*
> *Or who stretched the [measuring] line on it?*
> *⁶ "On what were its foundations fastened?*
> *Or who laid its cornerstone,......"* — **Job 38 AMP**

> *¹ Then the Lord said to Job,*
> *² "Will the faultfinder contend with the Almighty? Let him who disputes with God answer it." ³ Then Job replied to the Lord and said,*
> *⁴ "Behold, I am of little importance and contemptible; what can I reply to You? I lay my hand on my mouth.*
> *⁵ "I have spoken once, but I will not reply again— Indeed, twice [I have answered], and I will add nothing further......"* — **Job 40-AMP**

When we understand our place before God as Job did, we will never again question what He says; and we will come to respect His word forever. God doesn't need to ask our permission before

He does what He chooses - and besides, everything He does is perfect so it never has to change.

Could it be that God is not sure of which day He rested from His work of creation or that He's changed His mind on the day? Notice that the Sabbath is not just a day on which man is commanded to rest - God asked that we rest on the Sabbath because He first rested; not as though He was tired but the scripture explains that He ceased from His work of creation. When you look at it that way, you will realise that the argument that God changed His day of rest to Sunday is not only preposterous but I believe also very insulting to our God.

Do you have faith that God is the creator of the universe? To prove that you do, God says; "rest on the Sabbath". Your obedience to His command will prove to Him that you do have faith in Him - it is as simple as that, but remember, you are being tested.

HOW CAN WE BE SURE THAT SABBATH IS SATURDAY?

> *"For I am the Lord, I do not change…. — Mal 3:6*
> *Jesus Christ is the same yesterday, today, and forever*
> *— Heb 13:8*

Some people ask - "How can we be sure that the 1st day corresponds to Sunday and the 7th day corresponds to Saturday? What they really want to ask is; "how can we be sure that the Sabbath day is Saturday"? For the purpose of our discussion, let's put all our bias aside and see if scripture can help us find which day corresponds to which number.

When you go to the creation story as we notice from the scriptures below, we understand that God made the world in 6 literal days. His final creation was man who He made on the 6th day.

"Then God said, "Let Us make man in Our image, according to Our likeness; let them have dominion over the fish of the sea, over the birds of the air, and over the cattle, over all the earth and over every creeping thing that creeps on the earth." [27] *So God created man in His own image; in the image of God He created him; male and female He created them. ......* [31] *Then God saw everything that He had made, and indeed it was very good. So the evening and the morning were the sixth day". — **Gen 1:26-31***

"Thus the heavens and the earth, and all the host of them, were finished. [2] *And on the seventh day God ended His work which He had done, and He rested on the seventh day from all His work which He had done.* [3] *Then God blessed the seventh day and sanctified it, because in it He rested from all His work which God had created and made" — **Gen 2:1-3***

So the Bible is clear that God **FINISHED** His work [creation] on the **6th day** and on the **7th day;** He **blessed it**, **set it apart** and **RESTED.**

"And so it was, on the sixth day, that they gathered twice as much bread, two omers for each one. And all the rulers of the congregation came and told Moses. [23] *Then he said to them, "This is what the Lord has said: 'Tomorrow is a Sabbath rest, a holy Sabbath to the Lord. Bake what you will bake today, and boil what you will boil; and lay up for yourselves all that remains, to be kept until morning.'* *"* [24] *So they laid it up till morning, as Moses commanded; and it did not stink, nor were there any worms in it.* [25]

Then Moses said, "Eat that today, for today is a Sabbath to the Lord; today you will not find it in the field. [26] *Six days you shall gather it, but on the seventh day, the Sabbath, there will be none." — Exo 16:22-26.*

When God gave the manna - He commanded Israel to take twice as much as they needed on the 6th day because the following day would be their Sabbath of rest. This corroborates with the creation story which says that the 7th day was the day of rest [Sabbath]. There is consistency in these accounts.

According to the Bible, Jesus died on a day the Jewish folk called the Preparation day - it had that name because it was the day on which they prepared to enter God's rest, [Sabbath]. See the account below:

"Now there was a man named Joseph, a member of the Council, a good and upright man, [51] *who had not consented to their decision and action. He came from the Judean town of Arimathea, and he himself was waiting for the kingdom of God.* [52] *Going to Pilate, he asked for Jesus' body.* [53] *Then he took it down, wrapped it in linen cloth and placed it in a tomb cut in the rock, one in which no one had yet been laid.* [54] *It was **Preparation Day, and the Sabbath was about to begin" — Luke 23:50-54***

Again, we know from history that the day on which Jesus died was a Friday, the day they called Preparation day. This automatically tells us that the next day which they said would be the Sabbath was Saturday. So by allowing scripture to explain these things to us, we can safely say that the 1st day corresponds to Sunday; 2nd day corresponds to Monday, 6th day corresponds to Friday; and the 7th day corresponds to Saturday. Therefore, the 7th day God **blessed** and **set apart** and commanded that we **rest** on is no other day but **Saturday**.

But see what else is even more interesting in the detail of the events of both creation and redemption. The Bible tells us that Jesus is the creator - everything was created through Him and without Him nothing was created that has been created — **John 1:3**

What this means is that "On the **6th day**; Jesus **FINISHED** His work [of creation] and on the **7th day**, He **RESTED**.

Remember Jesus' last words on the cross on that 6th day [Preparation Day]? *"It is FINISHED"* - **John 19:30**. Do you suppose this is mere coincidence? And after He finished His work, the scripture says He was laid to **rest**. On which day do you suppose Jesus rested? *"53 Then he took it down, wrapped it in linen cloth and placed it in a tomb cut in the rock, one in which no one had yet been laid. 54 It was **Preparation Day**, and the **Sabbath was about to begin"** —* **Luke 23:53-54**. You guessed right - It was the Sabbath day*!*

So again and just as we saw in the event of creation, "On the **6th day**, Jesus **FINISHED** His work [of redemption] and on the **7th day**, He **RESTED**. Do you notice how consistent scripture is and also how Jesus has never missed one day of rest right from the time of creation?

On the other hand, notice how those who accused Jesus of breaking the Sabbath had no regard for the Sabbath command:

"The next day, the one after Preparation Day, the chief priests and the Pharisees went to Pilate. [63] *"Sir," they said, "we remember that while he was still alive that deceiver said, 'After three days I will rise again.'* [64] *So give the order for the tomb to be made secure until the third day. Otherwise, his disciples may come and steal the body and tell the people that he has been raised from the dead. This last deception will be worse than the first."* [65] *"Take a guard," Pilate answered. "Go, make the tomb as secure as you know how."* [66] **So they went and made the tomb secure by putting a seal on the stone and posting the guard"** — Matt 27:62-66*

On the day on which they were to cease from all labour; the custodians of the Law were themselves breaking God's Law. We see the Chief Priests and the Pharisees breaking the Sabbath command by going out and working. And yet they were quick at accusing others of sin. No wonder Jesus calls them hypocrites!

GOD'S HOLY LAW - Matters that truly matter!

18

CHANGE TO SUNDAY

While the earth remains, Seedtime and harvest, Cold and heat, Winter and summer, And day and night Shall not cease." — **Gen 8:22 NKJV**

Are you aware that there is no scripture that backs this notion of the day of rest [Sabbath] being changed to Sunday? Do we forget Jesus admonishing us against the thought that He came to change the Law? *"Do not think that I came to destroy the Law or the Prophets. I did not come to destroy but to fulfill"* — **Matt 5:17**. So if Jesus didn't want us even thinking that He came to set the Law aside, won't it be hypocritical of Him to have it changed?

Are you also aware that long before the decree to change the day of rest from Saturday to Sunday; God had shown Daniel in a vision that it would happen? Let's look at the account in **Daniel 7.25** — *"He shall speak pompous words against the Most High, Shall* *persecute the saints of the Most High, **And shall intend to change times and law**. Then the saints shall be given into his hand For a time and times and half a time".*

History helps us identify a time under Pagan Rome when Emperor Constantine I in worship of the pagan sun god, **decreed Sunday to be the day of rest** in place of God's Sabbath. The 'Sunday Sabbath' [if there should be anything like that] is man-made and the Roman Catholic Church stands behind it 100% till today - they even go as far as saying that God gave them the authority to make changes where they saw fit. Here are a few quotes you can refer to:

> *"The Pope has power to change times, to abrogate laws, and to dispense with all things, even the precepts of Christ"* — **Decretal De Translat. Espiscop. Cap.**

> *"We hold upon this earth the place of God Almighty"* — **Pg 304, The Encyclical Letters of Pope Leo XIII"**

> *"Sunday is our mark of authority. The Church is above the Bible, and this transference of Sabbath observance is proof of that fact."* — **Catholic Record; Sept 1, 1923**

> *"Perhaps the boldest thing, the most revolutionary change the Church ever did, happened in the first century. The holy day, the Sabbath, was changed from Saturday to Sunday not from any directions noted in the Scriptures, but from the Church's sense of its own power. People who think the Scripture should be the sole authority, should logically become 7th*

Day Adventist's, and keep Saturday holy." - **Saint Catherine - Catholic Church Sentinel, May 21, 1995**

"The civil authorities should be urged to cooperate with the Church in maintaining and strengthening this public worship of God, and to support with their own authority the regulations set down by the Church's pastor. For it is only in this way that the faithful will understand why it is Sunday and not the Sabbath day that we keep holy" — **The Roman Catechism 1985**

"In respecting religious liberty and the common good of all, Christians should seek recognition of Sunday's and the Church's holy days as legal holidays. It is time that we demonstrate our Catholic vitality and engage in the public policy debate. We have the power and the people to embark on this movement - a movement that will benefit all Americans." — **Catechism of the Catholic Church paragraph 2188, 1994 Edition.**

"Most Christians assume that Sunday is the biblically approved day of worship. The Catholic Church protests that it transferred Christian worship from the biblical Sabbath (Saturday) to Sunday and that to try to argue that the change was made in the Bible is both dishonest and a denial of Catholic authority. If Protestantism wants to base its teachings only on the Bible, it should worship on Saturday." — **Rome's challenge. [www. immaculateheart.com/maryonline]. Dec 2003**

In scripture, we learn that one is a slave unto him who he obeys or one under whose authority he serves - <u>Rom 6:16</u>. It therefore stands to reason that those of us who obey and or are eager and make excuses to observe the 'Sunday Sabbath' are obeying the institution who decreed it and or the person to whose honor it was decreed. Likewise those who observe the True Sabbath are obeying God.

Rather than watch for Rome to fall, Emperor Constantine decided to bring unity and make them strong by bringing together the two main opposing groups under the Roman Empire. These two opposing groups were Paganism and Christianity. Every leader knows that a kingdom/people divided against themselves can not stand [nor can they be strong] and so what Constantine did was a compromise so that the Christians and Pagans can unite for Rome to be strong again.

Constantine claimed to have converted to Christianity, but this was a very political move to save the Roman empire from collapse and thus making Christianity the State religion. The idea was to seek for ways that made it easier/comfortable for pagan worshippers to become Christians so that they who once persecuted the Christians were now one with them. This led to Rome becoming a "Christian" Nation and by so; allowing pagan rituals, man-made traditions and some rites and celebrations steeped in idol worship (including infant baptism; Christmas, Easter etc) to be introduced into the Church. You can read more about this in the **edict of Milan**.

According to history, Emperor Constantine in veneration of the pagan sun god Sol Invictus, **decreed Sunday to be the day of**

rest on **March 7 in the year 321**. Clearly, the reason Sunday was observed as the day of rest was not because Jesus rose on Sunday but rather in worship of the god of the sun - a reason steeped in idol worship, nothing to do with God. Let's pay close attention to Jesus words' to us regarding who we obey: *"No one can serve two masters; for either he will hate the one and love the other, or else he will be loyal to the one and despise the other. You cannot serve God and mammon.* — **Matthew 6:24**

So by lowering the standards of conversion [proven repentance by deeds and baptism for forgiveness of sins]; the Church in Rome grew in great numbers but at the same time, Spirituality went out of the door and the Church has grown weaker and weaker from that period till now. Unfortunately, the modern Church continues to make the same mistake of compromising so as to have more numerical growth. Contrary to what people may think, history teaches us that when the Church compromises on it's standards, the world doesn't get converted to the Church but rather the Church is converted into the world and into some form of fossilized customs and religion [having a form of godliness but denying its power]. God's Holy Spirit can not dwell in the Church that practices untruth, man-made traditions and or pagan practices.

The man of lawlessness' agenda is to covet the worship that belongs only to God and his main weapons are deception and counterfeiting. He diverts the minds of the world, especially followers of Christ, to believe the lie that God is behind changing the day of rest to Sunday. Unfortunately, many have bought into his lies, and worse, he makes them think the lie is rather the truth. He makes many to also think that it doesn't matter which day you observe the Sabbath when God was very clear on the day of rest from the beginning [by setting it apart and blessing it].

Truth is; we testify and acknowledge that God is Creator of the world by observing the true Sabbath - not observing the true Sabbath means that you don't acknowledge God as creator. The danger is; by not acknowledging God as creator, you CAN NOT have a relationship with Him. *"⁴⁴ You are of your father the devil, and the desires of your father you want to do. He was a murderer from the beginning, and does not stand in the truth, because there is no truth in him. When he speaks a lie, he speaks from his own resources, for he is a liar and the father of it. .....⁴⁷ He who is of God hears God's words; therefore you do not hear, because you are not of God."* — **John 8:39-47**. Like the Pharisees, those who live on lies are following after their father - the devil.

Another reason we can be certain that the day for the Sabbath observance did not change is from this scripture:

> *"¹⁵ "Therefore when you see the 'abomination of desolation,' spoken of by Daniel the prophet, standing in the holy place" (whoever reads, let him understand), ¹⁶ "then let those who are in Judea flee to the mountains. ¹⁷ Let him who is on the housetop not go down to take anything out of his house. ¹⁸ And let him who is in the field not go back to get his clothes. ¹⁹ But woe to those who are pregnant and to those who are nursing babies in those days! ²⁰ **And pray that your flight may not be** in winter or **on the Sabbath**. ²¹ For then there will be great tribulation, such as has not been since the beginning of the world until this time, no, nor ever shall be."* — **Matt 24:1-35**

Jesus is talking to His disciples about a future event - the destruction of the temple in Jerusalem which happened some forty years after His resurrection and ascension to Heaven. In this story, He asks the disciples to pray that their need to flee will not coincide with the winter or the Sabbath. So even in a time of war and disaster, Jesus expects that His followers would have to still obey the command of God. In other words, do not love your life even unto death or simply put - don't break God's Sabbath command even when your life depends on it. Friend, when you think of this, do you think we have a valid excuse to break God's Sabbath for the sake of any and all kinds of work?

You would think that in a time of war and distress, God would understand and excuse us but He rather tells us to pray to not encounter it at all. This means that God wants us to uphold His law at all times - we don't get an out for any and every reason. He is God, and when we come before Him with our challenging situations, He will help us - there is nothing that is impossible for God to do.

There is no doubt that Jesus knew all the details of the temple's destruction, He is the one who was and is and is to come - Jesus is God and therefore omnipresent as well as omniscient. If there was any such thing that the Sabbath would be changed to the first day of the week in commemoration of His resurrection - His statement would have read this way: *"Pray that your flight may not be in winter or the first day of the week"*. But that's not what He said; His disciples' understanding of the Sabbath could not have been different from what they had always been accustomed to - the 7th day Sabbath.

GOD'S HOLY LAW - Matters that truly matter!

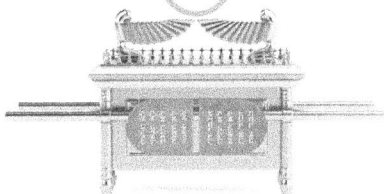

19

SCRIPTURES THAT SUGGEST EARLY CHRISTIANS WORSHIPPED ON SUNDAY

> *"It is not good for a person to be without much learning, and he who hurries with his feet rushes into sin.*
> — *Prov 19:2 NLV*

In this chapter, we will examine some scriptures that are mostly quoted to support the assumption that right after Jesus and in the time of the Apostles, the early Church started meeting on Sundays. I like the fact that the proponents of this theory do admit that such change happened after the death of Jesus; so before we even get into the scriptures they use to back up their theory - let's establish through scripture and law whether such change can be allowed.

First, according to **Heb 9:17**; *"For a testament is in force after men are dead, since it has no power at all while the testator lives"* - we learn that the 2nd covenant did not come into effect until after the death of Jesus. This means that the 2nd covenant came into force on the Friday that Jesus died on the cross. Again according to **Gal 3:15 TLB**; *"Dear brothers, even in everyday life a promise made by one man to another, if it is written down and signed, cannot be changed. He cannot decide afterward to do something else instead"* - this scripture clearly tells us that once Jesus died, no amendment of His will [covenant / testament] could be done. So if a clause or change was not in the contract at the time Jesus was living, nothing can be inserted after His death just as nothing can be taken from it after He is dead. This therefore is one clear reason we can be sure that any addition to the 2nd covenant which was made after the Friday Jesus died is null and void and can never be accepted. Even if such transference of the solemnity of the Sabbath to Sunday came on the resurrection Sunday, such inclusion came 3 days too late and can not be accepted according to the law of covenants and also as proved by scripture.

With the above explanation, we may not even need to go on to look at the scriptures often quoted to back Sunday observance - but let's do so for our learning.

There are about eight (8) instances where reference is made to the first day of the week in the New Testament - however, not once in all of these references does it mention that the day was kept sacred nor as a command as is in the case of the Seventh day Sabbath. The scriptures often quoted include Matt 28:1; Mark 16:2;9; Luke 24:1; John 20:1;19; Acts 20:7 and 1 Cor 16:2. Let's take a look at some of them.

1 Cor 16:2 - DOESN'T THIS SCRIPTURE SAY THE Church MET ON SUNDAYS?

One scripture that many quote to support the notion that the early Church stopped meeting on Sabbath and started meeting on Sunday is **1 Cor 16:2**. Let's look at this scripture in a bit more detail from several translations to see if what many are saying could be true.

KJV

Upon the first day of the week let every one of you lay by him in store, as God hath prospered him, that there be no gatherings when I come

NKJV

On the first day of the week let each one of you lay something aside, storing up as he may prosper, that there be no collections when I come.

CEB

On the first day of the week, each of you should set aside whatever you can afford from what you earn so that the collection won't be delayed until I come.

NIV

On the first day of every week, each one of you should set aside a sum of money in keeping with your income, saving it up, so that when I come no collections will have to be made.

NLT

On the first day of each week, you should each put aside a portion of the money you have earned. Don't wait until I get there and then try to collect it all at once.

AMP

On the first day of every week each one of you is to put something aside, in proportion to his prosperity, and save it so that no collections [will need to] be made when I come.

CEV

That is, each Sunday each of you must put aside part of what you have earned. If you do this, you won't have to take up a collection when I come.

TLB

On every Lord's Day each of you should put aside something from what you have earned during the week, and use it for this offering. The amount depends on how much the Lord has helped you earn. Don't wait until I get there and then try to collect it all at once.

Do you notice what is going on with the various translations? For instance in the KJV, NKJV and CEB; you notice that the text says a collection should be set aside (on the first day of the week). However, with all the other translations we have cited here - it suggests that the collection must be taken every first day of each week. Was it perpetual, how long was this collection to be taken? Also, do you also notice that only the TLB translation doesn't say first day or Sunday but calls the day the Lord's day? What do you say about that?

To understand the point I want to make on this; please read this statement below and answer the questions that follow:

"Hearing that Danny was at the hospital, Abigail quickly left the pot of soup she was making and rushed off to see him. The entrance of the hospital was packed full with people. Several others were calling on the phone to find out how Danny was doing - he was indeed a good man and had helped many people in his community".

Question:
1. Was Abigail Danny's wife or the sister or mother?
2. Was Danny a pastor or politician?
3. Was Danny involved in a car accident?
4. Were the people at the hospital coming to see Danny?

I am sure you are either asking - but how would I know? You need more information than what is provided or did you try to guess the answers? That's what happens when you pick scriptures out of context too. The story above was taken from a story I am developing to teach my kids. Without the rest of the text, you can never understand and therefore correctly answer the questions I posed.

Now see the rest of the text below:

"Abigail and Danny had known each other from their childhood, and got married right out of school. They were both part of the youth choir in the Baptist Church where Abigail's dad was the pastor. Ever since Danny excellently played the character of Jesus at their Church' Easter convention - he became the most

popular boy in the village. It was not surprising that he grew up to now be the pastor of the same Church they had been part of. He was such a joy to be around and dedicated all of his spare time to visit the people and teach them the word of God.

On that fateful day, he was visiting the homes of those who had recently lost their family members in the bush fire when a drunk driver sped into his car. It was as though the entire village had thronged to the hospital before Abigail got there".

With this other detail or portion of the story, I believe it makes it easy for you to answer all the questions right?

Similarly and as we have seen from this example, just taking <u>vrs 2</u> out of an entire letter Paul sent to the Corinthians will in no way tell you exactly what he was saying unless of course you read your own meaning into it.

But here is what we know from the text and also from history:

1. Paul does not mention anywhere in the text that the disciples were meeting on that particular first day of the week or any subsequent one. He only says that each disciple should set aside their contribution on the first day of the week. Also, notice that it is only the contemporary translations that use the phrase "The LORD'S day" - all the others simply say the first day of the week.

2. We also know that at the time of writing his first letter to the Corinthians (which is said to be possibly between the years 51 - 54AD, more probably in AD 55); Sunday was a working day.

3. According to History - Sunday was the day workers wages were paid.

> *"Sunday had become the day when wages were traditionally paid to workers, leading it to be seen as a day of celebration and thanks"*. **Credit:** **History.com**

With what is known - do you see the reason Paul said they should set aside their contribution on the first day? This was to ensure that before they even spent their wages, they would have set aside the contribution.

Further, no reference is given that the disciples assembled on the first day of the week - it only says they should set their money aside. It could very well be that someone would go round and take the contributions or they may bring it along at their next meeting.

WHAT OF ACTS 20:7

Another scripture often used to support the Sunday change is **Acts 20:7**. Before we get into that text, let's look at the background to this.

When the early Church started, we understand that they met daily, broke bread together in each other's homes and in the temple courts. It is not as if it was unusual for them to meet on the first day of the week (Sunday). These scriptures below confirm this:

> *"So continuing daily with one accord in the temple, and breaking bread from house to house, they ate their food with gladness and simplicity of heart, 47 praising God and having favor with all the people. And the Lord added*

[a]to the Church daily those who were being saved"
— **Acts 2:46-47**.

"And daily in the temple, and in every house, they did not cease teaching and preaching Jesus as the Christ"
— **Acts 5:42**.

Also, much earlier at the beginning of **Acts 20**; in **vrs 1-6** as well as the verses that follow; we notice that Paul was continuing his final missionary journey. There were places he visited and stayed for three months, like **Ephesus** and **Greece**; others he stayed for seven days like **Troas** and **Tyre**; he also stayed a day in **Ptolemais**; several days in **Caesarea** with Philip the Evangelist before finally ending in Jerusalem where he was arrested. Paul was taking advantage to see as many people as he possibly could and everywhere he got to, he made it a point to stay and spend the most time with the disciples there. He knew very well it was going to be the last time he saw them as he was sure of death awaiting him in Jerusalem. *"And indeed, now I know that you all, among whom I have gone preaching the kingdom of God, will see my face no more"* — **Acts 20:25**. With this background in mind, let's now read the scripture:

"Now on the first day of the week, when the disciples came together to break bread, Paul, ready to depart the next day, spoke to them and continued his message until midnight"
— **Acts 20:25.NKJV**

As we read the scripture by itself and without the background, we may be convinced that it gives us enough evidence of the disciples now meeting on Sunday. But notice that the fact of their meeting on this Sunday doesn't in any way suggest they no longer met on the Sabbath. And neither does it suggest they didn't meet on the other days. When you read the entire chapter, you will see the different days of the week that Paul met with disciples from other regions simply because that was the day he got there and or the time he could have with them.

Let me use the following text only as an illustration - consider the following scripture:

> *"When our days there came to an end, we left and proceeded on our journey, while all of the disciples, with their wives and children, escorted us on our way until we were outside the city. After kneeling down on the beach and praying, we told one another goodbye"* — **Acts 21:5 AMP.**

What if I say this scripture means *"all disciples have to go and pray at the beach with their families"*? Will you accept it just because the text is in the bible?

Without the context, anyone can make any scripture say or mean anything they want. So again, Let's encourage each other to read the scriptures contextually.

Further, when you read vrs 8-11; you notice the text says that Paul spoke until light dawned when he continued with his journey. This is the case where disciples had come to meet with Paul on Saturday evening (which according to Jewish timing would be the beginning of the next day) and Paul spoke with them late through midnight until the dawn of Sunday morning when he left. This explains why the text particularly says there were lamps in the room and also why Eutychus fell asleep.

WHAT OF JOHN 20:26?

There is no doubt that Jesus rose on the first day of the week [Sunday] and appeared to the disciples in the evening of that same day according to **John 20:19**. A lot of people would like us to believe that the next time Jesus met with the disciples was also on Sunday - they say this to further convince themselves and others that it must mean that Jesus endorsed that after His resurrection, the day on which disciples are to meet is on Sunday. But there is no text in the bible that suggests that the day of his next meeting with them was on Sunday except you [1] force the scripture; [2] calculate wrongly or [3] use one of such contemporary translations.

Let us scrutinize the scripture that this assertion is based on for ourselves as we've done with the others.

KJV
And after eight days again his disciples were within, and Thomas with them: then came Jesus, the doors being shut, and stood in the midst, and said, Peace be unto you

NKJV
And after eight days His disciples were again inside, and Thomas with them. Jesus came, the doors being shut, and stood in the midst, and said, "Peace to you!"

CEB
After eight days his disciples were again in a house and Thomas was with them. Even though the doors were locked, Jesus entered and stood among them. He said, "Peace be with you."

NIV

A week later his disciples were in the house again, and Thomas was with them. Though the doors were locked, Jesus came and stood among them and said, "Peace be with you!"

ISV

A week later, his disciples were again inside, and Thomas was with them. Even though the doors were shut, Jesus came, stood among them, and said, "Peace be with you."

EXB

A week later [LAfter eight days] the ·followers [disciples] were in the house again, and Thomas was with them. The doors were ·locked [shut], but Jesus came in and stood right in the middle of them. He said, "Peace be with you."

ERV

A week later the followers were in the house again, and Thomas was with them. The doors were locked, but Jesus came and stood among them. He said, "Peace be with you!"

What did you notice from reading the different translations? Is "after eight days" the same as "a week later"? Let's put this to some practical test by looking at the story below:

"The first case of coronavirus was reported in Washington DC on January 21, 2020 when a man in his 30's who had recently travelled to Wuhan was diagnosed. Eight days after, the WHO declared a global health emergency. Meanwhile, a week later from when the

first case was diagnosed in Washington DC; Europe confirmed its first case when a German man got infected by a work colleague".

From the above statement, let's see if we can answer the following questions:

a. On which date did the WHO declare a global emergency?
b. On which date did Europe confirm it's first case?
c. Are the two dates the same?

Alternatively, you may use **datecalculator.org** to find out if the two expressions ["a week later" and "after eight days"] are one and the same.

From the foregoing, and without sounding like a broken record, it is very obvious that when we restrict ourselves to just one translation of the bible, we will most certainly end up mis-interpreting what we read and or end in error.

Besides, the text and other related accounts in the Gospels clearly tell us that rather than having a resurrection service, the disciples were having dinner (Mark 16:14) of which they even gave some to Jesus (Luke 24:42) while behind locked doors because of fear of the Jews (John 20:19). You also notice that not all of them believed that Jesus had truly risen hence their being terrified when he appeared among them (Luke 24:37). Thomas also didn't believe until after he had seen Jesus (John 20:24-29). When you think through all these facts the Gospels present - could the disciples have been rejoicing over His resurrection they had not yet believed on that Sunday?

Putting all of it together, we can not by standing on a single verse like **1 Cor 16:2** and **Acts 20:7** or **John 20:26** or any other like it, draw the conclusion that after Jesus' resurrection, the day of meeting for Christians was changed to Sunday. We need more than that - If God wants to change His Law, He will say it in a way we won't miss it. Moreover, this is what God tells us about his Law:

> *"I will not violate my covenant or alter what my lips have uttered"* — **Ps 89:34**

In case we have forgotten, let's see what God's lips have spoken or what has come out of His mouth.

> *"And **God spoke** all these words, saying:*
> *2 "I am the Lord your God, who brought you out of the land of Egypt, out of the house of bondage. 3 "You shall have no other gods before Me............"* — **Exo 20:1-17**.

The Ten commandments [every one of them including the Sabbath command] came from God's own mouth and we have also learnt that He wrote them with His own **finger**. That makes His statement **in Ps 89:34** very strong and certain. He says, "I will not violate [set it aside] or alter [change] the commands l have given you" - (emphasis mine). Remember when Pontius Pilate was asked to change the title he had put on Jesus' cross? He, a mere human judge said to them; *"What l have written, l have written"* — **John 19:19-22**. Can you imagine then, that the Judge of the entire universe will make such a statement and then turn around on His own word?

> *"The **entirety** of Your word is truth, And **every one** of Your righteous judgments **endures forever**"* — **Ps 119:160** [emphasis mine].

Friend, Isn't it a big accusation we bring against God just by saying that He went contrary to His promise? And are we able to prove this case at all? Friend, let us patiently consider what we've been saying on this topic. My prayer is for God to open our eyes so we can fall at His feet, repent and cry out for His mercy; because it is a fearful thing to fall into the hands of the living God — **Heb 10:26-31.**

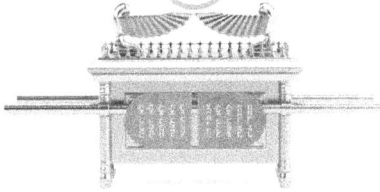

20

THE BLUE LAW

Do not fear any of those things which you are about to suffer. Indeed, the devil is about to throw some of you into prison, that you may be tested, and you will have tribulation ten days. Be faithful until death, and I will give you the crown of life — **Rev 2:10 NKJV**

The pilgrims, puritans and early settlers in America escaped Europe primarily because of religious freedom which was non-existent in Europe at the time. The persecutions drove them far out in search of a place where they could freely practice their faith. This is also why the first amendment to the US constitution states clearly that everyone in the United States has the right to practice their own religion or no religion at all.

The country's founders were very certain that the way to prevent what had been experienced in Europe in the days of Papal Rome when the Church and State were fused together to form the civil government was to separate Church from state. There was no other way to protect religious liberty than to ensure that the government will keep itself out of religion and not establish nor promote any religion.

History has shown us that anytime the government got involved in the issues of how people worshipped, who they worshipped and when they worshipped - it never ended well. The accounts in the book of Daniel of what happened in Babylon, and also what Europe experienced in our history are all recorded for us to learn from.

This is why we should all be very concerned whenever there are signs of civil government getting overly involved with the issues of religion. So while at this - let's see what else is happening around us [perhaps unbeknown to many].

With what you know of God, do you think there will ever come a time when God will 'beg' humans to worship Him? In the story of the triumphal entry, people were giving praise and worshipping Jesus saying *"Hosannah, blessed is He who comes in the name of the Lord"*. When some of the Pharisees present heard them praising Jesus, they asked that He stop them. Do you recall what Jesus said: *"But He said, "If they kept quiet, the stones would do it for them, shouting praise."* - **Luke 19:40 MSG.**

Interesting isn't it? When humans cease to praise God, the natural elements will sing His praises; God will never beg nor will He force men to give Him praise and worship. And yet, men have intended to promulgate and enforce worship and to make it a punishable offense if you don't adhere. Two questions arise;

(1) Do you think God, the creator of the universe will be behind such [forced] worship?

(2) Which day do you think they will be forcing people to worship on?

Blue laws, also known as Sunday laws, are laws designed to restrict or ban some or all Sunday activities for religious or secular reasons, particularly to promote the observance of a day of worship or rest. Blue laws may also restrict shopping or ban sale of certain items on specific days, most often on Sundays in the western world. Source: **Wikipedia**

You may not have heard but don't be surprised and you can be sure that it won't be long until we see the **blue law** legislated throughout the world [soon]. Ask yourself what agenda is being promoted by this Sunday law and to whose benefit - God or a god?

And need I talk about the timing too? How opportune, that in 2020, world leaders and the powers that be are advocating a one world solution to a global pandemic. They say global problems require global solutions. I believe we will soon be seeing the violation of constitutional laws on freedom to assemble as well as freedom of worship. God in His divine wisdom has already shown us what will happen at the end of time by telling us how the rulers at the time (Nebuchadnezer & Darius) set up an image to be worshiped [introducing false worship] and as well forbade everyone from their free worship respectively. It will be good to take some time to read the accounts in **Daniel 3** and **Daniel 6** as we look out for the recurrence of these events in our time. These violations will lead to the beginning of serious times of persecution for God's true people. When we see these signs, we won't have much time except a moment to flee - Jesus has warned of this in **Matthew 24:15-33** — *"33 So you also, when you see all these things, know that it is near - at the doors!"*

Daniel's vision also said concerning the beast: - *"He will attempt to change the times and law"* — **Dan 7:25**. We have already looked at the first part, let me use the time remaining to address the changing of the Law. Below, see a chart that shows the ten commandments as the scripture mentions them and what is said exists in the Roman Catholic Catechism:

Biblical Ten Commandments	Catholic Ten Commandments
1. You shall have no other gods before me.	1. You shall not have strange God's before me.
2. You shall not make for yourself an idol.	2. You shall not take the name of the LORD your God in vain.
3. You shall not misuse the name of the LORD your God.	3. Remember to keep holy the LORD's Day.
4. Remember the Sabbath day by keeping it holy.	4. Honor your father and your mother.
5. Honor your father and your mother.	5. You shall not kill.
6. You shall not murder.	6. You shall not commit adultery.
7. You shall not commit adultery.	7. You shall not steal.
8. You shall not steal.	8. You shall not bear false witness against your neighbor.
9. You shall not give false testimony against your neighbor.	9. You shall not covet your neighbor's wife.
10. You shall not covet your neighbor's house.	10. You shall not covet your neighbor's goods.
	"From Catechism of the Catholic Church"

CREDIT - preparingforeternity.com

The revision made to the 10 commandments by the Roman Catholic Church is quite obvious: the second commandment against idolatry has been taken out, and the tenth commandment against covetousness has been broken into two to keep the number of commandments still at the original 10. In this chart, the reading for the 4th commandment is rendered the "Lord's day" rather than the "Sabbath".

It won't be of much use for me to go into why the elimination of the 2nd command from the Roman Catholic Church' set of commands; because Roman Catholics argue that; their statues are not in the same 'class' of idols and images that the scripture refers to. They say their images aid in their worship of God just as Evangelicals use music as aid in worshiping God - both image and music are forms of art and either of them can be idolized.

In their rebuttal of it being a sin to bow to or worship an image, Catholics quote the scripture: *"Since you saw no form when the Lord spoke to you at Horeb out of the fire, take care and watch yourselves closely,* [16] *so that you do not act corruptly by making an idol for yourselves, in the form of any figure—the likeness of male or female,* [17] *the likeness of any animal that is on the earth, the likeness of any winged bird that flies in the air,* [18] *the likeness of anything that creeps on the ground, the likeness of any fish that is in the water under the earth."*— **Deut 4:15-18 NRSV**. They claim that the operative word in the above scripture is **"Since"** - which is a provisional word. It is attributed to a Catholic source as saying that at the time of this command; "God had not yet visually revealed Himself to mankind. However, Catholics believe that God did finally reveal Himself visually to mankind in the person of Jesus"

> *"He is the image of the invisible God, the firstborn of all creation"* — *Col 1:15*

> *"He who has seen me has seen the Father"* — *John 14:9*

Roman Catholics believe that when God revealed himself to mankind, He lifted the ban on making visual representations of him. Source: **catholicbridge.com**

What are we to make of their statements? I will leave that for you to debate.

God in His wisdom has shown us a time when the Blue Law will be promulgated all over the world and I would like you to know that we are already in those days. The event that must precede the promulgation of the blue law is a worldwide unity between the Roman Catholic Church (the beast), Apostate Protestantism (the false prophet) and other world religions.

Protestants is the term used to refer to those who broke off from the Catholic Church mainly because of their belief in one being saved by grace alone and not by human works as the Catholic Church endorses. Apostate Protestants refers to those who have fallen off or stopped protesting and have now embraced the opinions that were at one time repulsive to them. It is what the Apostle Peter refers to as "a dog going back to eat what it has vomited" - read what he says of it in **2 Pet 2:17-22**. The beast is working towards a unification of all world religions and it's hidden agenda is to use this unity to persecute God's true Church. Let's read the words of this prophecy:

> *"He was granted power to give breath to the image of the beast, that the image of the beast should both speak and cause as many as would not worship the image of the beast to be killed. 16 He causes all, both small and great, rich and poor, free and slave, to receive a mark on their right hand or on their foreheads, 17 and that no one may buy or sell except one who has [a]the mark or the name of the beast, or the number of his name"* — **Rev 13:15-17.**

When the scripture speaks of being granted power to give breath to the image - it is speaking of making it a law therefore making it a punishable offence if not adhered to. This is when true disciples of Jesus should remember and encourage themselves with the stories of Daniel; Shadrach, Meshach and Abednego and how they resisted such laws in their time as recorded in **Dan 3** and **Dan 6**. Many Christians are going to perish as a result of this law; but God will be glorified more in this way than in anyone giving in to worship the image of the beast.

THE GOLDEN CALF AND THE DAY OF THE SUN

There's a story in the Bible that closely resembles what Emperor Constantine did in choosing Sunday as the day to venerate the sun god. Read carefully the text below and let's compare both accounts:

> *"Now when the people saw that Moses delayed coming down from the mountain, the people gathered together to Aaron, and said to him, "Come, make us [a]gods that shall go before us; for as for this Moses, the man who brought us up out of the land of Egypt, we do not know what has become of him. "² And Aaron said to them, "Break off the golden earrings which are in the ears of your wives, your sons, and your daughters, and bring them to me." ³ So all the people broke off the golden earrings which were in their ears, and brought them to Aaron. ⁴ And he received the gold from their hand, and he fashioned it with an engraving tool, and made a molded calf. Then they said, "This is your god, O Israel, that brought you out of the land of Egypt!"⁵ So when Aaron saw it, he built an altar before it. And Aaron made a proclamation and said, "Tomorrow*

is a feast to the Lord." [6] *Then they rose early on the next day, offered burnt offerings, and brought peace offerings; and the people sat down to eat and drink, and rose up to play"*— **Exodus 32:1-6.**

Let's summarise a few things we learn from the scripture:

1. At the time; Moses had gone to meet God on the mountain top
2. Most of the people were not sure of Moses' return.
3. The current leader (Aaron) fashioned the calf to represent them as their god
4. What he chose as their "god" was something that God Almighty had made.
5. They ascribed worship to God's creature as their god
6. Aaron said that they were setting this day asde to worship the Lord.
7. They chose a particular day to venerate/worship the god.
8. They called the day - "the day of the LORD"

Now I want you to compare to when **Constantine decreed Sunday** in the year 321

1. At the time; Jesus had gone to God in Heaven
2. Most people were not sure of Jesus 2nd coming
3. The leader (Constantine) issued a decree making the sun represent them as God
4. What he chose as their "god" was something that God Almighty had made.
5. They ascribed worship to God's creature as their god.
6. Constantine said it was to be a "day of rest" for all the people to worship God

7. They chose a particular day to venerate/worship the god.

8. They called the day - "the LORD'S day"

Here is my question - in both accounts - which day did they choose? In the account with the Israelites, they said "Tomorrow". The text doesn't give further evidence except we can be sure that it was not the Sabbath because they wouldn't even have come out to work if it were. Also, we notice that the Levites didn't take part in this idol worship — **Exo 32:26-28**.

With Constantine, we know he chose Sunday. Also we know from history that after all three of the Barbaric tribes; Heruli, Vandals and Ostrogoths were uprooted and destroyed for heresy, the 3rd council of orleans (a synod of Roman Catholic Bishops of France on May 7, 538) established Sunday as the day of the Lord in place of the seventh day Sabbath. This is what is spoken of in Daniel 7:8 - "I was considering the horns, and there was another horn, a little one, coming up among them, before whom three of the first horns were plucked out by the roots. And there, in this horn, were eyes like the eyes of a man, and a mouth speaking pompous words"

Could there be any link in these two stories?

But what is most important is for us to know how God felt and reacted to this.

"And the Lord said to Moses, "Go, get down! For your people whom you brought out of the land of Egypt have corrupted themselves. 8 They have turned aside quickly out of the way which I commanded them. They have made themselves a molded calf, and worshiped it and sacrificed

to it, and said, 'This is your god, O Israel, that brought you out of the land of Egypt!' " [9] *And the Lord said to Moses, "I have seen this people, and indeed it is a [b]stiff-necked people!* [10] *Now therefore, let Me alone, that My wrath may burn hot against them and I may consume them. And I will make of you a great nation."* — **Exo 32:7-10**

"And the Lord said to Moses, "Whoever has sinned against Me, I will blot him out of My book" — **Exo 32:33**.

But let's even assume that what happened with the Golden Calf has nothing to do with Constantine's decree to make Sunday the day of worship and that there is nothing wrong with the Sunday worship. Is this something you want to have doubts about?

What we can be very sure about is: assuming Sabbath rest is no longer applicable to Christians under the new covenant - do you suppose God will blot your name out for observing it? There is no way we can go wrong following the customs of Jesus; and it was His custom to observe the Sabbath — **Luke 4:16**. On the other hand; we are not in any doubt of what God will do if He calls our Sunday worship idolatry. Friend, the ball is in your court; choose this day which way you'll follow - Jesus' way or an unsure way?

21

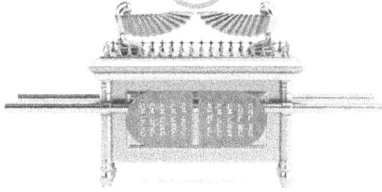

WAS THE SABBATH
FOR JEWS ONLY?

"The Sabbath was made for humankind
— Mark 2:27 NRSV

here are many who say that the reason Christians are not bound by the Sabbath command is because it was made for the Jews as shown in: *"17 It is a sign between Me and the children of Israel forever;..."* — **Exodus 31:12-17**. This notion is so far from the truth because God had established the Sabbath **(Gen 2:1-3)** way before the Law was given at Sinai, and even before there was a Jew on earth. See also Pharaoh's response to Moses in **Exo 5:5**, and how that gives us a clue that the Israelites [may] have been observing the Sabbath in Egypt until more work was forced on them. If this is so, it should only mean that the Patriarchs observed the Sabbath and passed on the practice to their children to do the same - further confirming that even before the Law was given, Sabbath observance was being practiced. This must have been the reason why God at the time of giving the Law just said: "Remember the Sabbath"; it's because it was already known to them and not a new command that God was now introducing them to.

Also, even when the Law was given, the law-giver clearly said that everyone in your household including slaves and strangers should observe it too — **Exodus 20:10**. Won't we be in error when we claim that the universe God made was for all mankind but then the Sabbath was only for the Jews? God commanded the day of rest and clearly stated that the reason behind it was that He rested after He completed all the work of creation - God didn't make the world only for Jews, therefore the rest He commanded could not have been for Jews only.

Further; God also says:

> *"⁶ Also the sons of the foreigner*
> *Who join themselves to the Lord, to serve Him,*
> *And to love the name of the Lord, to be His servants—*
> ***Everyone who keeps from defiling the Sabbath,***
> ***And holds fast My covenant—***
> *⁷ Even them I will bring to My holy mountain,*
> *And make them joyful in My house of prayer.*
> *Their burnt offerings and their sacrifices*
> *Will be accepted on My altar;*
> *For My house shall be called a house of prayer for all*
> *nations."* — **Isaiah 56:1-7**

Here in the above scripture, God makes it clear His intention of bringing all foreigners (Gentiles) together with the Jews - and don't miss this - My house shall be called a house of prayer for

ALL NATIONS!

It is important to notice that God's intention of taking the Jews as His chosen possession was to make them a model nation to show other nations how good God is (not that Israel was good). God's intent had always been that from that one man Abraham, all Nations on earth will come to faith in Him and as a result be blessed.

God held to His covenant with Abraham and so Israel was the way God chose to bless the inhabitants of this world and to show His goodness.

> *"Because Abraham obeyed me and did everything I required of him, keeping my commands, my decrees and my instructions"* — **Gen 26:5 NIV**

The above scripture shows that the Patriarch Abraham even before the nation of Israel was formed kept all of God's commands. Even though the scripture doesn't mention explicitly that Abraham observed the Sabbath - it must be implied if God Himself testified that Abraham kept His commands, laws and statutes.

In the same way, God also made it clear to Moses that all His commands and statutes are to apply to the foreigners as well as the Israelites. Notice in the scripture below:

> *"The community is to have the same rules for you and for the foreigner residing among you; this is a lasting ordinance for the generations to come. You and the foreigner shall be the same before the Lord:* ^{16} *The same laws and regulations will apply both to you and to the foreigner residing among you"* — **Num 15:15-16**

Going on to the early Church, notice it wasn't only Jews who observed the Sabbath; the Gentiles also kept the Sabbath:

> *"So when the Jews went out of the synagogue, the Gentiles begged that these words might be preached to them the next Sabbath. [43] Now when the congregation had broken up, many of the Jews and devout proselytes followed Paul and Barnabas, who, speaking to them, persuaded them to continue in the grace of God. [44] On the next Sabbath almost the whole city came together to hear the word of God* — **Acts 13:42-44**

> *"And on the Sabbath day we went out of the city to the riverside, where prayer was customarily made; and we sat down and spoke to the women who met there* — **Acts 16:13**

Luke who wrote the book of Acts was a Gentile and He wrote the book to Theophilus who was a Gentile too. He mentions in the above scripture that it was their custom to offer prayers and teach others on the Sabbath. Luke mentions the Sabbath several times in the book of Acts and never once does he refer to it as the Jewish Sabbath.

Moving on from Abraham, through the Israelites and through the Gospels, Paul in his writings also made it clear how in Christ, all are one. Let's look at a few of such scriptures;

> *"For there is no distinction between Jew and Greek, for the same Lord over all is rich to all who call upon Him"* — **Rom 10:12**

> *"There is one body and one Spirit, just as you were called*

in one hope of your calling; ⁵ one Lord, one faith, one baptism; ⁶ one God and Father of all, who is above all, and through all, and in [a]you all" — **Eph 4:4-6**

"where there is neither Greek nor Jew, circumcised nor uncircumcised, barbarian, Scythian, slave nor free, but Christ is all and in all" — **Col 3:11**

"Therefore remember that you, once Gentiles in the flesh—who are called Uncircumcision by what is called the Circumcision made in the flesh by hands— ¹² that at that time you were without Christ, being aliens from the commonwealth of Israel and strangers from the covenants of promise, having no hope and without God in the world. ¹³ But now in Christ Jesus you who once were far off have been brought near by the blood of Christ. ¹⁴ For He Himself is our peace, who has made both one, and has broken down the middle wall of separation, ¹⁵ having abolished in His flesh the enmity, that is, the law of commandments contained in ordinances, so as to create in Himself one new man from the two, thus making peace, ¹⁶ and that He might reconcile them both to God in one body through the cross, thereby putting to death the enmity" — **Eph 2:11-16.**

In the New Covenant, there is no more talk of Jew and Gentile but all have become one flesh because of Jesus death. So there is ONLY one body [the Church] which we all belong to now, just as it was in the days of the early Church where there was no separation between Jews and Gentiles.

We should also notice that God has foretold us and made it clear throughout scripture that; He will punish those who break His Law:

> *"If his sons forsake My law*
> *And do not walk in My judgments,*
> *[31] If they break My statutes*
> *And do not keep My commandments,*
> *[32] Then I will punish their transgression with the rod,*
> *And their iniquity with stripes.* — **Ps 89:30-32**

We can conclude therefore, that God didn't make the Sabbath for Jews only and we see evidence way back from Abraham observing all of God's commands through to the early Church that Gentile converts also kept the Sabbath. All of God's Law applies to every Christian in the very same way today as before - that is if we are part of Christ' body.

22

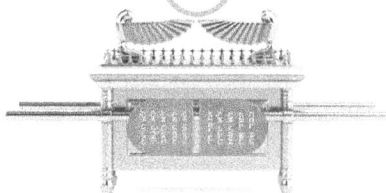

THE CHURCH [FALSE] & ANTICHRIST

A mysterious caption was written on her forehead: "Babylon the Great, Mother of Prostitutes and of Idol Worship Everywhere around the World
— Rev 17:5 TLB

First, it is important to note that the Church was created to serve man; man was not created for the Church. In that sense, the Church is a vehicle to achieve a purpose. The word "Church" means two or more people who are called out to separate themselves from others [the world] and group together for a common purpose. For us as Christians, that common purpose is to advance the Kingdom of God on earth. So the Church is an extension of God's Kingdom on earth, making people in the Church subjects of the King. Becoming a member of the Church requires the understanding of making Jesus the King [Lord] of your life - you are no longer going to be ruler of your life but Jesus becomes that ruler, master, King, Lord.

So in it's true sense or spiritually speaking, the Church is the body of Christ **(1 Cor 12:12-31)** where every Christian is a part by result of new birth [repentance for the forgiveness of sins and baptism to receive the gift of the Holy Spirit — **Acts 2:38-39**]. When a person is called out of the world, she/he becomes a part of the Spiritual and universal body of Christ. What we know as Church on earth is a local assembly of Christians to which we belong or join (voluntarily) for the express purpose of:

a. Living as subjects of the King
b. Reflecting the glory of Christ our King
c. To be fruitful and multiply and subdue the earth.

To achieve the Church' goal, individual disciples of Christ come together so as to:

1. Be in the company of like-minded people
2. Nurture/Equip each other for ministry
3. Edify each other (Help and support each other to grow in the Lord)

It shouldn't matter where a person has their local membership as long as <u>ALL</u> the other members and especially the leadership of the local Church are themselves committed and connected to Christ and worship the Father in Spirit and in Truth - this is the most important because two can not walk together except they agree. Two are better than one - one man can not be a local Church but two are enough to be a local Church because they can provide companionship for each other, nurture and edify each other towards reflecting the glory of Jesus and thus attract others to Christ.

By this statement, 1 am neither endorsing denominations nor disunity - the True Church [Body] of Christ is only One and is not divided by distance; race, ethnicity or tribe; gender; age; social & economic status, political affiliation or even the local congregation that one belongs to. Members of the True Church of Christ are connected in these key areas:

a. *They have repented and been baptized into Christ*
b. *They have made Jesus the LORD of their lives*
c. *They worship the Father in Spirit*
d. *Their worship is based on the truth of the word of God*
e. *They hear the voice of Jesus*
f. *They are known by Jesus*
g. *They obey & follow ALL the commands of Jesus [only]*
h. *They are led by the Holy Spirit (not their flesh/emotions/ others)*

This means that you and your spouse or any two people who meet the criteria described above can be a local Church and an extension of the body of Christ on earth. The scripture says - *"Two are better than one, because they have a good reward for their labor. 10 For if they fall, one will lift up his companion. But woe to him who is alone when he falls, for he has no one to help him up"* - Eccl 4:9-10. Although a Church of two is possible, it may not be the most ideal unless that's just the starting number; with a purposeful strategy to grow quickly. Notice that although Jesus' core group of disciples were twelve; He also appointed seventy-two others and that perhaps also gives us a lesson of strength in numbers. It was from this number that Jesus sent them out two-by-two to call others into the Kingdom of God — **Luke 10:1**.

Because Jesus' body (universal Church) is already a Mega Church, I doubt God is looking for another mega-Church on earth per se but rather, small units of local assemblies scattered all over where we use our individual gifts and resources to meet each others needs and to love each other so deeply that we reflect the image of Christ and attract the people of the world to become a part of Christ' body as well.

In Paul's writings, you are able to tell how much he knew and had personal relations with the people in all the Churches he planted and visited - these local assemblies were small enough to meet in each other's homes **[Rom 16:1-5 / Col 4:7-15]**. In such a set up; everyone's needs are met and each member plays an active role by using their gifts to serve others. That way, love is shown and felt and the communities around are able to witness and testify to God's love. By this kind of love, the world is able to know that such a group are truly Christ' disciples.

> *"12 So when He had washed their feet, taken His garments, and sat down again, He said to them, "Do you know what I have done to you? 13 You call Me Teacher and Lord, and you say well, for so I am. 14 If I then, your Lord and Teacher, have washed your feet, you also ought to wash one another's feet. 15 For I have given you an example, that you should do as I have done to you....34 A new commandment I give to you, that you love one another; as I have loved you, that you also love one another. 35 By this all will know that you are My disciples, if you have love for one another"* — **John 13:12-15;34-35**.

Although this is not a mark of membership, some advantages of smaller groups over larger mega Churches is that - other members know you rather than knowing of you; they know where you live; who your family are; where you work and or what you do. In my opinion, your connection to a local Church is not strong if others are not in your life, discipling you to be a better version of yourself and becoming all that God wants you to be. You are not connected to a local Church if you don't know other members' needs and are not there for them in the areas God has given you strength, ability and or talent in. Who is benefitting because you are part of your local Church?

Your membership should not be limited to warming the pew and being a financier only (offerings and special contributions). The Church is a family looking out for each other. Jesus said, His true family are the disciples; the Church - **Matt 12:46-50**. Do you see your local Church as your family? If not, why not? In the local Church; we all come in as volunteers to serve each other. Freely we have received from God so freely we give to others. While members may and should appreciate each other for the service performed, serving your fellow brother/sister is not a job or an opportunity to amass wealth and or gain power/control over them.

When you are part of Christ's universal body, no one can take you away except God Himself and or you decide to turn your back on God. A local assembly may disqualify you but that won't mean you are no longer part of Jesus' body. But when Jesus takes you out of His body - it doesn't matter how many local congregations you make yourself a part of. If God be for you, who can be against you? Jesus said He is able to keep those who God brings to

Him from falling but only if we stay connected to Him. We can't do anything by ourselves unless we stay connected to Him - John 15:1-10. But staying connected is a choice we make individually, by first entering through repentance and baptism and then hearing and obeying His voice.

We as humans can never even know what is in a man's heart, let alone convert it. *"The heart is deceitful above all things, And desperately wicked; Who can know it?"* — **Jer 17:9-10**. The responsibility of converting souls and adding to the Church is the work of God alone — **Acts 2:47**. God allows us as labourers to spread the seeds of His word and water the seed but only God causes the work of our evangelism to bear fruit — **1 Cor 3:6-7**.

Jesus spent time to help Peter so he will commit himself to love, keep, feed and protect His sheep from the evil one and from false teaching - that's the work of the local Church leaders - John 21:15-17. But some people have climbed and jumped over the fence into this space - they are thieves and hirelings and instead of doing what Jesus asked them; they rather fleece the sheep. This is because they themselves are not disciples of Jesus nor have they been equipped or given the responsibility to feed and protect Christ' sheep — **John 10:1-30**. If they are themselves not getting their food from Jesus, how can they pass some on to anyone? Instead of giving and feeding, they take and covet and steal from God's people.

The Pastors and leaders of our local Churches are men and women like us - they are not Jesus nor are they angels. They don't possess a higher power than any of us have access to. Jesus doesn't love any of the leaders more than He loves you; and they don't have any privileged access to God more than you do. The leaders, like everyone else don't have all the answers to every question as people make it to be; and then turn them into idols to be worshipped.

Your pastor is not there to pray for you; he may [and should] pray with you; encourage and also teach you how to pray; but you can't outsource your prayer request to pastors or prayer warriors (even if there were anything like that). Some people even go to the extent of "paying" people to fast & pray for them while they go about living lives of lawlessness. Some pastors are also luring and deceiving their members into thinking that by attending some "anointing service" or making special offerings, they can lay hands on them to receive God's favor and the gift of the Holy Spirit. Please read about Simon the sorcerer who thought he could buy the gift of God in Acts 8:9-24. If God won't listen to the prayers you pray, you can be sure that your Pastor can't change God's mind. One reason God says He doesn't hear our prayers is because of sin - so remove sin and God will hear your own prayers.

> *"1 Behold, the Lord's hand is not shortened, That it cannot save; Nor His ear heavy, That it cannot hear. ² But your iniquities have separated you from your God; And your sins have hidden His face from you,* **So that He will not hear...** *— Isaiah 59:1-14.*

It is very troubling and pathetic that our generation is fast going back to the days of the earthly High priesthood when he was the only one who could intercede for the people before God. That was in the old covenant which God found fault with - **Heb 8:7-9**. Now under the New Covenant; **the veil that separated God from us** has been torn down so Jesus wants everyone to come to

Him directly - **Heb 4:16**. No human pastor can lay their hands on you to receive the gift of the Holy Spirit as in the days of the Apostles, the Holy Spirit does not dwell in anointing oils. Unless one is born-again [repent of their sins and are baptized], they can never receive anything from God - read **John 3:3-6; Acts 2:36-41; 1 John 2:26-27**

Just as there are false Christians and false pastors, there are also false Churches. The role of the false Church is to be a false witness; distorting what God has said and causing deceit and promoting the works of the evil one. Satan works through his agents (beasts) who give the intoxicating wine of his teaching to the Church who then passes on that teaching to Church-goers to cause many to disobey God's command. Because there are true Churches and false Churches, we are admonished to find that which is true: *"Enter by the narrow gate; for wide is the gate and broad is the way that leads to destruction, and there are many who go in by it. **14** Because narrow is the gate and difficult is the way which leads to life, and there are few who find it"* - **Matt 7:13-14**. Jesus tells us that not every path or Church will lead us to His eternal Kingdom and only a few find the right way. This is why we need to put all our life in verifying whether or not we belong to a Church where Jesus is the [Only] Shepherd.

Let's look at the vision John described in Revelation to learn a few things about how the dragon and his beast(s) operate:

> *"Then I stood on the sand of the sea. And I saw a beast rising up out of the sea, having seven heads and ten horns, and on his horns ten crowns, and on his heads a blasphemous name. ² Now the beast which I saw was like*

a leopard, his feet were like the feet of a bear, and his mouth like the mouth of a lion. **The dragon gave him his power, his throne, and great authority.** *3 And I saw one of his heads as if it had been mortally wounded, and his deadly wound was healed. And all the world marveled and followed the beast. *4 So they worshiped the dragon who gave authority to the beast; and they worshiped the beast, saying, "Who is like the beast? Who is able to make war with him?" *5 And he was given a mouth speaking great things and blasphemies, and he was given authority to continue for forty-two months. *6 Then he opened his mouth in blasphemy against God, to blaspheme His name, His tabernacle, and those who dwell in heaven. *7 It was granted to him to make war with the saints and to overcome them. And authority was given him over every tribe, tongue, and nation. *8 All who dwell on the earth will worship him, whose names have not been written in the Book of Life of the Lamb slain from the foundation of the world. *9 If anyone has an ear, let him hear. *10 He who leads into captivity shall go into captivity; he who kills with the sword must be killed with the sword. Here is the patience and the faith of the saints. *11 Then I saw another beast coming up out of the earth, and he had two horns like a lamb and spoke like a dragon. *12 And he exercises all the authority of the first beast in his presence, and causes the earth and those who dwell in it to worship the first beast, whose deadly wound was healed. *13 He performs great signs, so that he even makes fire come down from heaven on the earth in the sight of men. *14 And he deceives those who dwell on the earth by those signs which he was *granted to do in the sight of the beast, telling those who dwell on the earth to make an image to the beast who was wounded by the sword and lived. [15] He was granted power to give breath to the image of the beast, that the image of the beast should both speak and cause as many as would not worship the image of the beast to be killed. [16] He causes all, both small and great, rich and poor, free and slave, to receive a mark on their right hand or on their foreheads, [17] and that no one may buy or sell except one who has the mark or the name of the beast, or the number of his name. [18] Here is wisdom. Let him who has understanding calculate the number of the beast, for it is the number of a man: His number is 666. — Rev 13*

In the above passage - the dragon [Satan] gives his power to a first beast [which we know from the book of Daniel as the Papal power]. Notice also that the second beast (**Rev 13:11-18**) exercises all the authority of the first beast and then causes an image to be set up in honour of the first beast causing many to worship the first beast and it's image. I know many stay away from the book of Revelation because of the many signs and symbols but it's a book of victory for God's people and l would encourage you to read it alongside the book of Daniel. If you've read **Daniel 7**, you will understand this passage even better; however, l am sure even without that study, you can still get the point l drive at the end. However, Daniel in his vision reveals the first beast as the Papal power or the Roman Catholic Church who took over power after pagan Rome fell - this is also quite clear from our own historical records. The second lamb-like beast spoken of refers to the USA.

Now, l need you to compare this account in **Rev 13** to what Paul warns of the man of lawlessness. He had also warned in **Acts 20:29-30** that after his departure, false Christians will find their way into the Church and some will rise from among them

"Concerning the coming of our Lord Jesus Christ and our being gathered to him, we ask you, brothers and sisters, ² not to become easily unsettled or alarmed by the teaching allegedly from us - whether by a prophecy or by word of mouth or by letter - asserting that the day of the Lord has already come. ³ Don't let anyone deceive you in any way, for that day will not come until the rebellion occurs and the man of lawlessness[is revealed, the man doomed to destruction. ⁴ He will oppose and will exalt himself over everything that is called God or is worshiped, so that he sets himself up in God's temple, proclaiming himself to be God. ⁵ Don't you remember that when I was with you I used to tell you these things? ⁶ And now you know what is holding him back, so that he may be revealed at the proper time. ⁷ For the secret power of lawlessness is already at work; but the one who now holds it back will continue to do so till he is taken out of the way. ⁸ And then the lawless one will be revealed, whom the Lord Jesus will overthrow with the breath of his mouth and destroy by the splendor of his coming. ⁹ The coming of the lawless one will be in accordance with how Satan works. He will use all sorts of displays of power through signs and wonders that serve the lie, ¹⁰ and all the ways that wickedness deceives those who are perishing. They perish because they refused to love the truth and so be saved. ¹¹ For this reason God sends them a powerful delusion so that they will believe the lie ¹² and

so that all will be condemned who have not believed the truth but have delighted in wickedness" — 2 Thess 2:1-12

From this scripture, there is no ambiguity that these two accounts of scripture are referring to the same person. Paul tells us that the "man of lawlessness" (**2 Thess 2:3-4**) who is spoken of as the "first beast" in **Rev 13:1-8** and as well referred to as the "little horn" in **Dan 7:8; 19-26**; will set himself up in the temple of God - this man is the "Papal power". Further down in **Rev 13:11-18**, the scripture speaks of a second beast [with two horns with the appearance of a lamb but speaks like a dragon] - but what is interesting is that it tells us that this second lamb-like beast comes out of "the earth" (**Rev 13:11**). When you read **Rev 12** especially in **vrs 13-17** - we notice that at the time when the dragon waged war through the first beast on the saints of God, "the earth" is mentioned as that which gave protection to the Church. History records that the first pilgrims fled to the USA for safety from the Papal power that was persecuting them. So the same USA which was a refuge for God's people is the same USA which is the second beast who during the last days will be used by the dragon to exercise both political and religious powers and as well become a persecuting power just like the first beast. It is important to look at what is happening and even more, what will be happening in the USA in the coming years as God's prophecy never fails.

Let's list the things we see in both scriptures:

a. Exalt himself above all
b. Blasphemes and speaks against God
c. Persecutes the Saints / disciples of God
d. Command worship to the dragon and the first beast

e. Performs signs, wonders and miracles
f. Speak lies and deceives
g. Leads astray those who give in to his lies
h. Sets up an image in honour of the first beast to be worshipped
i. When we don't believe the truth, God gives us over to delusions and to believe the lie of satan.

Now, as we've established earlier - we need to not only study scriptures contextually but also comparatively. Throughout scripture, whenever there's a revelation, we see it is also repeated and then expanded for us to understand. Do you remember the story of how the devil deceived Adam and Eve in the garden?

"Now the serpent was more cunning than any beast of the field which the Lord God had made. And he said to the woman, "Has God indeed said, 'You shall not eat of every tree of the garden'?" ² And the woman said to the serpent, "We may eat the fruit of the trees of the garden; ³ but of the fruit of the tree which is in the midst of the garden, God has said, 'You shall not eat it, nor shall you touch it, lest you die.' "⁴ Then the serpent said to the woman, "You will not surely die. ⁵ For God knows that in the day you eat of it your eyes will be opened, and you will be like God, knowing good and evil." ⁶ So when the woman saw that the tree was good for food, that it was [a]pleasant to the eyes, and a tree desirable to make one wise, she took of its fruit and ate. She also gave to her husband with her, and he ate". — Gen 3:1-6.

In this passage, the dragon [Satan] works through the beast

[serpent] who gives the intoxicating wine of his teaching to Eve [Church]. She, now acting as a false prophet [fallen Church] passes on the teaching to Adam [Christians] so as to disobey God's command. The wine of her teaching is to cast doubts [*"did God really say"*] in the mind of the believer regarding God's Law using false prophecies and saying: *"you will not surely die, your eyes will be opened; you will be like God"*. Do these sound familiar? Many Churches today are promising their members some supernatural powers and an ability to do things beyond what man can do. They focus on miracles, signs and wonders and false prophecies.

It doesn't seem like the devil is using any new tricks except that this time, we know that the deception is in the Church - a false Church for that matter. We learn that because the beast has the appearance of a lamb, he comes looking very familiar and many are unable to recognise him. By that, he subtly twists and changes God's Law so that even "Christians" are following his erroneous teaching; all the while thinking that they are still worshipping God. When Eve came to Adam, she looked familiar - there was nothing about her appearance that would make Adam think twice; except it was not the Eve he knew. She had bought into the devil's lies and was set up to deceive Adam and get him to disobey God's command.

In a similar way, your Church may look familiar because there are several aspects that seem fine and make you think it is genuinely praising God; but that may be far from the truth. Make no mistake, not everyone you see in Church is a Christian and not every Church is of Christ - even Jesus warned that the Church will have among them some who are of the devil - **Matt 13:41-42**. Does your Church teach that it is okay to break God's Law and that it is no longer applicable in our days? This is how Satan is working today in many Churches and God's word warns us to be vigilant.

There are many who say things like - "I feel the Spirit of God when I go to my Church". Friend, that is well and good, but notice what Jesus says will happen when His Spirit shows up: *"However, when He, the Spirit of truth, has come, He will guide you into all truth; for He will not speak on His own authority, but whatever He hears He will speak; and He will tell you things to come"* - **John 16:13**. The true Spirit of God will not compromise on truth, and can not stand falsehood. It can't be that your Church teaches a false doctrine and yet God's Spirit is there. Knowing this, how sure are you about the Church you belong to? Do you have a way to check whether it is a false witness masquerading as Christ Church?

Here is a list of a few things to look out for in your local Church:

- Does the Church believe and teach the word of God ONLY?
- Does the Church teach and proclaim Jesus as Lord and God as creator?
- Does the Church teach on repentance from sin leading to salvation or a wealth & health gospel?
- Does the Church teach you to live a daily life of righteousness based only on the power of the Holy Spirit?
- Is the doctrine of your Church based on human principles?
- Does the Church teach that God's laws are no longer applicable?
- Does the Church focus mainly on prophecies, miracles, signs and wonders?

- Is the Church confused with everyone claiming to be speaking in some "heavenly language" causing noise and disorder?
- Does the pastor have a Christ-like character and lead an exemplary holy life?
- Is there open access to the leadership or are they inaccessible to the congregation except a few and perhaps through some bureaucratic red-tape?
- Can you become a leader of your Church one day if interested and have the calling and what it takes (not a criteria set only by the current leader)?
- Does the Church have a program in place to deliberately train new Christians towards maturity? Is it working?
- Are members obviously growing in their relationship with God and becoming more and more like Christ as a result of the teachings?
- Is the Church active and getting all members engaged in winning souls for God [not merely interested in adding members] - or is soul winning by a few?
- Is your Church sincerely committed to meeting the needs of its members?
- Is your Church a "family business" where the Pastor is grooming his "son" to take-over?
- Have you checked your Church registration and constitution - do the assets of the Church "belong" to an individual or a group of individuals and are members of the Church automatically part of the "ownership"?
- Does your Church audit its accounts yearly - does it organise an AGM where members are presented with the audited accounts and allowed to question how funds

(members contributions and other income) are being spent?

● Does your Church have independent minded and spiritually strong elders and or a board that oversees the work of the presiding leader? Is a governing board in place to ensure checks and balances?

This is obviously not an exhaustive list but hopefully may give you some ideas into identifying a local assembly that is worth being a part of.

GOD'S HOLY LAW - Matters that truly matter!

23

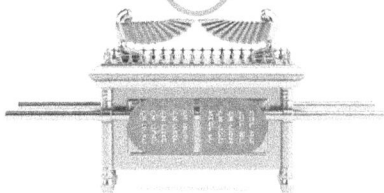

PATHWAY TO GOD

And you will seek Me and find Me, when you search for Me with all your heart — **Jer 29:13**

There are many who are sincerely looking for God and are asking, where do we go to find God? In this day and age where there are over 4000 different religions and an estimated number of about 34 thousand different denominations of Christian Churches alone [not to count other religious groupings] - which way truly offers the pathway to God? The choices presented are numerous and wide and each of them claim they are on the right path and have the truth.

If God is truly one, how come there are so many 'options' or are there truly that many options and could each one of them lead us to God? To make it even easy for us, let's just stick to Christian Churches. With so many differences and diverse theology and interpretations of the scriptures; yet each one claiming to be teaching the truth - which one is really true? The debate and conversations around this topic get so bad that people are beginning to get comfortable with being Atheist or Agnostic. Others are questioning - "if there is God, how come He is allowing all such confusion to go on?"

But can we blame God for the confusion? Or has He shown us the way except many are not understanding and or refusing to follow? So what is the pathway to God? And how do we approach God? A question like ours is asked in the book of Micah:

> *"With what shall I come before the Lord and bow down before the exalted God?*
> *Shall I come before him with burnt offerings, with calves a year old?* [7] *Will the Lord be pleased with thousands of rams, with ten thousand rivers of olive oil? Shall I offer my firstborn for my transgression, the fruit of my body for the sin of my soul?* [8] *He has shown you, O mortal, what is good And what does the Lord require of you? To act **justly** and to love **mercy** and to walk **humbly** with your God. —* **Micah 6:6-8** *[emphasis mine].*

Fortunately for us, **vrs 8** gives us a clue; we learn that we must be Just and love mercy and be humble. So the key character traits that will lead us to God are Justice, Mercy and Humility. Interestingly, this is what Jesus teaches in the beatitudes - **Matt 5:1-16**.

Justice and Mercy however look like opposites; it seems you can either be Just or be Merciful but not both. But is God both? And if so, at what point does He display His Justice and Mercy? Let's look at this together.

"And let them make Me a sanctuary, that I may dwell among them. ⁹ According to all that I show you, that is, the pattern of the tabernacle and the pattern of all its furnishings, just so you shall make it" — **Exo 25:8-9**

God in the old covenant had the Israelites build Him a sanctuary where He dwelt among them; and the Psalmist also tells us that the way to God is in His Sanctuary.

"Your way, O God is in the Sanctuary; who is so great a God as our God?" — **Ps 77:13**.

So in this chapter, we will study about God's Sanctuary to see how those who lived under the old covenant approached God and worshipped; and what we can learn from that which we know was only a type - the substance itself being Christ. It is very crucial for us as 21st century believers, to understand the purpose of the Old Covenant and particularly why the Holy Scriptures of the Old Testament have been preserved for us. Please see what Paul says of this in the following passages:

"For whatever things were written before were written for our learning, that we through the patience and comfort of the Scriptures might have hope" — **Rom 15:4**

"Now all these things happened to them as examples, and they were written for our admonition, upon whom the ends of the ages have come" — **1 Cor 10:11**

When we have this understanding, we will approach the scriptures with a lot of humility and patience; knowing that God has preserved them to teach us especially about how we relate with Him. With that mind-set; let's study the Sanctuary service.

In the Tabernacle as built by Moses and according to the pattern that God showed Him (details of which are recorded in Exodus 25 - Exodus 30); we notice that there were three areas namely;

[1] The Outer court - **Exo 27:9-19**
[2] The Holy Place - **Exo 26**
[3] The Most Holy place - **Exo 26:31-34**

THE OUTER COURT

The outer courts served as the main area where all Israelites could enter and bring their sacrifices. It is interesting to note that the entire structure of the tabernacle was to have only one entry point/gate - **Exo 27:16-17** & **Exo 26:36**. Once you enter, the first article you see is the **Altar of Sacrifice** where the sacrificial animal was burnt and it's blood poured at the base. Everyone in the community of the Israelites were permitted to come into the Outer court to present their sacrifices and offerings to God. When a person sins and brings a sacrifice - the priest would have the person lay their hands on the animal and then confess their sins on the animal. After, the animal will be slain and their blood will be sprinkled on the horns of the Altar of Sacrifice and the rest poured at the foot of the altar. So the base of the Altar of sacrifice always had blood as a record of sins that had been atoned for. See **Lev 4**

Just before entering the tent of meeting itself was the Bronze Laver which held the water that was used for ceremonial washing before the Priests could enter the first chamber of the Tent called the Holy Place. God warned that any priests who entered the Holy Place without the ceremonial washing of hand and feet would die - **Exo 30:21**. They washed to present themselves clean before going into the Holy Place to serve and they also washed when they came out to go serve the people.

THE HOLY PLACE

From the outer court, you could now enter the Tent of Meeting which had two chambers/apartments. The first chamber was the Holy Place and a veil separated the Holy Place from the Most Holy Place [Holy of Holies]. Only Priests could enter this Holy Place after the sacrifice on the Altar and the ceremonial cleansing at the Laver.

There were three (3) articles in the Holy Place. These were:

The **Table of ShowBread**

The **Gold Lampstand** which was the only light illuminating the room

The **Altar of Incense** was the last article. Notice that the altar of incense is placed just before the veil which separates the Holy Place from the Holy of Holies. And the altar of incense was burnt daily and perpetually (**Exo 30:8**.

In the case where the Priest sinned, in addition to pouring the blood at the base of the Altar of Sacrifice, they would also sprinkle some of the blood on the veil and also dip their fingers into the blood and put it on the horns of the Altar of Incense - Lev 4:1-12. Sprinkling the blood on the veil and the Altar of Incense also showed transferring the record of the Priests' sins unto the articles in the Holy Place. The priests ensured that the Light from the Lampstand would keep burning all the time and also a new batch of Showbread was brought to replace the old batch each Sabbath — **Lev 24:5-9**.

THE MOST HOLY PLACE

The third and final area of the Sanctuary is the Most Holy Place where there was only one article of furniture - The **Ark of the Testimony** also called the Ark of the Covenant. Unlike the other areas of the tabernacle - entry into The Most Holy Place was restricted and reserved for The High Priest and even there; he could enter once a year to cleanse the Sanctuary on the day of Atonement (Yom Kippur) and ask for pardon for all of God's people - See **Lev 16**. If he came there for any other reason, he would die - **Lev 16:2.**

The cover or lid on the Ark of the Covenant is called the atonement cover or the **Mercy Seat** where God sits enthroned between the two cherubim. Thus the mercy seat is the "Throne" of God, making this Most Holy Place His "Throne Room" where the Shekinah glory of God dwells.

> *"You shall put the mercy seat on top of the ark, and in the ark you shall put the Testimony that I will give you.* **22** *And there I will meet with you, and I will speak with you from above the mercy seat, from between the two cherubim which are on the ark of the Testimony, about everything which I will give you in commandment to the children of Israel"* — **Exo 25:21-22**.

The above scripture is very insightful - it tells us that beneath God's throne is the foundation of His justice; the Ten Commandments [God's Holy Law]. So the basis or foundation of God's judgement is the Decalogue. Also, we learn that the name God gives to His Throne is the Mercy seat. So already, we are drawing some connections. God is both Merciful and Just - and it is in His throne room that God's Mercy and Justice meet.

Because of this, God also wants His children to be both Merciful and Just. So what does it mean to be just? According to **Rom 1:17**; we learn that *"...the just are those who live by faith"* - [paraphrase mine]. In simple terms, this refers to those who take God seriously, who take God at His word; those who obey every command of God. So those who come to God must be humble; merciful and obedient. These are key character traits one must have if they are to find God.

Now that we have become a little familiar with the Sanctuary and it's furnishings, and what we need to have to find God; the logical question is to ask how it relates to our worship under the New Covenant.

First, let's draw some parallels by tracing our steps through the various chambers in the earthly Tabernacle. We know that the earthly sanctuary was only a copy of the one in Heaven where Jesus Christ has gone into and interceding for the children of God as our High Priest - **Heb 8:1-6**.

We first enter the gates into the courtyard with Thanksgiving and Praise - **Psalm 100**. In coming to God, we need to recognize Him as a good God who has done so much for us although He owes us nothing. It is out of His grace that He welcomes us; so we need to approach Him with fear and in humility but also with gratitude and joy in our hearts, and ready to obey all that He commands.

> *"Now it shall come to pass, if you diligently obey the voice of the Lord your God, to observe carefully all His*

*commandments which I command you today, that the Lord your God will set you high above all nations of the earth. ² And all these blessings shall come upon you and overtake you, because you obey the voice of the Lord your God" — **Deut 28:1-2***

In the outer court were the Altar of Sacrifice and the Laver which held the water. The Altar represents to us the Cross of Christ where we too come to lay your sins at the foot of His Cross through confession and repentance. Just as they poured the blood of their sacrifices at the foot of the Altar of Sacrifice; we too must come to the foot of Jesus' cross confessing all our sins. Only sins that we lay at the cross of Jesus are recorded. It is also at the foot of the cross we lay ourselves as Living sacrifices for God (**Rom 12:1-2**).

The Laver represents the water of baptism where we wash away our sins so we are cleansed from our past sins and made ready to be set-apart to begin good works which God prepared in advance for us. Without such cleansing, we are unable to go beyond the outer court into the Holy Place - remember how God warned Moses that the priests who don't cleanse themselves will die? In that same way, for us to serve before God, we too must be baptized to have all our sins forgiven (**Acts 2:38**); and as well continue to cleanse ourselves by confessing our sins and praying for each other [intercession] - **1 John 1:8-9; James 5:16**

It is very insightful that all the articles in the outer court were made of bronze. This also goes to show us that the outer court was only the beginning of all that was to be experienced in the Sanctuary service. It tells us that in our faith journey and as disciples of Christ, we shouldn't stop at the point of repentance and baptism; a better experience of gold awaits us only as we get closer into the Tent of meeting where all the articles were adorned with Gold.

Let's now proceed into the Holy Place. In the earthly sanctuary, only priests were allowed to enter; for that reason - God has made us who are followers of Christ the new priesthood. *"You are a chosen people, a Royal Priesthood, a Holy Nation...."* - **1 Pet 2:9** and also; *"And He has made us to be a Kingdom of priests to our God; and they will reign upon the earth"* - **Rev 1:6 / Rev 5:10**]. So now we who are in Christ have direct access into the Holy place and we have become the bridge between God and mankind in the same way as the old covenant priests offered sacrifices and made atonement for their people serving as the bridge between God and Israel. Paul says we are ambassadors of reconciliation - **2 Cor 5:18-20**.

Note that the service in the Holy Place was done daily - **Heb 9:6-7**. The articles in that room were the Table of Showbread, the Altar of Incense and the Lampstand. These articles represent to us; the word of God, Prayer and Witnessing (being light of the world) respectively.

This daily service in the Holy Place by Priests means that; Bible study; Prayer and Witnessing should be a daily devotion for a disciple of Christ. It serves also as a reminder to us of our relationship with each member of our Triune God - daily time with Jesus in His Word; daily prayer and communication to our Father; and constantly illuminating (reflecting) the Light of the Holy Spirit. Jesus is the Word made **flesh** which we have to feed on daily; Prayer is our communication with the Father, and both

Jesus and the Father are revealed to us by the illumination of the Holy Spirit who makes it possible for our light to shine in this dark world.

One more thing we saw with the priests when they sinned was that they sprinkled blood on the altar of incense as well as on the veil. I believe that teaches us that we too have to [as part of our daily worship] confess our sins to God and to lay it on the body of Christ.

All these aspects of the daily service are captured in the model prayer Jesus taught His disciples - **Luke 11:2-4**. We pray to the Father to give us our daily bread [word of God] and to forgive those who hurt or harm us and in that way; setting an example for those in the world to know how to live with each other. *"...Let your lights so shine before men, that they may see your good works and glorify your Father in Heaven"* — **Matt 5:14-16**.

Here are a few things to keep in mind from what we have seen so far:

Having only one gate and access point into the Tabernacle perhaps also endorses the fact that; it is not every road [religion] that will lead us to God, there is only one gate and that is through Christ - **John 10:9**.

Each Sabbath, the Showbread was replaced with a new batch. But why on Sabbath? Could it be that is when God rests with His people? How does it compare to what we are told will happen in the New Earth? *"From one New Moon to another and from one Sabbath to another, all mankind will come and bow down before me," says the Lord"* - **Isa 66:23**. How about also changing your bible study? **Heb 5:12-14**

The Altar of incense was to be burning perpetually. This reminds us to Pray without ceasing - **1 Thess 5:16-18**

The Lampstand was constantly being filled with o̲i̲l which represents the Holy Spirit. This tells us that we can not give light by ourselves and that without the oil of the Holy Spirit, our light will dim or be quenched [*"....Not by might nor by power, but by my Spirit,' says the Lord Almighty"* - **Zech 4:1-6**). The Christian life is not one that you can live on by yourself but only those who are led by the Spirit can - **Rom 8:14**. Are you growing in the fruit of the Spirit? **2 Pet 1:5-8** and **Gal 5:22-23**

The final area in the Sanctuary to look at is the Holy of Holies. Recall that it was only the High Priest who could enter this area and that, only once a year. We serve as priests and Jesus is our High Priest so clearly, this is not an area for us but interestingly; God has chosen for us to see what is going on not in the earthly sanctuary but the heavenly sanctuary so we can't neglect the opportunity. We are also exhorted in the book of Revelation to pay attention. In the beginning as well as at the end of the vision, John is told that the vision was about things which would soon take place:

> *"The Revelation of Jesus Christ, which God gave Him to show His servants - things which must shortly take place. And He sent and signified it by His angel to His servant John, ² who bore witness to the word of God, and to the testimony of Jesus Christ, to all things that he saw. ³ Blessed is he who **reads and those who hear the words of this prophecy**, and **keep those things which are written in it; for the time is near.** "— Rev 1:1-3* [emphasis added]

*"Then he said to me, "These words are faithful and true."
And the Lord God of the holy prophets sent His angel to
show His servants* **the things which must shortly take
place**. *⁷ "Behold, I am coming quickly! Blessed is he who
keeps the words of the prophecy of this book."— **Rev 22:6-
7*** [emphasis added]

So to understand what was going on in the Most Holy Place - let's
dive into the book of Revelation briefly to see what God is eager
to show us. It is very important to notice that; in John's vision,
he often switches from things he sees in Heaven and the things
he sees in the Sanctuary/Temple - please take note when you read
the book of Revelation so you don't get confused.

In this part of his vision, the Apostle John saw the ark of the
covenant in God's Sanctuary in Heaven - **Rev 11:19 AMPC**.
Recall that the Ark of the Covenant was in the Most Holy Place;
and it was on the Ark that God's throne [the Mercy Seat] is. This
tells us that the events John saw and described were taking place
in the Most Holy Place. What is perhaps most important for us to
note is that; the only time the High Priest enters the Most Holy
Place is on the day of atonement, apart from this one day in the
year, he won't know what is going on in the Most Holy Place.
So we need to be curious as to why God would give us a peep in
there - To what is God drawing our attention?

The scene that John saw when the throne room was open was
that of the seven angels with the seven plagues (**Rev 15:5-8** and
Rev 16:17-18). So there's no doubt that God allowed John to see
an event which was the most important on the calendar of Israel
(during the days of the earthly Sanctuary). When you follow the

events of his vision, you see that the first thing it discusses is the judgment of Mystery Babylon, the mother of all harlots.

Regarding judgement, Peter said that this will begin in the house of God [the Church].

> *"For the time has come for judgment to begin at the house of God; and if it begins with us first, what will be the end of those who do not obey the gospel of God? [18] Now "If the righteous one is scarcely saved, Where will the ungodly and the sinner appear?"* — **1 Pet 4:17-18**

Before we go ahead, it is important to take some time to explain what the day of atonement is and how different that day was from any other day in the life of those who worshipped in the days of the earthly Sanctuary.

THE DAY OF ATONEMENT

Unlike the other Holy Convocations of God's people in the Old Covenant; Yom Kippur [the day of atonement] was a day that all of Israel were to afflict themselves. Most or all of the other feasts of the Lord were happy celebrations where they would eat and be joyful - but not the day of atonement; this was a the day of their great fast [**Acts 27:9; Lev 23:26-32**] where they will be very solemn and fast from the time the High Priest entered the Most Holy Place till he returned the following day.

The day of atonement was the day when God goes over the records of all the sins that sacrifices have previously been made for at the altar throughout the year by the Israelite community. If God is satisfied by the sacrifices previously made for the sins, then these sins were completely blotted out from the records - which means completely forgiven. All their daily, weekly and monthly sacrifices were still not sufficient to wipe away their sins so this day was set aside for the final atonement of all sins for which blood had been shed throughout the year. On this day, the High Priest stood in as representative to seek reconciliation for himself, the priesthood and the entire people of God and to purify the sanctuary itself from all the sins confessed there during the year and thus the entire sanctuary was cleansed.

GOD'S HOLY LAW - Matters that truly matter!

Assuming there were sin(s) that had not been confessed and or sacrifices not made for; there will be no record of forgiveness which means that the sin would still be hanging on the sinner. In simple terms; God has books that keep records of different things everyone does; a book that keeps records of our sins; and another book that keeps records of Forgiven sins and also the book of Life. When you sin, it is recorded in the Sin Book; and when you confess your sin or make sacrifices for that sin, it is recorded in the Forgiven sins book. The book of Forgiven sins is kept in the Sanctuary (the blood of the sacrifice poured on the altar is how this record of forgiven sin is taken - Lev 1:5). When a person lays their hand on the animal and it is killed, with the blood poured on the altar, the person has transferred their sin unto the altar. The sinner is cleansed of the sin but now, the record of the sin is on the altar of sacrifice. This is how the Priest makes atonement for the sinner - **Lev 4:27-31**.

One key purpose the day of atonement achieves is to permanently cast away and destroy sin from the Israelite community. On the day of atonement, the records of the people's sins are permanently cleansed [blotted out] from the Sanctuary. The High Priest brings the atoning blood into God's throne room to ask for a final blotting out of the record of Israel's sins so there is no trace of sin and as though it never happened - **Isa 43:25; Isa 44:22; Ps 103:10-12**. To achieve this, the High Priest presents two goats, one which is sacrificed to cleanse the Sanctuary by sprinkling on God's Throne [Mercy Seat] and on the altar of sacrifice in the outer court - **Lev 16:16-19**. After this, the High Priest will lay both hands on the other goat and confess all the sins of the people on to it and then send the goat away from the community into the wilderness where there is no habitation - this is called the scapegoat which all sins are transferred unto and sent away - **Lev 16:10. 21**. God did this to eradicate sin entirely from the community once each year.

This day of atonement was a solemn day of fasting and prayer by the entire Israelite community who were anxious about whether God would accept their sacrifices or reject them - **Lev 16:29-34**. This was the day of the final judgment when God would review the books to see if for all sins committed; there are corresponding records showing that these sins have been forgiven (meaning; to see if appropriate confession and sacrifices have been made for the sins at the altar of sacrifice). If these two records tally, then one's name is transferred to the book of Life. But assuming there are sins with no matching records in the Forgiven sins book (unconfessed sins and those sins for which no sacrifice had been made) - one would be found wanting as their sin would still be on them after the High Priest has finished the work and the scapegoat has been let out to die in the wilderness.

If someone was found to be living in sin after this - the only way to get rid of that sin was to expel that person out of the community - **Deut 17:2-7 I 1 Cor 5**

So when we apply the day of atonement to we who are under the 2nd Covenant - the day of atonement is when God also reviews our books in the presence of our High Priest Jesus

Christ. When our Sin book is opened; Jesus our High Priest' would indicate that all our past sins have been paid for by His blood. But even after we become Christians, we continue to sin many times over. This is the reason we are to confess all our sins daily so that His blood cleanses us. However when we fail to acknowledge and confess our sins even after we have come to Christ; then His blood is unable to purify us.

> *"If we say that we have no sin, we deceive ourselves, and the truth is not in us. ⁹ If we confess our sins, He is faithful and just to forgive us our sins and to cleanse us from all unrighteousness. ¹⁰ If we say that we have not sinned, we make Him a liar, and His word is not in us"*
> — *1 John 1:8-10*

> *"For if we sin willfully after we have received the knowledge of the truth, there no longer remains a sacrifice for sins, ²⁷ but a certain fearful expectation of judgment, and fiery indignation which will devour the adversaries"*
> — *Heb 10:26-27*.

Unlike in the earthly Sanctuary where the day of atonement [Judgment] was once each year; scripture clearly indicates that Jesus will appear once at the end of the ages to atone for us - **Heb 9:25-28**. If any child of God still has unconfessed sins that they don't transfer unto Jesus [by acknowledgment, confession and repentance] before the close of probation, then Jesus' blood is unable to atone for such sins; and so whoever bears that sin would be found wanting after His final work of atonement before the Father in the Holy of Holies. To permanently cast out such sin then requires that the person is cast into the lake of fire (even though he may have at one point received Christ).

With this being clear, let's carry on from where we left off!

So going back to John's vision - we can now understand that John was being shown what was to take place on the day of judgment; and the details of his vision shows that judgment begins with "Babylon" [the apostate Church] just as Peter said. In bible prophecy, a woman refers to the Church. In speaking of the day of Judgment - Paul also told us in which state the Church would be by the time of the judgment. He says, it won't happen until at the time when the man of lawlessness has exalted himself and set himself as "God" using counterfeit miracles, signs and wonders to deceive the nations - **2 Thess 2:1-12**.

So we see that all of these three Apostles (John, Peter and Paul) are in agreement. I don't know your thoughts on this but it seems pretty obvious that the state of the Church today shows clearly that most are being "run" by the man of lawlessness - inciting followers of God against God's Holy Law and teaching strange man-made doctrines. This is exactly what John saw in his vision also - and this might be a good time to read the book of Revelation and especially to acquaint yourself on how this vision ends.

"Then the seventh angel poured out his bowl into the air, and a loud voice came out of the temple of heaven, from the throne, saying, "It is done!" [18] *And there were noises and thunderings and lightnings; and there was a great earthquake, such a mighty and great earthquake as had not occurred since men were on the earth* — **Rev 16:17-18**

Friend, without getting into the details which will fill up another book, it is important that we take notice of some instructions that John was given concerning the vision. Daniel saw a similar vision of judgement but at the time was told to seal it up until the end - **Dan 12:1-4**. But with John, he was told not to seal it up because it's time is near - **Rev 22:10-11**. This tells us that God wants us to know what is taking place now so we can prepare for it.

When Jesus finishes His work as High Priest before the throne of God; there will be no other chance for anyone to repent - that's why God enthroned said "**it is done**". The angel also tells John in **Rev 22:11**; let those who are righteous remain righteous and those who are filthy remain filthy still. There is nothing we can do when the verdict of judgment is pronounced and Jesus comes out of the Most Holy Place carrying His rewards - "no other sacrifice for sins can be made from that point onwards". Many people think they can wait until they see Jesus in the clouds and then get serious with their relationship with God; confess and repent of their sins and start living Godly lives. They have been taught wrongly about how the judgment will be; not realising that even now - judgment is taking place and Jesus is atoning for the sins we have confessed and asked forgiveness for.

Now is our only chance to confess all our sins, repent and obey God; we don't have tomorrow. Just as God always does; we can see a parallel to this story when the three angels were sent to **Sodom & Gomorrah** before it's sudden destruction; and where one of the angels told Abraham what was going to happen. In the same way, God has shown John what is soon to happen and he has made it known to us. Let us therefore take this as our final call to repentance as the three angels proclaimed in **Rev 14:6-12**.

> *"And behold, I am coming quickly, and My reward is with Me, to give to every one according to his work. [13] I am the Alpha and the Omega, the Beginning and the End, the First and the Last." [14] Blessed are those who do His commandments, that they may have the right to the tree of life, and may enter through the gates into the city. [15] But outside are dogs and sorcerers and sexually immoral and murderers and idolaters, and whoever loves and practices a lie. [16] "I, Jesus, have sent My angel to testify to you these things in the Churches. I am the Root and the Offspring of David, the Bright and Morning Star." — Rev 22:12-16*

So what does all of this mean for us? It points to us that we are in the day of "judgment", Jesus is before the Just and Merciful Father making atonement for the Church and this calls for us to afflict our souls - these are not times for merry-making nor to live our usual lives. God is showing us the times in which we are so that we can be sober, search our hearts; rid ourselves of everything that corrupts and set ourselves apart for Holy Living just as the Israelites would do during Yom Kippur. They lived this way with the hope that the sacrifice for their sins will be accepted by the Father and that the blood of the animals they sacrificed would plead for them. But we hold a better promise, with the blood of

Jesus **pleading on our behalf** (if indeed we have confessed and transferred all of our sins unto Him).

For a clue to those who are following a path that will lead to God; see what the angel says to John in **Rev 22:9** as well as what Jesus adds in **Rev 22:14**. I believe they re-echo the words of Jesus that He did not come to abolish the Law or the Prophets. The follower of God today can not be any different - we too must believe the prophecies and obey the Law.

When you study **Dan 1 & 2**; you learn that God gave special wisdom, knowledge and understanding to Daniel and his friends to interpret dreams and visions because they chose not to defile themselves but instead kept the decrees of God. I believe that when we stay pure and keep all of God's decrees and commands (*not so we will be saved but because we have been saved and in gratitude of our salvation*) - then God will also give us the gift of wisdom, knowledge and understanding of prophecy and the skill and ability to correctly interpret the Holy Scriptures. Then we can be sure of our 'sacrifices' being accepted and having a sure hope of inheriting His Holy City!

So to answer the questions we started with regarding the right pathway to God; we have found out that God has not changed - and just as it was under the old covenant

1. The way to God is only one and that is through Christ our High Priest
2. We in the new covenant should fully obey God's Law
3. We should confess our sins at the cross of Jesus and get baptized

4. We should as Priests continually offer prayers to God for ourselves and intercede for others; read God's word and be a witness [light] to the world.
5. We should constantly confess and renounce our sins so that Jesus' blood can atone for all our sins.

> *"And do this, understanding the present time: The hour has already come for you to wake up from your slumber, because our salvation is nearer now than when we first believed. [12] The night is nearly over; the day is almost here. So let us put aside the deeds of darkness and put on the armor of light. [13] Let us behave decently, as in the daytime, not in carousing and drunkenness, not in sexual immorality and debauchery, not in dissension and jealousy. [14] Rather, clothe yourselves with the Lord Jesus Christ, and do not think about how to gratify the desires of the flesh"* **— Rom 13:11-14.**

The evidence is very clear as we have seen - Judgment is currently on-going having started with the Church. This is the time for each person to afflict their souls, be humble, love mercy and obey all of God's Law which is the foundation of His Throne.

Christ is coming - Are you ready?

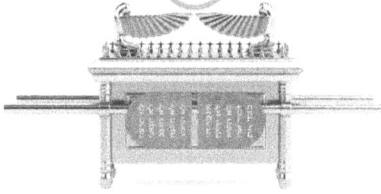

24

GOD'S SEAL

I will put My law in their minds, and write it on their hearts; and I will be their God, and they shall be My people — **Jer 31:33**

Many would like to argue that the Sabbath is no longer needed, but before we go down that path; we need to ask ourselves what purpose God made the Sabbath for?

"The Sabbath was made for man" — **Mark 2:27** - As we see, this day of rest that God set aside for QUALITY TIME with man was for man's benefit. In this day and age where over 70% of all doctors appointments and medications are as a result of stress, is it difficult to realize that the one thing that man needs more than perhaps anything else is a time of rest? And who better to rest with than God the creator Himself.

The Sabbath was made for all mankind not just Jews as some like to say. For instance, God also said; "It is not good for the man to be alone" and therefore He made woman for man. Do men still need women in our day or will we as well throw out women - have they also outlived their usefulness or purpose?

> *"Also the sons of the foreigner*
> *Who join themselves to the Lord, to serve Him,*
> *And to love the name of the Lord, to be His servants—*
> *Everyone who keeps from defiling the Sabbath,*
> *And holds fast My covenant"* — **Isa 56:6**

The Sabbath was a day that God set aside to really enjoy His relationship with all of man-kind and not just Jews; it was special and unlike any other day just like two people in a relationship; say a couple would set aside a day to go out on a date and spend quality time together. God also wants to spend quality time with each of His children; and so as our husband, He set the agenda and made a day special and Holy for that quality time with Him.

What is most interesting about the Sabbath is that it also is a seal (sign) that marks all His children.

> *"Moreover I also gave them My Sabbaths, to be a sign between them and Me, that they might know that I am the Lord who sanctifies them"* — **Eze 20:12**

In a seal; the three things that you will normally find are:

1. The name of the person
2. The title of the person
3. The territory the person controls

If you have seen the seal of the President on any letter or document, you will notice these three things - for example: DONALD TRUMP [NAME], PRESIDENT [TITLE] OF THE UNITED STATES OF AMERICA [TERRITORY]. Same as NANA ADDO DANQUAH AKUFFO-ADDO [NAME]; PRESIDENT [TITLE] OF THE REPUBLIC OF GHANA [TERRITORY].

CREDIT: Google Images.

It is interesting to note that in the book of Revelation; we are told that before the last seven plagues that destroy the world; 144,000 of God's people will be sealed on their foreheads. The account also mentions what the seal is, the name of God. Read **Rev 7:1-7** and **Rev 14:1-5**.

> *"1 Then I looked, and behold, a Lamb standing on Mount Zion, and with Him one hundred and forty-four thousand, having His Father's name written on their foreheads...."*
> *— Rev 14:1-5*

When you read the old testament, you come to learn of a time when God's people began ignoring His Law and were living in a state of indifference to His Law. At that time, God had all the wicked people slain with a sword but before that action occurred, He chose a man to go amongst the people and seal those who still worshiped Him and were hurting because of the ways that people were living against the will of God - **Eze 9**. These two accounts, in Ezekiel and in Revelation point to the same idea; one that happened in the time of the Old Covenant and another which will happen at the end of the ages.

"Then He called out in my hearing with a loud voice, saying, "Let those who have charge over the city draw near, each with a deadly weapon in his hand." ² And suddenly six men came from the direction of the upper gate, which faces north, each with his battle-ax in his hand. One man among them was clothed with linen and had a writer's inkhorn at his side. They went in and stood beside the bronze altar. ³ Now the glory of the God of Israel had gone up from the cherub, where it had been, to the threshold of the temple. And He called to the man clothed with linen, who had the writer's inkhorn at his side; ⁴ and the Lord said to him, "Go through the midst of the city, through the midst of Jerusalem, and put a mark on the foreheads of the men who sigh and cry over all the abominations that are done within it." ⁵ To the others He said in my hearing, "Go after him through the city and kill; do not let your eye spare, nor have any pity. ⁶ Utterly slay old and young men, maidens and little children and women; but do not come near anyone on whom is the mark; and begin at My sanctuary." So they began with the elders who were before the temple" — **Eze 9**

"After these things I saw four angels standing at the four corners of the earth, holding the four winds of the earth, that the wind should not blow on the earth, on the sea, or

on any tree. ² Then I saw another angel ascending from the east, having the seal of the living God. And he cried with a loud voice to the four angels to whom it was granted to harm the earth and the sea, ³ saying, "Do not harm the earth, the sea, or the trees till we have sealed the servants of our God on their foreheads." ⁴ And I heard the number of those who were sealed. One hundred and forty-four thousand of all the tribes of the children of Israel were sealed" — **Rev 7:1-8**

It is interesting to note from both accounts that everyone who did not have the seal of God on their foreheads, children, adults, male and female alike were slain - no one was spared.

This should make us curious of what the seal is so we can find out how we will get it too. Isaiah is told to seal God's disciples with the Law. *"Bind up the testimony, Seal the law among my disciples"* - **Isa 8:16**. This scripture mentions the Law of God being the seal which is set on God's people.

Today, not many people will argue the fact that if someone said they were traveling to the Holy Land; everyone would say Israel. If they said they were going to visit the Holy City, all will say it is Jerusalem. And if they went further to say that they were going to see the Holy Mountain; again all fingers will be pointing to Mount Zion. In Mt. Zion, if you were going to the Holy Place, they will lead you to the temple (now the remains of the temple). Recognize that in the days of the temple, there was also a place designated as the Most Holy Place or the Holy of Holies. In that chamber, there was only one article which was the Ark of the Covenant - and in the Ark of the Covenant was also the

Holy Law of God (the Ten Commandments or the Tablets of Testimony) together with Aarons rod and the manna. In all the ten commandments, there is only one that has the word Holy in it and that is the 4th commandment - "Keep the Sabbath Holy".

> "Remember the Sabbath day, to keep it **holy**. ⁹ Six days you shall labor and do all your work, ¹⁰ but the seventh day is the Sabbath of the Lord your God. In it you shall do no work: you, nor your son, nor your daughter, nor your male servant, nor your female servant, nor your cattle, nor your stranger who is within your gates. ¹¹ For in six days the **Lord made the heavens and the earth, the sea, and all that is in them**, and rested the seventh day. Therefore the Lord blessed the Sabbath day and hallowed it" — **Exo 20:8-11** [emphasis added]

I put an emphasis on the word Holy so you see that in all of God's Law, the Sabbath command is where He chose to put the word which best befits His character; *"You must be Holy because I am Holy"* - **Lev 11:44-45,Leviticus 19:2,Leviticus 20:7; 1 Pet 1:16**. This is interesting because if we are to look for the place where God is Holy, it points us to this one commandment. It is also interesting to find that, in the entire Law of God; the only one that has the characteristics of a seal - which are the name; the title and the territory of the person is found in this very commandment.

Boldly displayed in vrs 11: *"For in six days the **Lord** [NAME] made [TITLE - Creator] the heavens and the earth, the sea, and all that is in them [TERRITORY]._*

I mentioned in an earlier chapter that, when God created the World, no human-being was there and it is only by faith that we come to believe that He is indeed the Creator of the whole universe - **Heb 11:3**. In His command of the Sabbath; He also asserts His authority for which reason everyone must obey all His commands. In other words, God is saying that the reason you must [Honor me, do not bow to images, do not use my name in vain, honor your father and mother, do not murder, do not steal, do not kill, do not lie; do not covet your neightbours wife or property]; is because l am **JEHOVAH, CREATOR OF THE UNIVERSE** [His seal]. This is so powerful!

Knowing this, the devil's all time effort has been to attack this very commandment; the very command which God says we should "remember and keep Holy" is the one that the devil; having corrupted men including even some "Christians" are saying we should "forget" about. But should it come as a surprise that the one who is in competition with our Most High God would deceive the entire world into following [obeying] him rather than God?

> *'I will ascend into heaven,*
> *I will exalt my throne above the stars of God;*
> *I will also sit on the mount of the congregation*
> *On the farthest sides of the north;*
> ¹⁴ *I will ascend above the heights of the clouds,*
> *I will be like the Most High.' —* **Isa 14:13-14**

What is more, the crucial knowledge we are getting from all these scriptures put together is the fact that; the seal of God is really His 4th commandment and I believe it is this seal that will be marked on the foreheads of all of God's children before the destruction of the world. Notice that at the end of the age; everyone will be sealed, you will either have the seal of God [which scripture is giving us clues to see is the Sabbath] or you will have the seal of the beast which is the counterfeit of the mark that God gives us.

Let's take note of what is being said of this counterfeit seal which the Bible describes as the number of a man.

> *"Then I saw another beast coming up out of the earth, and he had two horns like a lamb and spoke like a dragon.* [12] *And he exercises all the authority of the first beast in his presence, and causes the earth and those who dwell in it to worship the first beast, whose deadly wound was healed.* [13] *He performs great signs, so that he even makes fire come down from heaven on the earth in the sight of men.* [14] *And he deceives [f]those who dwell on the earth by those signs which he was granted to do in the sight of the beast, telling those who dwell on the earth to make an image to the beast who was wounded by the sword and lived.* [15] *He was granted power to give breath to the image of the beast, that the image of the beast should both speak and cause as many as would not worship the image of the beast to be killed.* [16] *He causes all, both small and great, rich and poor, free and slave, to receive a mark on their right hand or on their foreheads,* [17] *and that no one may buy or sell except one who has [g]the mark or the name of the beast, or the number of his name.* [18] *Here is wisdom. Let him who has understanding calculate the number of the beast, for it is the number of a man: His number is 666"* — ***Rev 13:11-18***

The Roman Catholic Church has never shied away from boldly declaring that their faith and doctrine are based on both traditions and the scriptures. They mention that there were no other Churches until Martin Luther after ten (10) years of being a Catholic Priest broke off [protested] to form his own denomination in the year 1517. They boldly assert their authority for the transference of the solemnity of the day of worship being the Saturday Sabbath to Sunday.

It is interesting to note that in the Catholic Catechism which spells out what members should believe as they are baptized into the Catholic faith - among the questions asked is when the Sabbath is. For instance in page 50 of the Convert's Catechism (1977) - the question of why Catholics observe Sunday rather than Saturday is asked. Not only have the second commandment been completely taken off, making the Sabbath command the 3rd commandment in the Roman Catholic Catechism; but they boldly declare that the change from Saturday to Sunday was done with the authority of the Church.

Although there are no scriptures pointing to this change - the Roman Catholic Church says that' "because Sunday was the culmination of Jesus' work of redemption for mankind"; they transferred God's command of Sabbath rest and worship to Sunday to honor Jesus Christ. Below are a few statements that have been made over the years

> *"The pope is not only the representative of Jesus Christ, but he is Jesus Christ Himself, hidden under the veil of flesh"* - **Catholic National, July 1895**

"The Pope and God are the same, so he has all power in Heaven and earth" - **Pope Pius V, quoted in Barclay, Cities Petrus Bertanous, Chapter XXVII, p 218**

"To believe that our Lord God the Pope has not the power to decree as he is decreed, is to be deemed heretical" - **Pope John XXII, "Extravagantes", Ad Callem Sexti Decretalium, Tit. XIV, cap. IV (Paris, 1685)**

"The doctrines of the Catholic Church are entirely independent of Holy Scriptures" - **Familiar Explanation of Christian Doctrine by M. Muller (New York: Benzinger Brothers, 1876), pg 151**

"Like two sacred rivers flowing from paradise, the Bible and divine tradition contain the word of God... .Though these two divine streams are of equal sacredness....still, of the two, TRADITION is to us more clear and safe" - **Catholic Belief pg 33 Joseph Faa di Bruno**

"You may read the Bible from Genesis to Revelation, and you will not find a single line authorizing the sanctification of Sunday. The scriptures enforce the religious observance of Saturday" - **The Faith of our Fathers, pg 89**

"The authority of the Church could therefore not be bound to the authority of the Scriptures, because the Church had changed...the Sabbath to Sunday, not

by command of Christ, but by its own authority" -
Canon and Traditions, pg 263

"The sun was a foremost god with heathendom....
The sun has worshipers at this hour in Persia and
other lands. There is, in truth, something royal, kingly
about the sun making it a fit emblem of Jesus the Sun
of Justice. Hence the Church in these countries would
seem to have said, 'Keep that old pagan name. It shall
remain consecrated, sanctified and thus the pagan
Sunday, dedicated to Balder, became the Christian
Sunday, sacred to Jesus" - **The Catholic World,
March 1994, pg 809**

"Sunday is our mark of authority. The Church is
above the Bible, and this transference of Sabbath
observance is proof of that fact." - **Catholic Record;
Sept 1, 1923**

"Perhaps the boldest thing, the most revolutionary
change the Church ever did, happened in the first
century. The holy day, the Sabbath, was changed from
Saturday to Sunday not from any directions noted
in the Scriptures, but from the Church's sense of its
own power. People who think the Scripture should
be the sole authority, should logically become 7th
Day Adventist's, and keep Saturday holy." - **Saint
Catherine - Catholic Church Sentinel, May 21,
1995**

It is scary to see what Roman Catholics believe of their faith
and doctrine and how they can so confidently ascribe that much

power to the Pope and a man-made system as unto God. The devil is the only one known to be contesting the position of God (**Isa 14:14**); so to see that the Catholic Church believes that the Pope (a man) is a representative of God on earth is a bit scary; let alone to equate him to God and have authority to change what God has said concerning His Law and times.

> *"He shall speak pompous words against the Most High,*
> *Shall persecute the saints of the Most High,*
> *And shall intend to change times and law.*
> *Then the saints shall be given into his hand*
> *For a time and times and half a time"* — **Dan 7:25**

I don't think I need to go further but in conclusion; the bible says that the man who has understanding will be able to calculate the mark of the beast, it is the number of a man - **Rev 13:18**. And History; Prophecy and even what we witness in our times should point to us that the dragon [devil] is using the Roman Catholic Church as his beast to oppose everything that is God and of God. And gradually as the beast' **wounds have healed**, the dragon [devil] will unify the beast [Catholic Church] and the false prophet [Apostate Protestantism] under the seal set up by the beast which the bible describes as man-made (under the authority of man).

So let us remember that the devil has a counterfeit for everything that is of God. In Egypt, Pharaoh's magicians tried to replicate each of the miracles that Moses did and it is the same today; the devil does miracles, signs and wonders that make people marvel and so follow him. God reveals Himself to us in the form of an animal, the lamb; the devil comes as a wolf in sheep's clothing. In

Revelation; God's true Church is the woman clothed in white, the devil has a false Church in the form of a woman dressed in purple. God works as three persons - Father, Son and the Holy Spirit - the devil works through three agents; the dragon, the beast and the false prophet. Jesus is the true light; the devil masquerades as an angel of light.

So, just as God has a seal, the devil also has a seal - God's seal is a day that he has made Holy and set apart; the devil's seal is also a different day that by his authority has set apart - and do you wonder that he will make his seal as close to that of God as possible to deceive even some who are of God?

> *"For false christs and false prophets will rise and show great signs and wonders to deceive, if possible, even the elect"* — **Matt 24:24**

Friend, the end is so near - we need to watch and pray as Jesus told His disciples. He said that the day will be just like in the days of Noah - so we need to watch the days of Noah and how those who survived the disaster that happened in the world were only those who entered the Ark. Today, our Ark is the Ark of the Covenant in which the Holy Law of God is and we are being admonished to obey His commandments.

> *"This is how we are sure that we have come to know Him: by keeping His commands. 4 The one who says, "I have come to know Him," yet doesn't keep His commands, is a liar, and the truth is not in him"* — **1 John 2:3-4**

More than knowing Christ is He knowing us. We don't want Jesus to say to us: *"And then I will declare to them, 'I never knew you; depart from Me, you who practice lawlessness!"* - **Matt 7:21-23**.

But that's what happens to those who claim to know Him and yet do not keep ALL His commandments.

When Jesus said *"For the Son of Man is Lord even of the Sabbath"* - **Matt 12:8** - we need to think carefully about what He was saying. I believe the devil is behind advocating that God has changed the original Sabbath to Sunday, and hiding behind Jesus' resurrection as the reason; although no one is able to provide a single scripture reference to back the assertion of the transference of the Holy day to Sunday. Jesus says that His Lordship also covers the Sabbath. That means if you call Him Lord [master], then be sure that He is calling you to keep the Sabbath Holy as well. Being Lord over the Sabbath also tells us that if anyone would have more knowledge or understanding or be able to interpret it more accurately and without error, then it will be Jesus and not anybody else - that's what being master of something means. So the question you need to ask is - where in scripture does Jesus [Lord of the Sabbath] give us any idea or command to discard the original Sabbath for Sunday? And if the Lord is not saying so - then who have you been listening to and obeying?

"What good does it do for you to say I am your Lord and Master if what I teach you is not put into practice?" — **Luke 6:46 TPT**

WHEN TO OBSERVE THE WEEKLY SABBATH

Before we close this chapter, let's establish when we should observe the Sabbath.

> *"And on the seventh day God ended His work which He had done, and He rested on the seventh day from all His work which He had done"* — **Gen 2:2**

It is clear in the above scripture that God rested on the Seventh day and that's the day we must observe. The below scripture however gives us some details of how the people of Israel who experienced God first-hand also observed the Sabbath.

> *"And Moses said, "Let no one leave any of it **till morning**." [20] Notwithstanding they did not heed Moses. **But some of them left part of it until morning**, and it bred worms and stank. And Moses was angry with them. [21] **So they gathered it every morning**, every man according to his need. **And when the sun became hot, it melted**. [22] And so it was, **on the sixth day**, that they gathered twice as much bread, two omers for each one. And all the rulers of the congregation came and told Moses. [23] Then he said to them, "This is what the Lord has said: '**Tomorrow** is a Sabbath rest, a holy Sabbath to the Lord. **Bake what you will bake today, and boil what you will boil; and lay up for yourselves all that remains, to be kept until morning.'** " [24] **So they laid it up till morning**, as Moses commanded; and it did not stink, nor were there any worms in it. [25] Then Moses said, "**Eat that today, for today is a Sabbath to the Lord; today you will not find it in the field**. [26] Six days you shall gather it, but on the seventh day, the Sabbath, there will be none." [27] Now it happened that some of the people went out on the seventh day to gather, but they found none. [28] And the Lord said to Moses, "How long do you refuse to keep My commandments and My laws? [29] See! For the Lord has given you the Sabbath; therefore He gives you on the sixth day bread for two days. Let every man remain in his place; let no man go out of his place on the seventh day." [30]*

*So the people rested on the seventh day" — **Exo 16:19-30**
[emphasis mine].

The above scripture is very helpful in our understanding of when the Sabbath was observed. It clearly tells us that they collected the manna every morning; by afternoon when the sun was hot, it melted. That alone tells us that people won't be out in the afternoon looking for manna. But on the sixth day, they collected twice as much as they needed and kept part till morning of the seventh day and yet it did not stink. What they kept from the sixth day is what they ate on the Sabbath (seventh day). Again, notice that some people went out on the seventh day (must have been in the morning as they usually did) but did not find any manna. So if the manna fell on the morning of a day and was good throughout the day even till the evening and night but went bad only by the morning of the following day (except for the seventh day) - then perhaps we can deduce that the Sabbath was observed throughout the entire Seventh day.

There is also evidence from scripture that in the days of Jesus; the people started to prepare for the Sabbath by the time of sundown of the sixth day (Friday). We notice that from the text below where they referred to Friday as the preparation day but rested on the seventh day Sabbath:

> "This man went to Pilate and asked for the body of Jesus. 53 Then he took it down, wrapped it in linen, and laid it in a tomb that was hewn out of the rock, where no one had ever lain before. 54 That day was the Preparation, and the Sabbath drew near. 55 And the women who had come with Him from Galilee followed after, and they observed the tomb and how His body was laid. 56 Then they returned

and prepared spices and fragrant oils. And they rested on the Sabbath according to the commandment"
— *Luke 23:52-56*

Finally, it was very early in the morning at dawn that the women woke up after the Sabbath rest; to go and apply the spices on Jesus' body. Some have argued that, if Sabbath had ended by sundown of the seventh day, they sure would have gone to anoint Jesus' body at that time for fear that His body might decay quickly (with no spices on). But all we know is that the women waited till the following morning on the first day of the week (Sunday) to go and do that work. See the text below:

"Now on the first day of the week, very early in the morning, they, and certain other women with them, came to the tomb bringing the spices which they had prepared"
— *Luke 24:1*

I must add that, in speaking of the day of atonement (which was one of the seven annual feasts of the Lord), God instructed Moses on when the Sabbath was to begin and end:

"It shall be to you a sabbath of solemn rest, and you shall afflict your souls; on the ninth day of the month at evening, from evening to evening, you shall celebrate your sabbath."
— *Lev 23:32 NKJV*

Many Jews even in this age, observe the Sabbath from sundown of Friday to sundown of Saturday. What is extensively clear from scripture is that the seventh day is Saturday, and I believe we won't go wrong when we learn from these accounts from both the Old and New Testaments.

HOW SHOULD WE OBSERVE THE SABBATH?

The command of the Sabbath is to keep it Holy by resting. At the core of the Sabbath command is a test of our faith in God.

A good reference is the story told of Mary and Martha.

> *"Now it happened as they went that He entered a certain village; and a certain woman named Martha welcomed Him into her house. ³⁹ And she had a sister called Mary, who also sat at Jesus' feet and heard His word. ⁴⁰ But Martha was distracted with much serving, and she approached Him and said, "Lord, do You not care that my sister has left me to serve alone? Therefore tell her to help me."⁴¹ And Jesus answered and said to her, "Martha, Martha, you are worried and troubled about many things. ⁴² But one thing is needed, and Mary has chosen that good part, which will not be taken away from her" — Luke 10:38-42*

I believe on the Sabbath; God knocks on our doors hoping to be welcomed in as Martha opened up her home to Jesus. In this story, we see that the practice Jesus commended was what Mary did - Mary chose to sit still at the feet of Jesus to be taught and to enjoy His' presence while Martha was busy working and distracted although she was actually the one who invited Jesus. You also notice that Jesus spoke well of Mary showing that she allowed her attitude to reflect goodness as a result of spending time with Jesus - she became a good witness that Christ pointed to.

When Jesus visits us; He doesn't do it so we show Him around our garden/home or to enjoy a good meal or to prove anything to Him; He visits only for a brief moment to enjoy us just as you would want your partner to make quality time for you on a date.

Sabbath is our moment to do away with distractions so we can be with Jesus, worship Him but most importantly to rest in Him knowing that because He is with us, we won't need to worry about anything. Everything else in the world can wait till after God has left our home [although He never leaves us]. All God wants to do while we rest in Him is encourage us and let us know that He loves and cares for us and will take care of all our needs - thereby building our faith in Him. Sabbath is a time of resting from our work (all that we normally do in the six days God gives us) and possibly while resting, we can immerse ourselves into God's word and in prayer and also use every opportunity we have to witness to people around us - letting our lives shine by our good works for the world to notice that we have been with Jesus - **Matt 5:14-16**.

But the key thing to remember about our Sabbath rest is to understand that "living on earth is a matter of having FAITH in God" - that He alone is the creator and redeemer and we won't achieve much by our own works as the Psalmist says.

> *"Unless the Lord builds a house, the builders' work is useless. Unless the Lord protects a city, sentries do no good. [2] **It is senseless for you to work so hard** from early morning until late at night, fearing you will starve to death; for **God wants his loved ones to get their proper rest"** — **Ps 127:1-2 TLB** [emphasis mine]*

See also below:

> *"Then he said, "This is God's message to Zerubbabel: 'Not by might, nor by power, but by my Spirit, says the Lord Almighty—**you will succeed because of my Spirit, though you are few and weak.'** [7] Therefore no mountain, however high, can stand before Zerubbabel! For it will*

flatten out before him! And Zerubbabel will finish building this Temple with mighty shouts of thanksgiving for God's mercy, **declaring that all was done by grace alone.**" — **Zech 4:6-7 TLB** [emphasis mine].

THE MEANING OF THE SABBATH REST

I must also take the time to emphasize that; God doesn't rest because He is tired (Isa 40:28). God didn't also call man to rest from being weary because Adam & Eve had not done any work when God asked them to rest a day after they were created - **Gen 2:1-3.** When we understand this, it leads us to the main purpose of Sabbath and what the "rest" it talks about really means. Our Holy God set aside the seventh day Sabbath so man could come and worship Him as the creator of everything, sustainer and also redeemer of all life.

Quite apart from the many scriptures in the book of Acts that speak of the early Church coming together with other believers on Sabbath to worship God, we notice also that it was Jesus custom to attend the convocations in the synagogues during His time (Luke 4:16). James also intimated that the Gentile believers would join in the synagogue worship on the Sabbath - Acts 15:21. Another scripture that clearly helps us to see that God commanded the Sabbath to be a day of holy assembly for worship is:

> *"And the Lord spoke to Moses, saying, ² "Speak to the children of Israel, and say to them: 'The feasts of the Lord, which you shall proclaim to be holy convocations, these are My feasts. ³ 'Six days shall work be done, but the seventh day is a Sabbath of solemn rest, a holy convocation. You*

GOD'S HOLY LAW - *Matters that truly matter!*

*shall do no work on it; it is the Sabbath of the Lord in all your dwellings". — **Lev 23:1-3***

In this scripture above, you see God clearly commanded that there should be a holy convocation on the Sabbath.

Isaiah also prophesied that in the future, every one who makes it into Heaven will come together to worship God on the Sabbath.

> *"And it shall come to pass*
> *That from one New Moon to another,*
> *And from one Sabbath to another,*
> *All flesh shall come* to worship before Me," says the Lord" — ***Isa 66:23 NKJV***

So it is very clear from scripture that the rest that God calls us to have on the Sabbath is not to sleep but rather to cease everything and worship Him as creator and redeemer.

Unlike the other feasts where the Israelites would all go to the place of the temple, the weekly Sabbath meetings were held in people's homes or in synagogues and in close communities or proximity so there would not be the need to travel long distances and get weary. This explains why there was the Sabbath day's walk.

I believe it is becoming clearer that the day God has sanctioned for His children to come together to worship Him is not the day that man has appointed but the day that He alone has chosen, set apart and made Holy. No human can in any way create a day, let alone make it Holy - so we can't choose any other day and say that is the day we want to come together to worship the God of the universe. God made it clear to the people of Israel that they should not worship him in the manner that the nations surrounding them worship their gods - for more on this, please take a very careful read on what God commanded in Deut 12.

> *"You shall not worship the Lord your God in that way; for every abomination to the Lord which He hates they have done to their gods; for they burn even their sons and daughters in the fire to their gods. 32 "Whatever I command you, be careful to observe it; you shall not add to it nor take away from it" — Deut 12:31-32* [emphasis mine]

It is God [in His wisdom] who has chosen the Sabbath as a day for His worship and do you as man dare change it or come to Him on your terms? If we fear God as should be and claim to obey His commandments, then we will lay everything aside and keep His Sabbath Holy!

25

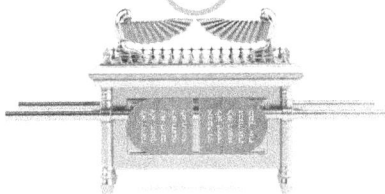

THE UNPARDONABLE SIN

> *For it is impossible for those who were once enlightened, and have tasted the heavenly gift, and have become partakers of the Holy Spirit, ⁵ and have tasted the good word of God and the powers of the age to come, ⁶ if they fall away, to renew them again to repentance, since they crucify again for themselves the Son of God, and put Him to an open shame* — **Heb 6:4-6**

For the son of man came to seek and to save that which was lost.... Even so, it is not the will of your Father in Heaven that one of these little ones should perish. These are recorded in **Matt 18:11,14**. When you think of these statements; we are certain that God and Jesus Christ are interested in the redemption of all mankind. It goes in line with the most recognized scripture in the entire bible - **John 3:16**. So if that is the case; why did Jesus say that there is a sin that will not be forgiven both in this life and in the life to come; and what exactly is this sin?

Let's look at it together in this chapter from God's word contextually and comparatively as we have done other scriptures.

> *"Then the Pharisees went out and plotted against Him, how they might destroy Him. ¹⁵ But when Jesus knew it, He withdrew from there. And great multitudes followed Him, and He healed them all"* — **Matt 12:14-15**

Up to this point, Jesus has been having some dialogues with the Pharisees and "putting them in their place". Jesus calls the people to come to Him for true rest (the truth about the Sabbath) after refuting the Pharisee's hypocrisy in the man-made rules and traditions they had added to make the Sabbath command unbearable for the people. Rather than repent of their sins, the Pharisees now sought to kill Jesus (read from **Matt 11 & Matt 12** for the context).

In following Jesus to witness all that He was doing, there was no doubt that Jesus was truly the anointed one sent by God with Power to do all the miracles (healings) that He was doing. Yet because of their wickedness and intent to call Him a bad name so that they could kill Him; they wouldn't admit that Jesus is truly from God.

So with this background, let's now look at the scripture that discusses the unpardonable sin.

> *"Therefore I say to you, every sin and blasphemy will be forgiven men, but the blasphemy against the Spirit will not be forgiven men. ³² Anyone who speaks a word against the Son of Man, it will be forgiven him; but whoever speaks against the Holy Spirit, it will not be forgiven him,*

either in this age or in the age to come" — ***Matt 12:31-32***

First, Jesus establishes that every sin and blasphemy will be forgiven - this means that all types of sin (transgressing God's command); be it fornication and or adultery and all the sins relating to sex and perversion, stealing, idolatry, coveting, murder, bearing false witness, breaking the Sabbath, dis-honoring parents, making vows in God's name etc etc - everything that is contrary to God's command - all types and manner of sins can be forgiven. So we know that the blasphemy against the Holy Spirit is not limited to any particular sin because all sins are forgive-able.

One time, Peter came to Jesus with a question. The story doesn't say who had angered or hurt him but from his question, it is obvious that someone had persisted in doing him wrong. Jesus tells Peter to forgive 70 x 7 times; in other words, keep on forgiving always. Jesus uses this opportunity to tell of God's goodness and how much He forgives His subjects and because of which; He expects that all His subjects will equally forgive each other. When you understand God's character from what Jesus shared - you know that God is always willing to forgive whatever sin we commit when we ask.

> *"Then Peter came to Him and said, "Lord, how often shall my brother sin against me, and I forgive him? Up to seven times?"* [22] *Jesus said to him, "I do not say to you, up to seven times, but up to seventy times seven.* [23] *Therefore the kingdom of heaven is like a certain king who wanted to settle accounts with his servants.* [24] *And when he had begun to settle accounts, one was brought to him who owed him ten thousand talents.* [25] *But as he was not able*

to pay, his master commanded that he be sold, with his wife and children and all that he had, and that payment be made. ²⁶ The servant therefore fell down before him, saying, 'Master, have patience with me, and I will pay you all.' ²⁷ Then the master of that servant was moved with compassion, released him, and forgave him the debt. ²⁸ "But that servant went out and found one of his fellow servants who owed him a hundred denarii; and he laid hands on him and took him by the throat, saying, 'Pay me what you owe!' ²⁹ So his fellow servant fell down at his feet and begged him, saying, 'Have patience with me, and I will pay you all.' ³⁰ And he would not, but went and threw him into prison till he should pay the debt. ³¹ So when his fellow servants saw what had been done, they were very grieved, and came and told their master all that had been done. ³² Then his master, after he had called him, said to him, 'You wicked servant! I forgave you all that debt because you begged me. ³³ Should you not also have had compassion on your fellow servant, just as I had pity on you?' ³⁴ And his master was angry, and delivered him to the torturers until he should pay all that was due to him. ³⁵ "So My heavenly Father also will do to you if each of you, from his heart, does not forgive his brother [c]his trespasses." — Matt 18:21-35

From this parable; you notice two servants, each of them were in debt - let's call them Jada and Mareya. Jada owed her master and couldn't pay so even though it was the Master's intention to have her sold with her family to retrieve his money, he relented, had compassion and forgave all that she owed when Jada came to fall at his feet and ask for his masters' patience.

Interestingly, Jada was also owed by Mareya who also came, fell at Jada's feet and begged for patience to pay (just as Jada had done earlier with her master). But Jada refused to forgive and had Mareya thrown into prison.

Although Mareya acted in the very same way that Jada did towards her own master ([1] came over to acknowledge her debt; [2] knelt down to demonstrate sorrow and repentance; [3] begged/asked for time to pay); which caused the Master to have compassion on her and forgive her debt; Jada didn't act the same way of her Master (have compassion) but rather threw her fellow servant into prison. Jada's wicked attitude caught the attention of the other servants who reported her back to her master who then asked for payment for everything she had previously been forgiven of.

This parable teaches us many lessons but I would like to highlight a few to focus on:

1) If we acknowledge our sins, the Father will always have compassion on us
2) Being forgiven by God depends on how we forgive others

It is important that we learn from the text that the servant was forgiven because he demonstrated remorse and came to ask for pardon. The scripture also alerts us that the servant owed a lot (his sins were many); but that notwithstanding, God was ready to forgive all. Do you imagine what the Master would have done if the Servant came and argued with the Master on how much he owed? That would obviously have infuriated the Master and make him not relent but throw him into prison.

*"**If** we say that we have no sin, we deceive ourselves, and the truth is not in us.* [9] *__If__ we confess our sins, He is faithful and just to forgive us our sins and to cleanse us from all unrighteousness.* [10] *__If__ we say that we have not sinned, we make Him a liar, and His word is not in us"*
— *__1 John 1:8-10__* [emphasis added]

What 1 would like to emphasize in the above scripture is the word "if". "If" is a conjunction used to introduce a conditional statement. In the above three verses, the emphasis is on the condition that; a party's response will be determined by what the other party does. In this case, God's response to our sins will be dependent on whether we acknowledge our sins, and confess our sins. This scripture expands on how God forgives us. The reverse is equally true that; "If we do not acknowledge and confess our sins, God will not forgive us".

"If I had cherished sin in my heart, the Lord would not have listened" — *__Ps 66:18__*

"He who covers his sins will not prosper,
But whoever confesses and forsakes them will have mercy"
— *__Prov 28:13__*

Here, the Psalmist and the wise-man Solomon help us to see another condition for God answering us or forgiving our sins is when we forsake/renounce our sins - again notice the conditional clause. God's forgiveness of our sin is dependent on if we will renounce it - that means it is not enough to just acknowledge our sin and even to confess it, we also have to repent of it. Repentance means a complete change of mind and attitude. When we renounce our sins, it means we are no longer engaged in the things we used to do.

> *"But when he saw many of the Pharisees and Sadducees coming to where he was baptizing, he said to them: "You brood of vipers! Who warned you to flee from the coming wrath?* [8] *Produce fruit in keeping with repentance"*
> *— Matt 3:7-8 NIV*

> *"First to those in Damascus, then to those in Jerusalem and in all Judea, and then to the Gentiles, I preached that they should repent and turn to God and demonstrate their repentance by their deeds" — Acts 26:20 NIV*

> *"Now there were some present at that time who told Jesus about the Galileans whose blood Pilate had mixed with their sacrifices.* [2] *Jesus answered, "Do you think that these Galileans were worse sinners than all the other Galileans because they suffered this way?* [3] *I tell you, no! But unless you repent, you too will all perish" — Luke 13:1-3 NIV*

In all three scriptures above; the emphasis on proving repentance is based on the fruit, in other words; our life after we claim to have repented. Repentance is not just stopping sin but renouncing it such that it is no longer something you dabble in.

So far, we have seen that God will forgive us of every type and or kind of sin but His forgiveness is conditional and dependent on us:

1. Acknowledging our sins
2. Confessing our sins
3. Renouncing our sins / Repent of our sins and show our repentance by our deeds

Now; to understand what constitutes blasphemy against the Holy Spirit - we must look at the work of the Holy Spirit, who He is, what He does and that will lead us to determine how we can speak or act against Him [blasphemy].

> *"But the Helper, the Holy Spirit, whom the Father will send in My name, He will teach you all things, and bring to your remembrance all things that I said to you"*
> — *John 14:26*

> *"But when he, the Spirit of truth, comes, he will guide you into all the truth. He will not speak on his own; he will speak only what he hears, and he will tell you what is yet to come"* — *John 16:13*

In introducing the third member of the God-head; Jesus told His disciples what He was going to be doing. He said that the Holy Spirit will be our teacher and also remind us of what we know. Also; everything that He (the Holy Spirit) makes known to us (anyone) will be what He receives from the Father and from Jesus; and His major intent was to point us to the truth. The Holy Spirit doesn't speak or judge by Himself; He comes to tell us what God/Jesus wants us to know and of course, what He says is the Truth.

Please notice in both scriptures the emphasis on **ALL** - He will teach us ALL things, He will guide us into ALL Truth. So the Holy Spirit doesn't reveal some truth and or teach us some of the things but all. The Holy Spirit won't teach some truth and some untruths; He won't mix truths and lies for us - therefore we can trust that if whatever we are being led into is not the truth or has some untruth in it; then it is not the Holy Spirit. The Holy Spirit may choose to reveal truth incrementally as and when He notices our readiness - all truth may not come to us at once but where you find that there is some truth and some lies mixed together - you can be sure that's not where the Holy Spirit operates. I am stressing this point because too often; you see and hear people doing all sorts of things in the name of being "slain" by the power of the Holy Spirit. The Bible admonishes us to test all spirits and one sure way to do that is by looking into God's word to see what it says because; Jesus said the Holy Spirit will only take from God/Him and make it known to us - therefore; the Holy Spirit will not contradict God's Word [Jesus].

> *"Beloved, do not believe every spirit, but test the spirits, whether they are of God; because many false prophets have gone out into the world" — **1 John 4:1***

Another thing Jesus says about the role of the Holy Spirit is to convict us of sin, righteousness and judgment. Which means that our ability to discern right from wrong is through the power of the Holy Spirit.

> *"When he comes, he will prove the world to be in the wrong about sin and righteousness and judgment: [9] about sin, because people do not believe in me; [10] about righteousness, because I am going to the Father, where you can see me no longer; [11] and about judgment, because the prince of this world now stands condemned" — **John 16:8-11***

So again, putting it all together; the Holy Spirit is our aid in this world pointing us on the path of Truth to make it to God and to convict our hearts of wrongdoing. When we have such understanding of the role of the Holy Spirit, our response towards Him must be nothing short of obedience.

We therefore need to check:

1. Is there some knowledge and truth He is leading me into that I am resisting?
2. Is He convicting me of sin, righteousness and judgment that I am ignoring?

The way we sin against the Holy Spirit is remaining on a continual course of sin even when He has shown you the Truth and cherishing whatever sin He warns you against but still refusing to repent. When we do that, we resist the Holy Spirit. Sometimes, we know the truth but we procrastinate our repentance; other times, we become presumptuous of God's mercy.

I recall having a conversation with a friend and telling her about a decision she wanted to take which she knew God was not happy with - but she persuaded herself by saying; "God is merciful, He will understand". Friend, that is being very presumptuous - that is one way we resist the Holy Spirit - see the scripture below.

> *"Then the word of the Lord came to Zechariah, saying,* [9] *"Thus says the Lord of hosts: 'Execute true justice, Show mercy and compassion everyone to his brother.* [10] *Do not oppress the widow or the fatherless, The alien or the poor. Let none of you plan evil in his heart against his brother.'* [11] *"But they refused to heed, shrugged their shoulders, and stopped their ears so that they could not hear.* [12] *Yes, they made their hearts like flint, refusing to hear the law and the words which the Lord of hosts had sent by His Spirit through the former prophets. Thus great wrath came from the Lord of hosts.* [13] *Therefore it happened, that just as He proclaimed and they would not hear, so they called out and*

*I would not listen," says the Lord of hosts" — **Zech 7:8-13***

When we turn a deaf ear to God's word and still think in our hearts that He will show mercy - we forget what price Jesus had to pay for our sins. The anguish and torment; His best friends sleeping on Him when He needed them to pray with Him; the blood that oozed from his veins as a result of the emotional pain he suffered; the betrayal kiss from Judas; His eyes falling on Peter when the cock crowed three times as he denied ever knowing Him; the physical pain He endured from being beaten and tortured; the piercing of the thorns from the crown they put on His head; the weight of the cross He carried up-hill to Golgotha, the nails they drove through His hands and feet, the shame as they spat on Him, ridiculed Him and took of His robes where He hang naked on the cross; His separation from His Father in that moment.

Just think through all the things Jesus had to go through to secure our atonement - and do we trample on Him and make His blood a common thing - and deliberately sin?

> *"One who turns away his ear from hearing the law,*
> *Even his prayer is an abomination" — **Prov 28:9***

God takes it very seriously when we know what He expects us to do but we just decide not to do so in the hope of Him being merciful to us. Of this, Samuel tells Saul that God wants us to obey rather than sin and then offer a sacrifice.

> *"Has the Lord as great delight in burnt offerings and sacrifices, As in obeying the voice of the Lord? Behold, to obey is better than sacrifice, And to heed than the fat of rams" — **1 Sam 15:22***

It is as a result of such willful sins that God's Spirit departed from Saul - **1 Sam 16:14**. If we keep resisting the Holy Spirit; He will depart from us too.

> *"Therefore, to him who knows to do good and does not do it, to him it is sin"* — ***James 4:17***

When you look at scripture, the Holy Spirit being part of the God-head is also long suffering just as is said of God and Jesus. So He gives us many chances until we finally abuse Him - that's when He leaves us to ourselves. The Bible discusses four progressive stages of how we treat the Holy Spirit in our disobedience which leads us to losing Him but also blaspheming and sinning against Him.

Sometimes; we know God's word and still go against it - usually it starts by us putting off the Holy Spirit one time, the bible describes this as "**quenching the Spirit**". This progresses and it becomes more and more easier to put Him off more often and set aside the knowledge and truth He reveals to us so we can do our own things - the bible refers to this second stage as "**grieving the Spirit**". As sin masters us, the next stage is when we flat out disregard Him - the bible calls this third stage "**resisting the Spirit**". The final stage is when we abuse Him and become very presumptuous, even thinking to indulge Him in the sin we are participating in - the bible refers to this fourth stage as "**insulting the Spirit**".

The four stages are:

Do not quench the Holy Spirit - **1 Thess 5:19**
Do not grieve the Holy Spirit - **Eph 4:30**
Do not resist the Holy Spirit - **Acts 7:51**

Do not despise / Insult the Holy Spirit — **Heb 10:29**

Whenever we come to hear some truth and or have some knowledge in God's word; we respond to it in one of four ways. Jesus discusses a parallel in the parable of the four soils recorded in **Matt 13:1-23**.

1. We obey immediately
2. We become indifferent to the truth
3. We procrastinate our actions or lastly
4. We become complacent and do nothing.

But whereas we have seen that our response should always be to obey; sometimes we just behave indifferently. Winston Churchill said it best when he said; ***"Men occasionally stumble over the truth, but most of them pick themselves up and hurry off as if nothing happened"***. Unfortunately, some people will be shown the truths in this book and disregard it. Pontius Pilate was one such person who behaved this way - His encounter with Jesus was so remarkable; and it could have led him to change but he chose to wash his hands off.

Others will procrastinate the actions they know they should take as a result of the truths the Holy Spirit has guided them and opened their hearts to see - they tell themselves they are waiting for a more convenient time to make the move. One would say - "I am just waiting until after COVID"; yet another will say - "I will change when my spouse changes or when my Pastor changes or when my Church accepts this 'new' teaching". One such person who kept his decision to later was King Felix who heard Paul's case.

"Now as he reasoned about righteousness, self-control, and the judgment to come, Felix was afraid and answered, "Go away for now; when I have a convenient time I will call for you." — Acts 24:25

You see clearly what Paul was discussing with Felix - how the Holy Spirit convicts us of Righteousness, Sin and Judgment. But rather than act immediately - King Felix like many put off the decision to another day which never came for him.

Still others just stay in their state of spiritual complacency - although they know the truths of God, they neither acknowledge the truth nor repent from their evil ways. The Pharisees who Jesus was speaking to were in this category. Everything pointed to the fact that Jesus was the Christ and yet they decided in their hearts to discredit Him. Their minds were made up that they were not going to accept Jesus' message no matter what and they were planning to kill Him. These Pharisees were so wicked that they would much rather give praise to the devil for the miracles Jesus was doing among the people than to accept the truth.

Jesus knowing their hearts then told them that God could never forgive their sin because they were:

1. Insulting the Holy Spirit by constantly resisting the truth He was showing them
2. They would not repent in the light of significant truth

So in conclusion, blasphemy against the Holy Spirit does not refer to any one particular distinct sin like idolatry or murder or fornication, breaking the Sabbath, lying or stealing or any of such. Rather, it is living in sin or deliberately breaking a command of

God even when we know the truth but choose to be indifferent, procrastinate our action and or just continue to be comfortable in our sinful state without regard to God and or presumptuous of His mercy.

To my shame; I have resisted the Holy Spirit many times in the past and quite often too; and I am only begging for God's mercy as I have resolved in my heart to follow His leading into all the Truth He guides me into from now on. It is when we produce fruit in accordance with our repentance [after we have come into knowledge of the truth]; that we will not be guilty of the unpardonable sin.

How about you? How will you respond to the Truths that you have stumbled on in this book? Will you acknowledge, confess and repent and ask for God's forgiveness; or will you plod on staying comfortable as was the case of the Pharisees?

26

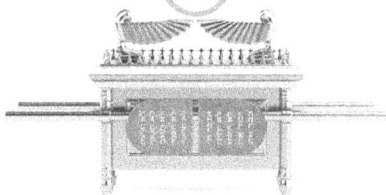

COME OUT OF HER
MY PEOPLE

Don't let anyone fool you. "Bad companions make a good person bad
— 1 Cor 15:33

In his 2nd letter to the Corinthians, Paul admonishes the followers of Jesus to come out of among unbelievers; he asks them not to be unequally yoked with such people - **2 Cor 6:14-18**. Though most often, this scripture is quoted to warn people of getting married to those outside the Church, we are certain it was not marriages that Paul was referring to. He never once asked believers who were already married to unbelievers to divorce - he had already addressed that in his first letter - **1 Cor 7:10-16**. And while l am not faulting the application, l believe it will serve us better when we first seek to understand the context before we apply it.

In his first letter to the Corinthians [**1 Cor 8; 1 Cor 10**], Paul addresses the issues of idolatry so we know that this was a problem as some who used to be idol worshipers have now become Christians. Unfortunately, these ex idol worshipers who are now Christians [supposedly] are still keeping fellowship with their "old friends" and perhaps are even engaging some of the things they used in idol worship for Christian worship also. Paul warns that by indulging in food that is sacrificed to idols or using to worship God items that have previously been devoted to idol worship - we provoke God's jealousy and we are not stronger than Him.

So Paul asks them - "What do believers have in common with unbelievers for which they would be yoked in fellowship?". He further goes on to describe the two groups as "*righteous and lawless*"; "*light and darkness*"; "*Christ and Belial [wicked or worthless]*", the "*Temple of God and idols*" respectively. That helps us to understand that those who Paul refers to as idol worshipers, those in darkness, followers of Belial include those who are also not obeying the Law [lawless] - everyone serves a master so if you are not serving God, then you must be serving an idol [some kind of a man-made religion]. So the question, Can the infidel and the believer worship the creator of the universe in the same acceptable way? By application, let's ask - Can the non law abiding (lawless/unbeliever) and the law abiding (the Christian) work toward the same end when they are traveling in different directions? That's what Paul was asking and 1 believe the same question applies to us today.

Now, before you probably start thinking that the text is referring to people in the world, people who have not made any commitment to follow Jesus, permit me to share another scripture which will clear this up; so you have no doubts that Paul is referring to supposed followers of Jesus but are lawless, unbelievers, idolaters etc. Earlier in his first letter, Paul explained this:

> *"I wrote to you in my epistle not to keep company with sexually immoral people.* [10] *Yet I certainly did not mean with the sexually immoral people of this world, or with the covetous, or extortioners, or idolaters, since then you would need to go out of the world.* [11] *But now I have written to you **not to keep company with anyone named a brother, who is sexually immoral, or covetous, or an idolater, or a reviler, or a drunkard, or an extortioner—not even to eat with such a person.*** [12] *For what have I to do with judging those also who are outside? Do you not judge those who are inside?* [13] *But those who are outside God judges. Therefore "put away from yourselves the evil person."* — 1 Cor 5:9-13*

So it is quite clear that Paul is referring to "Disciples" who are lawless. Surprisingly, there were people like that in his days, so don't get stunned hearing the same in our day. So what is Paul advising or rather what message did God want Paul to give them? His final exhortation to them is: *"Therefore; "**Come out from among them And be separate**, says the Lord. Do not touch what is unclean, And I will receive you."* 18 *"**I will be a Father to you, And you shall be My sons and daughters**, Says the Lord Almighty."* - 2 Cor 6:17-18

Interesting that we see repeated here, the very words God uses whenever He made a covenant with people [*"I will be your God*

and you will be my people"]. This is **God's covenant promise** we
see throughout scripture - see for example where else this phrase
is used:

- **Exodus 6:7** - Before God delivered the Israelites from
Pharaoh and makes His covenant with them
- **Jeremiah 31:33; Jer 32:38** - When God fore-told Jeremiah
of the new covenant He was about to establish with His
people
- **Hebrews 8:10** - Referring to the 2nd covenant
- **Rev 21:3** - After God has destroyed the present earth and
the new Jerusalem is brought down from Heaven.

God has promised to dwell among His people and that's the
most important reason there should be a separation between **the
people of God** and **people who claim to be of God but are not
following the way**! He implores that His people be Holy. *"I will
bring you out from the peoples and gather you out of the countries
where you are scattered, with a mighty hand, with an outstretched
arm, and with fury poured out"* - ***Eze 20:34***. Further; *"I will accept
you as a sweet aroma when I bring you out from the peoples and
gather you out of the countries where you have been scattered; and I
will be hallowed in you before the Gentiles."* — **Eze 20:41**.

Being Holy means being separated for the service of God, not
in fellowship with those who choose to be lawless or follow the
doctrines and commandments of man; man-made religion and
especially those who do not acknowledge that God is the creator
of the universe and or who will not submit to His will. It's not
just Paul who encounters such people but Peter also warns of such
people in **2 Pet 2**. Paul again talks about those **having a form
of godliness but denying its power** - **2 Tim 3:1-9**. These were

all people in the Church, not outside - they were referred to as brothers and sisters and some played significant and leading roles in the Church too; yet were unbelieving, immoral, idolaters etc. That was their way of life.

Such was the case with the religious leaders in the days of Jesus - Who did Jesus teach His disciples to be wary of? The Pharisees and Sadducees. Doesn't it amaze you that those Jesus referred to as lawless/unbelieving are the very ones who were 'acclaimed' to be knowledgeable about God's word and His ways? Therefore, do not be surprised if the lawless and unbelieving of today are not necessarily the people of the "world" although that will certainly include them. It very well also includes people and groups you may never suspect - recall that Jesus said the majority of people are lost. How sure are you of where you stand?

I think what makes it harder to see who belongs to this category is that; we are not always quick to remember or realise that God doesn't look at things the way we look at them. While we may think that there are numerous religions including Islam, Hinduism, Buddhism, Jewish, Atheists etc; to God, there are only two groups in the world - His people and the others - there's nothing in between - like in the old where there was only Jew or Gentile, today we are either the Israel of God or Lost; One is either Sheep or Goat. So there is either true worship or false worship. If you are not found to be with God's true people, it's no use splitting hairs as to which of the other ones you belong to.

The good news is, in the book of Isaiah, God foretells what He will do before the second coming of Jesus and prior to He making the new Heaven and Earth. You can read the story in Isaiah 66, a chapter that talks about True and False worship. Particularly in vrs 18-21; He talks of how He will gather back to Himself from everywhere those who are His (the True Israel). I believe this speaks of God's true people coming out of false religion [false worship and or false Churches] just as Paul also speaks of those in Corinth.

> *"For I know their works and their thoughts. It shall be that I will gather all nations and tongues; and they shall come and see My glory.* [19] *I will set a sign among them; and those among them who escape I will send to the nations: to Tarshish and Pul and Lud, who draw the bow, and Tubal and Javan, to the coastlands afar off who have not heard My fame nor seen My glory. And they shall declare My glory among the Gentiles.* [20] *Then they shall bring all your brethren for an offering to the Lord out of all nations, on horses and in chariots and in litters, on mules and on camels, to My holy mountain Jerusalem," says the Lord, "as the children of Israel bring an offering in a clean vessel into the house of the Lord.* [21] *And I will also take some of them for priests and Levites," says the Lord"* — **Isa 66:18-21**

The references shown above are not the only places God speaks to us to come out of the "idolatrous Church or false worshippers". Perhaps the strongest warning is sounded when we most need it and closest to the time of Jesus 2nd coming [*which is now more than ever, imminent*]. In the book of Revelation before the final hour, we hear: *"And I heard another voice from heaven saying, Come out of her, my people, **lest you share in her sins, and lest you receive of her plagues." - Revelation 18:4**. Here, God sends a strong warning because as He says, those who don't "come out" will share in the plagues that are reserved for the lawless, the unbelieving and disobedient.

It may seem as though I am picking on the Sabbath and trying to make most people guilty who don't obey that command; but realise I am only pointing out what the bible says - this is not an original message from me. Although I am hoping to reach as many people as God will allow who haven't as yet paid much attention to God's moral laws - I see that a majority of the people who sincerely love God happen to fall in the category who do well to keep the other 9 laws but desecrate the Sabbath. Let us not be unaware of the devil's schemes for he knows quite well that when he gets us to fail in one aspect of the Law, we are guilty of all *"10 For whoever shall keep the whole law, and yet stumble in one point, he is guilty of all….."* — **James 2:10-12**

Some say it is legalistic to preach Sabbath observance and that it shouldn't matter which day on which you rest - any day one chooses is okay and should be acceptable to God is what we say. But notice, just as God didn't let Adam choose which of the fruits he will not eat but God did, God also specifically chose the day He wanted man to rest on - plus because that was the day on which He rested; our choice can not nullify the fact that God rested on the 7th day and He wants us to observe it in memory of His rest after creation. Is it okay for God to want something and ask His creatures to reserve or observe it for Him? Our generous God says; "I have given you six days on which you can do all your work but reserve the 7th day for me". But we tell Him; "No you must take this one that we want to give you, you can't have that which you want" - thus we compete with God - can you imagine that?

"Woe to those who quarrel with their Maker, those who are nothing but potsherds among the potsherds on the ground. Does the clay say to the potter, 'What are you making?' Does your work say, 'The potter has no hands'? [10] *Woe to the one who says to a father, 'What have you begotten?' or to a mother, 'What have you brought to birth?'* [11] *"This is what the Lord says - the Holy One of Israel, and its Maker: Concerning things to come, do you question me about my children, or give me orders about the work of my hands?*
— **Isaiah 45:9-11**

It came a time when Cain and Abel brought offerings to God; Abel brought what God required [a lamb] but Cain decided to bring to God what he chose [the fruits of his own labor]. Cain's offering and worship represents the self righteousness of our own works while Abel's offering and worship represents righteousness by grace which God requires. We know the story as told in **Gen 4:3-6** and how Cain and his offering was rejected. God said to Cain - *"Why are you angry? Why is your face downcast…. If you do what is right, will you not be accepted?"* The Psalmist says:

[10] *Some sat in darkness, in utter darkness, prisoners suffering in iron chains,* [11] *because they rebelled against God's commands and despised the plans of the Most High…..* [17] *Some became fools through their rebellious ways and suffered affliction because of their iniquities.*
— *Psalm 107*

Rebellion is choosing to live your life free from what God commands. Iniquity means the same - being lawless, living contrary to the Law. The Psalmist says those who live in rebellion will suffer affliction - but they are responsible for what they suffer because it's a choice they make. God doesn't force a choice on us. God is love and love can not be forced or demanded. We have complete freedom as to what we choose - Cain chose to rebel and so got rejected; he could also have chosen to obey to get God's acceptance - we live in a world of cause and effect. So just like God did with Cain, we too can be sure that God will reject us, our offering and our worship when we choose to rebel against Him by offering Him what we want rather than what He requires. Only remember; Sin [rebellion] is crouching at your door and desires to master you.

Let's look at it from another story; could God not have asked for Ishmael? Why did He ask Abraham to sacrifice Isaac, the promised heir? Difficult as it was and much as it didn't make sense to him, Abraham who God had earlier called to come out of from among his people, did not withhold his precious son, but rather because He feared God and trusted Him, he was willing to obey and offer God exactly what He asked for [without question] - **Gen 22:12**. Righteousness was credited to Abraham because he was willing to give God what He requested. He too, like David knew God's secret; *"17 Then the Lord said, "Shall I hide from Abraham what I am about to do?"* - **Gen 18:17**. Faith, backed by obedience to His command [out of our love for God] is our key to having the right relationship with God our creator.

One of the events the world will soon experience is the coming together of all religions starting with the unification of the Catholic Church and apostate Protestantism. While many may think of this as a victory, it is the tell-tale signs of the beginning of a worldwide persecution of God's true people before the end of the world. Jesus foretold us of this event:

> *"Therefore when you see the 'abomination of desolation,' spoken of by Daniel the prophet, standing in the holy place" (whoever reads, let him understand),* [16] *"then let those who are in Judea flee to the mountains.* [17] *Let him who is on the housetop not go down to take anything out of his house.* [18] *And let him who is in the field not go back to get his clothes.* [19] *But woe to those who are pregnant and to those who are nursing babies in those days!* [20] *And pray that your flight may not be in winter or on the Sabbath.* [21] *For then there will be great tribulation, such as has not been since the beginning of the world until this time, no, nor ever shall be.* [22] *And unless those days were shortened, no flesh would be saved; but for the elect's sake those days will be shortened.* [23] *"Then if anyone says to you, 'Look, here is the Christ!' or 'There!' do not believe it.* [24] *For false christs and false prophets will rise and show great signs and wonders to deceive, if possible, even the elect.* [25] *See, I have told you beforehand" — **Matt 24:15-31***

While there will be [temporary] security and relief for those who will be part of this world-wide [false] Church system, God's true people will be going through intense persecution and killings. But God's judgment will finally fall on Babylon, the harlot, the false Church which Satan is putting together in these last days.

Friend, if you are serious about your salvation - this is the time to separate yourself and be Holy to the Lord, allowing His Holy Spirit to guide you to worship Him not only in Spirit but also in Truth and according to God's word. Not false worship, not worship with roots steeped in idolatry and in conflict with the word of God; and not worship that is fossilized - putting new wine into old wineskins; mixing the teachings of Christ with tradition. But worship that follows the unchanging law of God.

Is God calling you to come out of a false Church or union - will you heed His call today?

GOD'S HOLY LAW - Matters that truly matter!

27

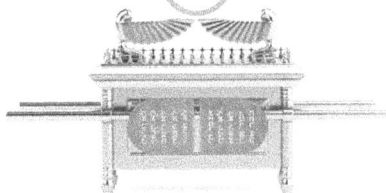

SELF APPLICATION

If your hand or your foot makes you sin, cut it off and throw it away. It is better for you to lose part of your body and have eternal life than to have two hands and two feet and be thrown into the fire that burns forever.
— **Matt 18:8**

So how do we "Come out of Babylon" according to the command? For some, it may be as simple as taking time to evaluate the practices, rituals and traditions imported into the Church and throw off those that are offensive to God. Just as Paul told the Corinthian believers, they too must give up on their idolatrous and immoral practices; to not provoke God's jealousy and anger by offering Him that which has been offered to idols. For others, it may be to come out completely of false Churches and false worship. God doesn't want us to mix true worship with false worship - it arouses his anger.

At a party he threw for his royals, Belshazzar king of Babylon requested that the gold and silver vessels which had been taken from God's temple in Jerusalem be brought to the party so he and his guests would drink from. A pagan king having a wild party with his wives and girlfriends were going to use the same vessels which were used to serve a Holy God. How far people would want to go to kindle God's wrath, by mixing that which is holy with that which is unholy. Immediately after drinking from the vessels, a finger wrote on the wall passing judgement on Belshazzar and that same evening, the entire kingdom of Babylon was overthrown by the Medes & Persians. God's judgment was swift when the unholy was mixed with the holy - you can read the story in **Daniel 5**.

In the same way, we can trust that God's judgment will come on the [false] Church who "flirts" and commits "fornication" with the world; the Church which is lukewarm [partly hot, partly cold]; the Church which has mixed "idol worship" with God's true worship - having a little bit of God and a little bit of the world's ways; the counterfeit Church which poses as the bride of the lamb and deceives the world, even the elect. God's true people must make a clear separation from everyone including Churches that don't take a stance for God alone - the two can not mix. Do you think it is a coincidence that God called the idolatrous Church in the end time "Babylon" - **Rev 18**? Just as physical Babylon of the Old Testament fell swiftly, the counterfeit or apostate Church [Spiritual Babylon] which is mixing true worship and idol worship is going to fall, and swiftly too! That is why God commands everyone who is His' to "come out of her".

So we need to examine ourselves as well as the Church we belong to, to know if it is true or the fallen Church or a counterfeit. There are many false prophets, disciples and Churches that act, feel and on the surface seem genuine but are not. And many will follow the anti-Christ thinking He is Christ. It behoves on you [personally] to make every effort to check the lives for evidence of obedience to God and His commands as is done by those who love Him. What God wants is obedience, not sacrifice; as we learn from several accounts in both the Old Testament (**Cain, Saul**) and New Testament (**Martha, Ananias & Sapphira**).

Remember the admonition:

> *"If we deliberately keep on sinning after we have received the knowledge of the truth, no sacrifice for sins is left, ²⁷ but only a fearful expectation of judgment and of raging fire that will consume the enemies of God. ²⁸ Anyone who rejected the law of Moses died without mercy on the testimony of two or three witnesses. ²⁹ How much more severely do you think someone deserves to be punished who has trampled the Son of God underfoot, who has treated as an unholy thing the blood of the covenant that sanctified them, and who has insulted the Spirit of grace? ³⁰ For we know him who said, "It is mine to avenge; I will repay," and again, "The Lord will judge his people." ³¹ It is a dreadful thing to fall into the hands of the living God." — Heb 10:26-31*

God loves us, and doesn't want any of His children to perish. But a righteous God is both merciful and just. His character requires that He does what He says - that's why He calls all of us to repent. We must not keep off longer anymore because we can never be sure what tomorrow holds. Many plans have had to be shelved because of nCOVID-19; it didn't announce it's coming and took all by surprise. If a tiny virus which can't even be seen with our naked eye can disrupt our world this way, then how much more a God who holds the entire world in the palm of His hands?

> *"There were present at that season some who told Him about the Galileans whose blood Pilate had mingled with their sacrifices. ² And Jesus answered and said to them, "Do you suppose that these Galileans were worse sinners than all other Galileans, because they suffered such things? ³ I tell you, no; but* **unless you repent you will all likewise perish**. *⁴ Or those eighteen on whom the tower in Siloam fell and killed them, do you think that they were worse sinners than all other men who dwelt in Jerusalem? ⁵ I tell you, no; but* **unless you repent you will all likewise perish**.*" — Luke 13:1-5.*

Let us heed this message that Jesus says to us and turn away from our lawless ways. Jesus died a painful death so we can have a relationship with God. We make His death of no benefit to us when we continue to live in a state of sin even after we have come to know the truth. Do you have an excuse to continue deliberately breaking God's Law?

> *"I am the Lord your God; follow my decrees and be careful to keep my laws. ²⁰ Keep my Sabbaths holy, that they may be a sign between us. Then you will know that I am the Lord your God." — Eze 20:19-20*

In the story Jesus told of the prodigal son - we notice that immediately the young man came to his senses, he decided to run back to his father. He didn't hesitate and neither did he allow anything to stop him from going back to his loving father. We too must be quick to act when we come to realize that we have gone off the track that we were supposed to walk on. And we can be sure that our loving father will run towards us when he sees us a far way off.

> *"When he came to his senses, he said, 'How many of my father's hired servants have food to spare, and here I am starving to death!* [18] *I will set out and go back to my father and say to him: Father, I have sinned against heaven and against you.* [19] *I am no longer worthy to be called your son; make me like one of your hired servants.'* [20] *So he got up and went to his father. "But while he was still a long way off, his father saw him and was filled with compassion for him; he ran to his son, threw his arms around him and kissed him" —* **Luke 15:17-20**

How would you like to respond today? And what is it that might be holding you back from running into the arms of your loving Father?

GOD'S HOLY LAW - Matters that truly matter!

28

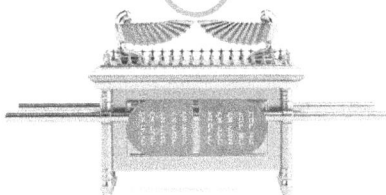

OBSTACLES TO OBEDIENCE

It is the same for each of you. You must leave everything you have to follow me. If not, you cannot be my follower.
— **Luke 14:33**

I t is possible that you may have come to realise the truth and want to make some changes in your Christian journey - but have you considered what might stand in your way and or make it difficult for you to obey God's word? There are quite a number, such as pride, self reliance and many others. Let us discuss a few of them.

FEAR

Many of us live in fear of what others think of us - hence our entire lives are lived unconsciously seeking the approval of others. In a way, our religious world makes us too conscious of others. Whether it is lifting our hands in prayer or joyfully dancing in praise and worship of God, we are quick to look around to see who's watching us. This is not just in the area of doing something right. It's the same behaviour we put up when we do something we know is wrong also. You may have noticed how people will look around to see who's watching before they throw out some trash or urinate where they are not supposed to or cross the red light. Whether right or wrong, fear of people seems to have such a high influence in our lives more than God. We are people of sight and not of faith - we are afraid of the physical more than we are of the Spirit.

I recall a remark my brother made recently about corruption - He said, "if we would ask suspects to swear by their local gods/idols rather than God, corruption would be reduced drastically or even be eradicated completely".

This sadly is the true state of the world we live in, even among Christians. We tend to think God is so far removed from the world and therefore act as though He can not see anything we do. So we show a lot more fear, respect and reverence for our local authorities and powers that be, than we show God the creator of this world, who lives in unapproachable light before whom nothing we do is ever hidden from His sight. It is so sad what sin has done to man who God gave dominion over all things He made. Sin has so reversed the roles that man is now afraid of things that he should have power/authority over. Many bow to stones, wood and images they have made to be their gods and are more afraid of these things than they would ever be afraid of God. While we may think we are not in that category of people, we need to ask ourselves whether fear of a pastor, a leader or an institution, even our Church, would ever stop us from pursuing the truth we have come to understand?

Fear is real and almost everyone has had a fear at one point or the other. Before they received the Holy Spirit, the Apostles who walked and talked with Jesus were very fearful of the ruling religious leaders (including the Pharisees, Sadducees and Scribes). Moses at the time of being sent to Pharaoh was full of fear, likewise Joshua and Gideon. Indeed records show that all the great men that God used, were once very fearful people. So fear is not the problem, it is what we do about our fears that matter.

We know from the stories of the Apostles that they overcame their fear. At one point when the religious leaders wanted to intimidate them to not speak anymore in the name of Jesus - they responded by saying:

*"Then they called them in again and commanded them not to speak or teach at all in the name of Jesus. [19] But Peter and John replied, "Which is right in God's eyes: to listen to you, or to him? You be the judges! [20] As for us, we cannot help speaking about what we have seen and heard."[21] After further threats they let them go. They could not decide how to punish them, because all the people were praising God for what had happened." — **Acts 4:18-21**.*

Up until this time, all the Apostles were seized with fear and hiding behind closed doors for fear of the Jews - **John 20:19**. It took the Holy Spirit and great courage for the Apostles to step out of their fear and comfort zone and begin to preach the gospel of Jesus. The Apostles honored God by their action - to stand up for God even when they knew they'd endure punishment and hardships from the bullies.

In **Matthew 10**, Jesus speaks to His disciples about a future time of persecution and He tells them that their faith will be tested. Whoever is able to stand through the persecutions and still confess His name and the truth will overcome and the same person, Jesus will also confess before God. He leaves them with these words that we too should ponder over:

> *"Whatever I tell you in the dark, speak in the light; and what you hear in the ear, preach on the housetops. [28] And do not fear those who kill the body but cannot kill the soul. But rather fear Him who is able to destroy both soul and body in [h]hell.* — **Matthew 10:27-28**.

The people (or man-made idols/gods) we are so afraid of are not able to do to us what God can do to us - therefore the one we need to fear is rather God and not Man (parents, pastors, local authorities, etc.).

When he was tempted with an offer that may have seemed to benefit him greatly, (after all, agreeing to go to bed with his master's wife could have enhanced his status of being a slave, it would have boosted his ego, he may have gotten what he wanted from Mrs. Potiphar as long as he kept quiet about the secret affair); the fear of God made Joseph flee from the scene. He knew very well that no matter the consequence he was likely to face (jail or death); it was preferable than being wrong with God. Joseph feared God greatly and would not let what man could do to him make him disobey God. He honored God with his choice and so fled from sin. Look up the story in **Genesis 39**.

Christianity is not for the faint-hearted; there will come times in your journey where you may become fearful of what might happen to you by standing up to the truth - will you give in to your fears or will you act boldly and fearlessly to honor God like Joseph and like the Apostles?

What fear are you feeling right now as you consider obeying God's word of truth? Is it fear of your pastor/Church leader; fear of parents; fear of loss of people's approval; fear of loss of relationships? The Bible teaches us that *"The fear of God is the beginning of wisdom"* — **Prov 9:10**. This tells us that the wisdom we need to make it past the cross-road we are in, is to fear God. A lot of people today have prayed asking God for wisdom, they desire to have wisdom in the situations they find themselves in but God promises to give His wisdom to those who fear Him. Fearing God means honoring Him and obeying His commands.

If you are afraid about the decision to make, pray to God to fill you with His Holy Spirit and wisdom, and meditate on stories of people who in spite of their fears stood up for God and did what was right and honored God. Do not allow fear of people make you sit on the fence or worse, even continue in a state of being lawless.

No matter what you are afraid of - remember that when God is for you, no one can be against you. When you put your trust in God, you will overcome your fears. That's what the one who had the testimony of being "the man after God's own heart" did whenever he felt fear.

> *³ But when I am afraid,*
> *I will put my trust in you.*
> *⁴ I praise God for what he has promised.*
> *I trust in God, so why should I be afraid?*

What can mere mortals do to me?
⁹ My enemies will retreat when I call to you for help.
This I know: God is on my side!
¹⁰ I praise God for what he has promised;
yes, I praise the Lord for what he has promised.
1¹ I trust in God, so why should I be afraid?
*What can mere mortals do to me? — **Psalm 56***

INFLUENCE

Sometimes, that which causes us to do wrong is the influence of other prominent people in our lives - people like our parents, spouses, children, pastors, and bosses; other times, it may be because of financial inducement. Suppose you are a pastor of a Church and you have come to the realization that some practices in your Church are wrong or false - what do you do? Or suppose you are the son or daughter of the leader of the Church - how easy will it be for you to walk away or point out the false practice? Oftentimes, your livelihood depends on the salary you take at the end of each month to take care of your own family. It may be much more difficult for such people than it would be for an ordinary member to take the decision to walk away. As a result, there are many that have succumbed to the influence of people they regard highly or even money and have had to keep mute over practices or doctrines that they know are false.

At one point when a large crowd followed Jesus, He turned and told them that whoever does not put Him first, can not be His disciple — **Luke 14:25-27**.

Once when Moab was going to go to war with Israel, Balak the king of Moab had tried to influence Balaam to curse the Israelites.

Balaam's response should be one that we follow when we are enticed. *"If Balak were to give me his house full of silver and gold, I could not go beyond the word of the Lord, to do good or bad of my own will. What the Lord says, that I must speak?"* — **Numbers 24:13**

The temptation for Pastors and Church leaders [especially] are very high when it comes to influence (be it from money or their superiors or sometimes their own congregations) to keep doing things the same way even when they have come to knowledge of the truth. But if Balaam being a diviner would not be enticed by all that King Moab could give him, and had deep convictions about sticking to God's word - then what excuse do you have if your salary or the influence of others keep you from speaking and teaching the truth of God's word? Do you imagine standing next to Balaam on judgment day - what will you say to Jesus?

Paul warned Timothy of a time when people will pay people to teach/preach to them what they want to hear and not necessarily the truth - as you can tell, we are already in those times. *"³ For the time will come when they will not endure sound doctrine, but according to their own desires, because they have itching ears, they will heap up for themselves teachers; ⁴ and they will turn their ears away from the truth, and be turned aside to fables".* — **2 Tim 4:1-5**. He entreats Timothy to endure hardships and to do the work God has called him to do. Yes, there will be challenges when you stand for the truth - but what's the alternative? Would you rather fall in the hands of God for doing evil?

Should you find yourself in this situation, let Paul's words be your encouragement.

2 But we have renounced the hidden things of shame, not walking in craftiness nor handling the word of God deceitfully, but by manifestation of the truth commending ourselves to every man's conscience in the sight of God.......

*[16] Therefore we do not lose heart. Even though our outward man is perishing, yet the inward man is being renewed day by day. [17] For our light affliction, which is but for a moment, is working for us a far more exceeding and eternal weight of glory, [18] while we do not look at the things which are seen, but at the things which are not seen. For the things which are seen are temporary, but the things which are not seen are eternal" — **2 Cor 4**

Paul says that when the truth about God appeared, out went the hidden things, craftiness, and deceptions. We have an obligation to follow God's truth once He reveals them to us. The good news however is that, whatever challenge we encounter as a result of standing for the truth can never compare to the glory that awaits us. Let us throw off every weight of influence so we can persevere to the very end to receive the crown of glory that God has for us.

TRADITIONS

"This is how we've always done it" - how often do you hear that? Many people are so accustomed to tradition it hurts. You can laugh when you visit a village or even places in a developing country and see people doing things in ways you did some twenty years ago. But there are some situations that don't evoke laughter in you but anger and frustration - "why would an educated person act the way they are acting"? Not all traditions are bad but there are many that don't make any sense in our 21st century and yet, generations after generation endure without question.

In our day and time of much religiosity, you would think that truth would be as widespread as we see Churches scattered all over and at every intersection in our cities, but it is very sad that people are very quick to defend their old antiquated traditions over even God's truth. Traditions are very difficult to break - even when they are not achieving the right results.

The leadership of the Church should be warning members as well as correct errors and speak of the danger that lies ahead if not corrected - in some cases however, the leadership supposed to warn are not even aware of the wrong being perpetrated. The situation may be one that they have inherited and yet, it is the leaders responsibility to make the right changes. One day, God will call into account all that the Spiritual leadership allowed in the house of God. Moses, Daniel, Nehemiah and the Prophets were not necessarily involved in the apostate state they found Israel in, but they individually took steps to address whatever wrong there was, asked God for forgiveness on behalf of the people and took active measures to bring changes. Do you find wrong traditions in your Church - what are you doing about it?

When Jesus took a little break and sat at Jacob's well - He encountered a woman who was so steeped in tradition. The entire conversation shows how we can miss the promises of God when we don't come out of our "traditional mode". Observe how the conversation goes; first she discusses the ways the Jews and Samaritans have been at logger-heads from the past, second in talking about living water that Jesus would give her, her mind is only on how water has always been drawn - from a well - so Jesus not having a cup/bowl can't give her the living water He's promising. Third, Jesus points out that she's repeating the same error jumping from man to man thinking that's how she will find fulfillment. This is a woman who after the first marriage, she jumps on to man number two, that doesn't fulfill her so she keeps going - that's the only way she knows how. Fourth, her form of worship is what was handed on from her ancestors - that's the way they did it, that's how we should do it.

The fact that things have always been done a particular way doesn't mean we should continue to do them the same way (especially when they are not even achieving the results) - we need to search for the truth; that's what Jesus seems to be telling her.

> *"But the hour is coming, and now is, when the true worshipers will worship the Father in spirit and truth; for the Father is seeking such to worship Him.* [24] *God is Spirit, and those who worship Him must worship in spirit and truth." — John 4:23-24.*

I encourage you to read this beautiful story as it plays out in **John 4:1-42.**

Perhaps Jesus is saying to us that rather than dutifully follow our old and known way of doing things, we need to question/test everything in line with the truth we have come to know - that's what liberates. Do you know the truth - are you following the truth? Or are you for the sake of tradition (*how it has always been done*) following the kind of worship you are involved in? Sadly, that is what can be said for some of us - we haven't questioned it, we haven't taken time to find the truth and we've been caught up in following tradition.

There's a classic account in scripture where Jesus teaches not to allow traditions to nullify God's commands. There are some traditions that may not harm us, but there are others that will take us away from God. We need to identify all of such and get away from them immediately!

> *"Then the scribes and Pharisees who were from Jerusalem came to Jesus, saying,* ² *"Why do Your disciples transgress the tradition of the elders? For they do not wash their hands when they eat bread."* ³ *He answered and said to them, "Why do you also transgress the commandment of God because of your tradition?* ⁴ *For God commanded, saying, 'Honor your father and your mother'; and, 'He who curses father or mother, let him be put to death.'* ⁵ *But you say, 'Whoever says to his father or mother, "Whatever profit you might have received from me is a gift to God"—* ⁶ *then he need not honor his father [a]or mother.' Thus you have made the [b]commandment of God of no effect by your tradition.* ⁷ *Hypocrites! Well did Isaiah prophesy about you, saying:* ⁸ *'These people draw near to Me with their mouth, And honor Me with their lips, But their heart is far from Me.* ⁹ *And in vain they worship Me, Teaching as doctrines the commandments of men.' " — **Matt 15:1-9***

The Pharisees and Scribes approached Jesus with the aim to condemn His disciples for not washing their hands, Jesus uses the opportunity to show them how their doctrines were full of **commandments of men**. Jesus reserved the harshest of His words for those who claimed to know better and yet surprisingly, they were the ones who had knowingly **set aside God's commands for the sake of tradition**.

Jesus bluntly told them that they were **hypocrites** and their worship was in vain - it achieved or amounted to nothing. This is something that most Christian denominations and Churches must consider seriously - where they are merely following tradition [especially when they have come to the knowledge of the truth].

What will Jesus say about your Church' worship? Will he acknowledge it or call it vanity - a waste of your time and everyones? Come out of vain worship - it won't take you anywhere!

To be a true follower of Jesus, He expects us to put Him first, above people and certainly above tradition. He also wants us to give up on everything that holds us back from having true fellowship with Him. Jesus says; *"whoever does not renounce/forsake everything, can never be my disciple"* — **Luke 14:33**. Idolatry is when you put anything (people, money, business, possessions etc..) before God; when the love of the things of this world causes you to say No to Jesus. Jesus said that friendship with the world is enmity towards God — **James 4:4**.

I am not sure what may be holding you back from fully giving yourself to follow Jesus [in the way He wants, not what you have wanted to give]. Jesus is not so desperate to take anything that you offer as we have noted earlier - He's specific on the criteria of worshipers He is after - those who have given up everything to worship in Spirit and in Truth.

So while you and other men (pastors, Church leaders etc) may acknowledge the efforts you have made so far, Jesus is asking about the areas you have not as yet made Him Lord over. I encourage you to write down whatever they may be and work on them immediately like your salvation depends on them.

LET GO AND BE SAVED

In the part of Africa where l live, those who hunt for monkeys have an interesting way of catching these animals. Their strategy has proved successful for all time not so much because of the strategy itself but because of the unchanging nature of these monkeys - they are very predictable. Not only are they greedy, but also very unwise - they don't let go of the trappings and so be saved. The hunters, knowing monkeys like nuts, put nuts in a gourd bottle that has a small opening and large base and then bury the gourd in the ground exposing only the top opening. When the monkeys see this, they put their empty hand in it to see what they can find. There, they find these nuts and so grab all that they can which makes their fists larger and so unable to draw out of the bottle's small opening. They are stuck, unable to free themselves. You would think that the monkeys at this point will just let go of the nuts and free themselves. But no, they keep at it for hours trying to figure out other ways to bring their hands full of the nuts out. That's when the hunters come and seize them.

> *"For l take no pleasure in the death of anyone, declares the Sovereign LORD, Repent and live!"* — ***Eze 18:32.***

We can laugh at the folly of these animals but please pause and examine yourself - are you stuck and unable to free yourself because of pride, fear of finances or people, influence, tradition or other trappings of this world? I encourage you my dear friend to let go of anything that is holding you down so you can be saved.

> *"With many other words he warned them; and he pleaded with them, "Save yourselves from this corrupt generation."* — ***Acts 2:40.***

GOD'S HOLY LAW - Matters that truly matter!

29

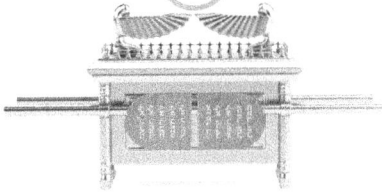

HOW SHOULD WE RESPOND TO THIS REALISATION?

But when he [finally] came to his senses, he said, 'How many of my father's hired men have more than enough food, while I am dying here of hunger!
— Luke 15:17

The question that may be on our minds is - in view of what we have heard (assuming any of this is new to us); how should we respond? Fortunately, God doesn't leave us to ourselves but guides us in His word. Let's read an account we find in scripture to see what we can learn from there.

"Then Hilkiah the high priest said to Shaphan the scribe, "I have found the Book of the Law in the house of the Lord." And Hilkiah gave the book to Shaphan, and he read it. ⁹ So Shaphan the scribe went to the king, bringing the king word, saying, "Your servants have gathered the

money that was found in the house, and have delivered it into the hand of those who do the work, who oversee the house of the Lord." ¹⁰ *Then Shaphan the scribe showed the king, saying, "Hilkiah the priest has given me a book." And Shaphan read it before the king.*

¹¹ *Now it happened, when the king heard the words of the Book of the Law, that he tore his clothes.* ¹² *Then the king commanded Hilkiah the priest, Ahikam the son of Shaphan, Achbor the son of Michaiah, Shaphan the scribe, and Asaiah a servant of the king, saying,* ¹³ *"Go, inquire of the Lord for me, for the people and for all Judah, concerning the words of this book that has been found; for great is the wrath of the Lord that is aroused against us, because our fathers have not obeyed the words of this book, to do according to all that is written concerning us."*

¹⁴ *So Hilkiah the priest, Ahikam, Achbor, Shaphan, and Asaiah went to Huldah the prophetess, the wife of Shallum the son of Tikvah, the son of Harhas, keeper of the wardrobe. (She dwelt in Jerusalem in the Second Quarter.) And they spoke with her.* ¹⁵ *Then she said to them, "Thus says the Lord God of Israel, 'Tell the man who sent you to Me,* ¹⁶ *"Thus says the Lord: 'Behold, I will bring calamity on this place and on its inhabitants—all the words of the book which the king of Judah has read—* ¹⁷ *because they have forsaken Me and burned incense to other gods, that they might provoke Me to anger with all the works of their hands. Therefore My wrath shall be aroused against this place and shall not be quenched.'"'* ¹⁸ *But as for the king of Judah, who sent you to inquire of the Lord, in this manner you shall speak to him, 'Thus says the Lord God of*

Israel: "Concerning the words which you have heard— [19]
because your heart was tender, and you humbled yourself
before the Lord when you heard what I spoke against this
place and against its inhabitants, that they would become
a desolation and a curse, and you tore your clothes and
wept before Me, I also have heard you," says the Lord. [20]
"Surely, therefore, I will gather you to your fathers, and
you shall be gathered to your grave in peace; and your eyes
shall not see all the calamity which I will bring on this
place."' " So they brought back word to the king"
— 2 Kings 22:8-20 NKJV

In this account, God's people find the book of the Law after a very long time of living in transgression. The King's reaction was one of Godly sorrow and deep humility. He quickly sends to find out what must be done to remedy the situation - just as Paul teaches the Corinthians -

"Even if I caused you sorrow by my letter, I do not regret it.
Though I did regret it—I see that my letter hurt you, but
only for a little while— [9] *yet now I am happy, not because*
you were made sorry, but because your sorrow led you to
repentance. For you became sorrowful as God intended
and so were not harmed in any way by us. [10] *Godly sorrow*
brings repentance that leads to salvation and leaves no
regret, but worldly sorrow brings death. [11] *See what this*
godly sorrow has produced in you: what earnestness, what
eagerness to clear yourselves, what indignation, what
alarm, what longing, what concern, what readiness to see
justice done. At every point you have proved yourselves to
be innocent in this matter" — 2 Cor 7:8-11 NIV

HOW SHOULD WE RESPOND?

Because the King was sorrowful about how God's Law had been transgressed and seeks to correct the situation immediately; God also promises to spare him from the calamity that is to come on the people.

God has already promised that; "if His people will **humble themselves** and **pray** and **seek His face** and repent from their wicked ways [lawlessness], He will hear us from Heaven and forgive our sins" - **2 Chron 7:14**. I believe when we are quick to act as King Josiah did; God will also spare us from any disaster that will come on the lawless. Let us all repent and spare ourselves from the wrath of God.

> *"21 But if a wicked man turns from all his sins which he has committed, keeps all My statutes, and does what is lawful and right, he shall surely live; he shall not die. 22 None of the transgressions which he has committed shall be remembered against him; because of the righteousness which he has done, he shall live"* — *Eze 18:21-22*

Please notice in this scripture that God says - "keeps **ALL** my statutes" - the scripture doesn't say some of His commands but all. God's Law is not presented to us like a buffet station where we get to choose which foods appeal to us - it's rather an à la carte service; so we take it or leave it. James the brother of Jesus tells us that when we break one of the commands, we are guilty of all — **Jam 2:10-12**.

Perhaps you have been a faithful disciple of Jesus but God has through this presentation opened your eyes to some new truths that you are convicted by and you are asking - what is the next step for me? Such was the situation with the disciples Paul met

334   GOD'S HOLY LAW - Matters that truly matter!

when he arrived in Ephesus. You notice that these disciples had previously been baptized but they didn't hesitate to be re-baptized on account of the new truth that they had found. You can read the story in **Acts 19:1-5**. So there is a precedence in the bible that you could follow. And if you choose to do so, be assured that you are on the right path. Baptism is an opportunity to have your sins forgiven and be given a clean sheet and more than that, a new beginning in your walk with Christ. So as you come to Jesus, ask Him to give you a new heart and renew a right spirit within you to serve Him wholeheartedly; in spirit and in truth.

If this is your plan or what you have done, l wish you a great life in Christ!

GOD'S HOLY LAW - Matters that truly matter!

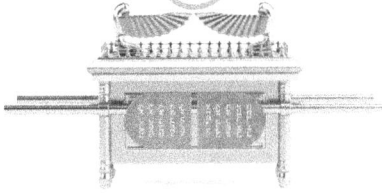

30

FINAL REMARK

For we must all appear before the judgment seat of Christ, so that every person may receive the works of his body, according to what he has done, whether it be good or bad — **Eccl 12:13-14 TLB**

When sin entered the world, God had three options to choose from - He could have simply let man die as a result of their sin; He could also have taken away His Law because if there is no law, there won't be any sin. But we know the story; He didn't choose any of these two options but went for a third one - He let His own son come to die in our place.

Friends, let's think carefully about this - God didn't take away His Law but rather watched for Jesus to die a very painful death. In the garden of Gethsemane, the shame, the guilt and the sin of all humanity was placed on Jesus. The weight of our sins was so heavy it was crushing the life out of Him; to the extent that His capillaries burst open and blood started oozing out of His pores. It was no ordinary pain and emotional anguish that Jesus felt as a result of your sin and my sin.

But what made it worse was the fact that; for the first time; He was being separated from His Father. Jesus; who knew well that He would rise again on the third day, couldn't bear the pain of a moment's separation from His source. So He tells us:

> *"Therefore I will judge you, O house of Israel, every one according to his ways, declares the Lord God. Repent and turn from all your transgressions, lest iniquity be your ruin* ³¹ *Cast away from you all the transgressions that you have committed, and make yourselves a new heart and a new spirit! Why will you die, O house of Israel?* ³² *For I have no pleasure in the death of anyone, declares the Lord God; so turn, and live."* — **Eze 18:30-32 ESV**.

On the cross, Jesus was forsaken because the penalty for breaking God's law [sin] is death. The fact that He died shows that God will not set aside His Law (holy and eternal); which confirms that; if God did not spare Jesus, then He won't spare any of us who transgress His Holy Law. And yet, He doesn't want to see us die. So we see Jesus, His intense love for humanity pinning Him to the cross, to die in our place so that you and I can have a second chance to receive God's forgiveness. What manner of love is this?

Be assured that when God reveals His truth to us, He doesn't do so to embarrass us nor does He intend to condemn us - His word like a mirror exposes our faults and what we are like to us, so that we can repent and turn to Him, so He can save us. God has given us enough reasons and proof that His word is living and active and not dead or altered as we may have thought - **Heb 4:12-13**. When God shows us the truth; He doesn't do so to give us head knowledge but wants to transform our hearts so we can be workers of righteousness. So here is the BIG question - "what will you do as a result of the knowledge you have received through this presentation"? When God asks the question about following His unchangeable Law - will you have a good answer to give Him?

Let us come before God in humility and repentance; and allow His word to examine our hearts and take away from us anything that doesn't please Him. And let us surrender fully to Him so He can forgive us and set us free to live with Him into eternity. So he bids us to open our hearts and welcome Him, to come in and give us eternal life; for that's why He came. And we can receive this free gift when we repent [and get baptized]. Let us not allow the enemy of our souls to steal this gift from us.

Please take some time to ask yourself the following questions:

- Who do my choices and decisions show l am following - God or Man?
- Do l have Jesus and am I sincerely following Him or paying Him lip service?
- Is my Christian life marked by Tradition or God's Truth?
- Is there a part of me that l have not fully surrendered to God?
- Am I guilty of disobeying God's moral Law [any part thereof]?
- Which aspects of God's Law of liberty do l need to (re) consider?

- Am l caught up in false worship or a false Church?
- If Jesus scrutinized my worship, will He say it is pleasing to Him or vain?
- Do I realize God is sounding His final warning and gathering His people?
- If Jesus came right now, will you make it with Him?
- Am I truly broken about my failure to observe any part of God's Law?
- Will I heed God's call today and "come out" of false worship/Church/religion?

If today you hear His voice, do not harden your heart; do not arouse God's anger by breaking His Law deliberately after you have come to know the truth. Please take time to meditate on **Heb 3** - where God shows us that our forefathers did not enter His rest because of unbelief [lack of faith]. They could not obey God because, even though they saw everything He did and heard everything He said, they still did not trust that He is who He said He is. *"And to whom did He swear that they would not enter His rest, but to those who did not obey?* ¹⁹ *So we see that they could not enter in because of unbelief." — **Heb 3:18-19 NKJV***.

Don't you find it interesting that when Moses asked how he should introduce God to the people of Israel, His answer was **"I AM WHO I AM"**. God doesn't end there, He tells Moses that it is the name by which He will be known throughout all generations and it will be a reminder to them forever - **Exodus 3:13-15 NKJV**. God is telling us to trust Him for who He says He is - the biggest test to our faith. Though all His qualities are there for all to see, unfortunately many still don't have faith in Him - see how Paul captures it in **Rom 1:18-32**. Only by works is faith made perfect, therefore works of faith become the leveler, the tool God uses to separate His sheep from the goats. When we are confident that He is who he says He is, we will love Him, and when we love Him, we will obey all that He commands us to do.

Friend, understand this, Satan is an angel, he used to be one of the two **covering cherubs** for that matter (**Isaiah 14:12-15**). We also know that Humans were created as lower beings than the angels - **Ps 8:3-5**. So if Satan [an angel] got **kicked out of Heaven** because he broke God's holy Law, what makes you [a mere man] think you can make it up there when you break God's Law?

Moses was one who did so much for God's people - if not for him, God would have destroyed the entire generation of Jews who came out of Egypt when they made the calf and declared a day to worship it. Several times, they provoked God and kindled His anger against them. But Moses always intervened on their behalf - **Exodus 32:7-14**. And yet, for not following God's specific instructions; God prevented Moses from entering the promised land - **Numbers 20:1-12**. This thought should keep us humble and teach us that it will take us taking God seriously and at His word, striving and making every effort, to obey completely what He tells us so as to enter through the narrow gate. This is not the time to entertain the doubts that Satan casts on us regarding what God has commanded.

Now all has been heard; here is the conclusion of the matter: **Fear God** and **Obey His commandments,** for this is all that man is here on earth to do! For God will bring **every work into judgment** including every secret thing, whether good or bad - **Eccl 12:13-14** - [emphasis mine]. When we go back to the beginning, we come to understand that the reason God created man was so that we will worship Him and do His bidding. Contrary to everything else we come to learn here on earth or what others' may tell us; our principal purpose is to bring glory to God through everything we do - **1 Cor 10:31.** So if that is our purpose here on earth - then let us faithfully live to obey God as He says.

May God bless you for taking your time to read, may He lead you to make decisions that will honor, please and glorify Him and may He prepare you for His coming. May His favour be on you for choosing to discuss this material among your small group/ fellowship/Church while you pray for God to use it to guide all who are His to the truth of His word. Please pray also, that God's warning will reach all who fear Him and desire a relationship with Him, and that they will come out of false worship and escape the wrath stored up for the lawless.

Based on God's word regarding what will happen in the last days; please pray for God's wisdom so we may understand the times, and to use our time wisely in acting as watchmen, and to faithfully minister His truth to the world around us. And finally, please pray that God gives us His strength so we may endure the persecution that is soon to break out on Christians the world over - pray that we will keep our good confession and won't love our lives even to death.

The Lord bless you and keep you;
The Lord make His face shine on you, and be gracious to you;
The Lord turn His face toward you and give you peace.

Shalom!

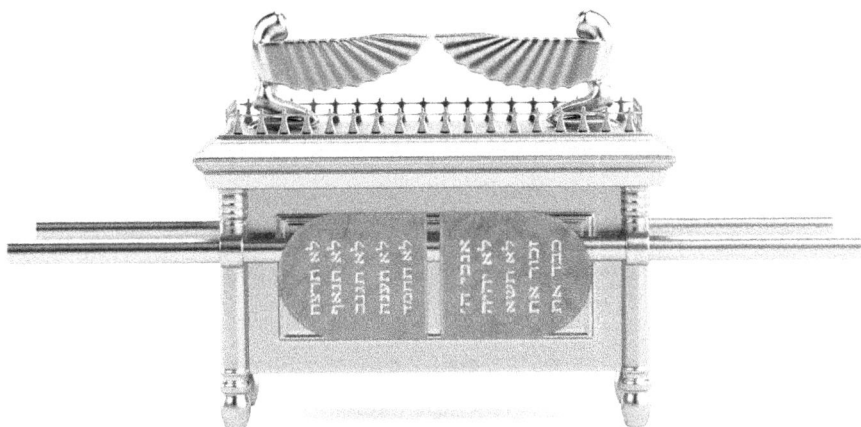

THE END

EPILOGUE

In a conversation with a friend, she mentioned that the difficulty with having the sort of relationship she'd like to have with God is because life gets in the way. *"Often, I plan to spend quality time in scripture reading and prayer but almost all the time - I realize there are other things that need my attention and I've got to skip my plan to attend to the urgent things of life - that which ultimately takes care of me and pays my bills"* - she said.

When she said that - I immediately remembered the times I felt and thought this way too. And this is very true for the kingdom of the world we are in - except that being a Christian is actually meant to belong to a different kingdom; God's kingdom. In God's kingdom; things work quite differently - it is not like in our world where your effort is what puts food on the table and pays your bills. While meritocracy is the way to get ahead in this world - the opposite is true in the kingdom of God. In God's kingdom, we only need to seek His interest and all these needs we have are given to us for free; not on merit but because the King loves his subjects.

Christianity introduces us to living in the kingdom of God where things are entirely different - and so we can't have the same mind set of this world and hope that we will function well in God's Kingdom.

God tells us that it is in turning away [from our ideas, methods and plans] and resting in Him that we will be saved — **Isa 30:15 NLV** [Paraphrased]. So in God's kingdom, only one thing truly matters - and Jesus says when you discover and choose it; it will not be taken away from you. That good thing which Mary found was to rest at the feet of Jesus and not be distracted by the world.

> *"And Jesus answered and said to her, "Martha, Martha, you are worried and troubled about many things. [42] But one thing is needed, and Mary has chosen that good part, which will not be taken away from her." — **Luke 10:41-42*** [emphasis mine].

When you live in God's kingdom, you rest while He provides. I don't know about you but that sounds like a super great deal to me. This is why I am choosing to obey all that the King says - and I invite you to come alongside; there's plenty of room here!

www.ingramcontent.com/pod-product-compliance
Lightning Source LLC
Chambersburg PA
CBHW062359090426
42740CB00010B/1333